MINDJACKED: How AI Hijacks Social Media, Controls Your Thoughts, and Manipulates the Masses

Introduction: The Invisible War You're Already Losing

In January 2024, thousands of New Hampshire voters picked up their phones to hear what sounded exactly like President Biden telling Democrats not to vote in the state's primary. "We know the value of voting Democratic when our votes count. It's important you save your vote for the November election," the voice on the line said with the familiar cadence and tone of the President.

But it wasn't Biden. It was a deepfake created with artificial intelligence—a perfect digital forgery designed to suppress voter turnout in a critical early primary. The voice was indistinguishable from the real thing, the message crafted to sound plausible, and the delivery timed for maximum impact just days before the election.

This wasn't some elaborate operation requiring a government intelligence agency or millions in funding. A single political consultant with access to publicly available AI tools created it. He was eventually caught, fined $6 million by the FCC, and faced criminal charges—but not before thousands heard the message and had to question whether their own president was telling them to stay home on election day.

Welcome to the new battlefield of the 21st century. It's not defined by geographical borders or conventional weapons. It's fought in the digital spaces where billions of us now live significant portions of our lives—on social media platforms, messaging apps, news sites, and search engines. The weapons aren't bombs or bullets but bytes, bots, and beliefs. And you're already losing this war, whether you realize it or not.

For most of human history, our senses were reliable guides to reality. We could trust what we saw with our own eyes and heard with our own ears. That fundamental assumption—the bedrock of human experience—is now crumbling beneath our feet. As William Marcellino, a senior behavioral scientist at RAND, puts it: "Human beings have spent hundreds of thousands of years interacting with our environment through our senses. Now those senses can be fooled."

This book is about how artificial intelligence has transformed social media from a communication tool into a weapon of unprecedented power—one being wielded by governments, corporations, extremist groups, and lone actors to manipulate public opinion, sow division, and undermine democracy itself. It's about how the same technologies that help us connect, create, and share are being exploited to deceive, divide, and control.

The Scale of the Threat

In 2019, a Chinese academic named Li Bicheng published a paper that should have set off alarm bells worldwide. In it, he outlined a plan for using artificial intelligence to flood the internet with fake social media accounts. These wouldn't be the crude bots of years past, easily spotted by their broken English and strange posting patterns. These would be sophisticated AI personas that looked real, sounded real, and could nudge public opinion without anyone noticing. His co-author was a member of the Chinese military's political warfare unit.

Li's vision was science fiction in 2019. Then, three years later, ChatGPT and other large language models burst onto the scene, and suddenly his blueprint became not just possible but practical. These AI systems, trained on trillions of words of human text, can mimic human writing with uncanny accuracy. They can generate content in specific regional dialects, engage in back-and-forth debates, respond to cultural references, and even create photo-quality images.

The threat isn't theoretical. In 2024, investigators took down a sophisticated Russian "bot farm" using AI to create fake accounts on X (formerly Twitter). These accounts had individual biographies, profile pictures, and could post content, comment on other posts, and build followers. The programmers behind the effort called them "souls." Their purpose, according to law enforcement officials, was to "assist Russia in exacerbating discord and trying to alter public opinion."

The scale of the problem is staggering. According to a 2024 poll by Deloitte, more than one in four executives revealed that their organizations had experienced one or more deepfake incidents targeting financial and accounting data in the previous year. Half of all respondents expected a rise in attacks. The Financial Crimes Enforcement Network (FinCEN) has observed "an increase in suspicious activity reporting by financial institutions describing the suspected use of deepfake media in fraud schemes." Deloitte's Center for Financial Services predicts that generative AI could enable fraud losses to reach US$40 billion in the United States by 2027.

And these are just the incidents we know about. As Nathan Beauchamp-Mustafaga, a China expert and senior policy researcher at RAND, warns: "If they do a good enough job, I'm not sure we would know about it."

The Psychological Battlefield

What makes this new form of warfare so insidious is that it targets the most vulnerable aspects of human psychology. Our brains evolved in an environment where seeing was believing. We're hardwired to trust our senses and to give special credence to information that confirms what we already believe. AI manipulation exploits these cognitive vulnerabilities with surgical precision.

Consider the case of Steve Beauchamp, an 82-year-old retiree who drained his retirement fund and invested $690,000 in a scam after seeing a deepfake video of Elon Musk promoting a cryptocurrency investment. "I mean, the picture of him—it was him," Beauchamp told The New York Times. "If somebody had said, 'Pick him out of a lineup,' that's him."

Even when told the video was fake, victims often struggle to accept it. "They still look like Elon Musk. They still sound like Elon Musk," said another victim after rewatching the same videos that had deceived her, despite having since learned they were AI-generated fakes.

This psychological vulnerability extends beyond individual scams to society-wide manipulation. In India's 2024 elections, AI-generated memes flooded WhatsApp, depicting opposition leader Rahul Gandhi as a "stupid thief" imagining all the money he would steal if elected. In Indonesia, the political party Golkar used AI to reanimate Suharto, the longtime dictator who died in 2008, to endorse their candidates. Shortly after, Suharto's son-in-law—who had Golkar's support—was elected president.

In the United States, Elon Musk shared a fake ad in which an AI clone of Kamala Harris's voice described herself as "the ultimate diversity hire," without disclosing the video was originally posted as a parody. Donald Trump posted a cartoonish AI image purporting to show Taylor Swift endorsing him—which she never did.

These examples reveal a crucial insight: the most dangerous AI manipulations aren't necessarily the ones trying to fool you completely. They're the ones that exploit existing biases, amplify emotional reactions, and gradually shift perceptions through repeated exposure. As Zeve Sanderson of NYU's Center for Social Media and Politics notes, this use of AI is not meant to change people's minds, but to "make their preferred candidate look patriotic or noble [or] to make their opposing candidate look evil."

The Actors Behind the Curtain

Who's waging this invisible war? The cast of characters is diverse and growing:

Nation-states lead the charge. Russia's Internet Research Agency pioneered modern digital influence operations during the 2016 U.S. election. China has dramatically increased its capabilities, with U.S. officials believing fake Chinese accounts tried to sway congressional races in the 2022 midterms. The most recent U.S. threat assessment notes that China is demonstrating a "higher degree of sophistication" in its influence operations and warns that "the PRC (People's Republic of China) may attempt to influence the U.S. elections in 2024 at some level."

Corporations have discovered the power of synthetic influencers and covert marketing. AI-generated personalities with millions of followers promote products without disclosing their non-human nature, creating parasocial relationships with consumers who feel genuine connections to digital phantoms.

Political campaigns and partisan groups deploy AI-generated content to energize supporters and demonize opponents, often without clear disclosure of the artificial nature of their messaging.

Criminal organizations have embraced deepfakes for fraud on an industrial scale. In one case, a British engineering company lost over $25 million when an employee was tricked by a deepfake CFO during a video conference call.

Lone actors with minimal technical skills but access to increasingly user-friendly AI tools can now create convincing fakes that would have required a Hollywood studio just a few years ago.

The democratization of these technologies means the barrier to entry for sophisticated influence operations continues to drop. What once required state-level resources is now available to anyone with a laptop and an internet connection.

The Stakes

Why does this matter? Because democracy depends on a shared reality. When we can no longer trust what we see and hear, when every piece of information becomes suspect, the foundations of democratic society begin to crumble. Citizens cannot make informed choices if they cannot distinguish fact from fiction. Institutions cannot function if public trust evaporates. Social cohesion breaks down when we no longer agree on basic facts.

> The personal stakes are equally high. Financial security, reputation, and psychological well-being are all threatened in a world where anyone can be impersonated, any statement fabricated, and any image manipulated. An AI-manipulated audio clip of a school principal making racist and antisemitic remarks went viral in January 2024, accumulating almost two million views within hours. The principal was put on paid administrative leave pending an investigation, his reputation damaged by words he never spoke.

Navigating the New Reality

This book is your guide to understanding and navigating this new reality. In the pages that follow, we'll explore:

- How AI is transforming propaganda and psychological operations
- The technologies behind deepfakes, synthetic media, and AI-driven influence
- The social media ecosystem that amplifies and rewards manipulation
- The major players in this new form of warfare
- The tools and techniques being used against you right now
- How to protect yourself, your family, and your community
- The future of this battle and what it means for society

The goal isn't to induce paranoia but to foster resilience. Knowledge is the first line of defense in this new kind of conflict. By understanding how these technologies work, who's using them, and why, you gain the ability to recognize manipulation attempts and protect yourself against them.

As Robert Weissman, president of the advocacy group Public Citizen, warned after the Biden deepfake incident: "The political deepfake moment is here. Policymakers must rush to put in place protections or we're facing electoral chaos."

But we can't wait for policy solutions alone. Each of us must develop our own defenses against manipulation. This book will show you how.

Read on, before the next thought you have isn't really your own. # Chapter 1: The Digital Theater of War

From Propaganda to Psyops 2.0

On a crisp autumn morning in 2016, residents of the small town of Twin Falls, Idaho, awoke to find their community at the center of a national firestorm. Social media platforms were ablaze with stories claiming that Syrian refugees had gang-raped a five-year-old girl at knifepoint while filming the attack. The story spread like wildfire across Facebook groups, Twitter feeds, and alternative news sites. Local officials were bombarded with angry calls. Death threats poured in. Armed militia groups began patrolling the streets.

There was just one problem: the story wasn't true.

Yes, there had been an incident involving children, but it bore little resemblance to the viral narrative. There were no Syrians involved. No knife. No gang rape. No filming. But by the time local authorities could respond with facts, the damage was done. The community was torn apart. Trust in institutions crumbled. And somewhere, far from the pain and confusion in Twin Falls, the architects of this disinformation campaign celebrated another successful operation in the digital theater of war.

This is the new face of propaganda—a sophisticated blend of truth, half-truth, and fiction, precisely targeted at specific communities, designed to exploit existing tensions, and delivered through the very platforms we use to connect with friends and family. It represents a fundamental transformation in how influence operations are conducted, a shift so profound that it requires us to rethink everything we thought we knew about propaganda.

To understand this transformation, we must first look backward. The story of propaganda is as old as human civilization itself. From the monuments of ancient Egypt to the speeches of Roman senators, from religious texts to royal proclamations, those in power have always sought to shape public perception. But for most of human history, propaganda was a blunt instrument—mass messages delivered to mass audiences through limited channels.

The systematic study of propaganda as we understand it today didn't emerge until the Industrial Revolution brought mass production and raised hopes of immense profits through mass marketing. As the 20th century dawned, researchers began studying consumer motivations and responses to various kinds of salesmanship and advertising. By the 1930s, "consumer surveys" similar to public opinion polls were commonplace. Almost every conceivable variable affecting opinions, beliefs, and behavior was being investigated across different groups and cultures.

World War I marked a turning point. For the first time, modern industrial nations deployed propaganda on an unprecedented scale. The British created the Ministry of Information. The Germans established the War Press Office. The Americans formed the Committee on Public Information. These institutions employed artists, writers, filmmakers, and psychologists to craft messages that would maintain morale at home and demoralize enemies abroad.

In 1927, American political scientist Harold D. Lasswell published "Propaganda Technique in the World War," a dispassionate analysis of these massive propaganda campaigns. This groundbreaking work, along with studies by Walter Lippmann and insights from Sigmund Freud's "Group Psychology and the Analysis of the Ego," laid the foundation for our modern understanding of how propaganda works.

The Nazi period, World War II, and the subsequent Cold War between the United States and Soviet Union saw propaganda elevated to a science. Governments, political movements, and businesses employed researchers to design carefully controlled experiments, attempting to quantify the effectiveness of different propaganda approaches. Joseph Goebbels, Hitler's propaganda minister, famously declared: "Propaganda becomes ineffective the moment we are aware of it." This insight—that the most effective propaganda is that which doesn't appear to be propaganda at all—would prove prophetic in the digital age.

By the second half of the 20th century, every significant government, political party, interest group, and large business had developed specialized corps of "opinion managers" (sometimes euphemistically called information specialists, public relations experts, or strategic communications professionals). The most skilled among them were trained in history, psychiatry, politics, social psychology, survey research, and statistical analysis.

But even as propaganda became more sophisticated, it remained fundamentally a top-down affair. Messages flowed from centralized sources through controlled channels to relatively passive audiences. The propagandist spoke. The public listened. This dynamic was about to change dramatically.

The Digital Paradigm Shift

The internet was supposed to democratize information. By removing gatekeepers and enabling direct peer-to-peer communication, many early internet pioneers believed they were creating a more informed, more connected world. Stewart Brand, founder of the Whole Earth Catalog, captured this techno-utopian vision with his famous declaration that "information wants to be free."

What actually emerged was something far more complex and troubling. Rather than a democratic paradise of enlightened discourse, the internet evolved into a battlefield where information itself became weaponized in ways previously unimaginable.

The fundamental distinction between traditional and digital propaganda lies in the difference between passive and participatory forms of information consumption. When reading newspapers, watching television, or listening to radio, we are largely passive observers. We maintain a certain psychological distance from the content, creating space for skepticism and doubt. Traditional propaganda always faced this obstacle—the fact that those subject to it retained enough distance to question what they were being told.

Digital media changed this dynamic entirely. When we post, comment, like, share, and search online, we are active participants in information processing and knowledge formation. We become invested in narratives not just as consumers but as co-creators. As researchers at the Lowy Institute have noted, "In the same way that students learn more effectively by doing, it's the *doing* part of contemporary digital media that is distinct. Participation is a type of cognitive investment."

This participatory nature makes digital propaganda fundamentally different from its predecessors. Modern influence operations rarely aim to change what people believe. Instead, they confirm and amplify existing beliefs—what Alicia Wanless and Michael Berk describe as a "Participatory Propaganda" model. Rather than trying to convince someone of something new, digital propagandists flood them with confirmation bias for beliefs they already hold while starving them of opportunities to encounter contradictory information.

The echo chamber effect—where users are increasingly exposed only to information that confirms their existing views—was a key component of Russian interference in the 2016 U.S. election. By identifying politically polarized communities and feeding them increasingly extreme content that aligned with their existing beliefs, Russian operatives didn't need to change minds. They simply had to deepen divisions that already existed.

This approach requires little of the sophistication of traditional psychological operations. It's more about amplification than persuasion, more about triggering emotional responses than making logical arguments. And it's devastatingly effective.

The tools and techniques of digital influence have evolved rapidly. "Captology"—the study of computers as persuasive technologies—emerged as a field in the mid-1990s, pioneered by Stanford University professor B.J. Fogg. Research into human-computer interaction (HCI) has revealed how digital interfaces can be designed to shape behavior in subtle but powerful ways. Governments worldwide have established "nudge units" that deploy these insights to influence public behavior, while private companies use the same techniques to maximize engagement and profit.

What makes digital propaganda particularly dangerous is its unprecedented combination of scale, precision, and participation:

Scale: A single message can reach billions of people instantly, crossing national borders and language barriers with ease.

Precision: Micro-targeting based on vast amounts of personal data allows propagandists to tailor messages to specific psychological profiles, delivering different content to different users based on their vulnerabilities.

Participation: Users themselves become unwitting vectors for propaganda, spreading messages through their networks and lending them credibility by association.

Algorithmic Amplification: Platform algorithms designed to maximize engagement naturally boost emotional, divisive content, creating a feedback loop that rewards the most inflammatory messages.

Blurred Authority: In the digital environment, traditional markers of credibility are absent or easily faked, making it harder to distinguish reliable sources from unreliable ones.

Persistence: Digital content remains accessible indefinitely, allowing propaganda narratives to resurface and gain new life long after they've been debunked.

Cross-platform Coordination: Modern influence operations work across multiple platforms simultaneously, creating an immersive information environment that surrounds targets from all sides.

Automated Deployment: Bots and AI systems can operate 24/7, responding to events in real-time and adapting messages based on audience response.

Feedback Loops: Digital platforms provide immediate data on what's working, allowing propagandists to refine their approaches continuously.

The result is a propaganda environment unlike anything we've seen before—one where the line between authentic communication and manipulation has become almost impossible to discern.

Memes, Movements, and Misinformation

In 1976, evolutionary biologist Richard Dawkins coined the term "meme" to describe a unit of cultural transmission—an idea, behavior, or style that spreads from person to person within a culture. Little did he know that decades later, this concept would become central to understanding how information spreads in the digital age.

Internet memes—typically images or short videos with text overlays that convey humorous or pointed messages—have emerged as powerful vehicles for propaganda. They bypass rational thought processes by packaging complex ideas into easily digestible, emotionally resonant formats. Their effectiveness stems from several key characteristics:

They use humor to lower cognitive defenses, making recipients more receptive to embedded messages.

They simplify complex issues into binary narratives that often reinforce existing biases.

They trigger emotional responses—outrage, fear, amusement, pride—that encourage sharing.

They create in-group/out-group dynamics, reinforcing tribal identities and polarization.

They're easily modified for different audiences while maintaining core messaging.

Consider the "Biden deepfake" mentioned in our introduction—a fabricated audio clip of President Biden telling Democrats not to vote in the New Hampshire primary. This wasn't just a technological feat; it was a meme in audio form, designed to spread rapidly through social networks and influence behavior. The creator understood that the message would resonate with existing narratives about election manipulation and would trigger emotional responses that would drive sharing.

Social movements, too, have been transformed by digital influence operations. Authentic grievances and legitimate causes are increasingly exploited and amplified by actors with hidden agendas. Extremist voices are elevated over moderates. Opposing sides are pushed toward greater polarization. What appears to be organic coordination may in fact be orchestrated by sophisticated influence campaigns.

The 2011 Arab Spring initially seemed to demonstrate social media's potential to empower democratic movements against authoritarian regimes. But the same tools that allowed protesters to organize in Tahrir Square were soon being used by governments to identify dissidents, spread disinformation, and manipulate public opinion. What began as liberation technology quickly became a tool for surveillance and control.

This pattern has repeated across numerous movements worldwide. The line between authentic grassroots activism and manufactured outrage has blurred to the point of invisibility. When thousands take to the streets, how many are responding to genuine conviction, and how many to algorithmically amplified rage? The answer is rarely simple.

The misinformation ecosystem that enables these operations consists of four key components:

Creators: Those who produce false or misleading content, including state actors, political groups, profit-seekers, and true believers.

Amplifiers: Those who boost the signal, including bots, influencers, unwitting participants ("useful idiots"), and algorithm manipulation.

Consumers: The general public who receive and potentially spread misinformation further.

Legitimizers: Those who add credibility, including compromised experts, media outlets, and public figures.

This ecosystem doesn't require central coordination to function effectively. Each component can operate independently while still contributing to the overall impact. A false story created by a fringe website can be amplified by bots, picked up by consumers who share it with their networks, and eventually legitimized when a public figure references it—all without any direct connection between the original creator and the ultimate legitimizer.

The case of the Twin Falls incident mentioned at the beginning of this chapter illustrates this ecosystem in action. The initial incident—a true but mischaracterized event involving children—was seized upon by anti-refugee activists who distorted the facts. These distortions were amplified by social media algorithms that reward emotional content. Consumers shared the inflammatory version without verification. And ultimately, the story was legitimized when it was covered by national media outlets and referenced by political figures.

By the time local authorities could respond with accurate information, the false narrative had already taken root. The damage to community trust and social cohesion was done. And the playbook for this operation was refined for use in future campaigns.

This is the new digital theater of war—a space where truth and fiction blur, where emotions trump facts, where algorithms amplify division, and where we all unwittingly become soldiers in battles we didn't choose to fight. Understanding this theater is the first step toward defending ourselves against those who would manipulate us within it.

As we move forward in this book, we'll explore the specific technologies that enable these operations, the actors who deploy them, and the strategies they use. But perhaps most importantly, we'll examine how individuals and societies can build resilience against these new forms of manipulation. Because in this invisible war, awareness is the first line of defense.

Chapter 2: What Is AI… and Why It's Dangerous Here

LLMs, GANs, NLP, and Emotion Modeling

In 2016, a Microsoft chatbot named Tay was released on Twitter as an experiment in conversational understanding. Designed to learn from its interactions with users, Tay was supposed to become more natural and personable over time. Within 24 hours, Microsoft had to shut it down. The bot had transformed from an innocent AI into a hate-spewing entity, parroting the most toxic viewpoints it encountered online. Microsoft hadn't anticipated how quickly their creation could be weaponized.

This cautionary tale illustrates a fundamental truth about artificial intelligence: the same technologies that power helpful virtual assistants, creative art generators, and efficient search engines can be repurposed for manipulation, deception, and harm. The difference isn't in the technology itself, but in how it's deployed.

To understand why AI is particularly dangerous in the context of social media manipulation, we need to first understand what these technologies are and how they work. In this chapter, we'll explore the key AI technologies driving social manipulation—Large Language Models, Generative Adversarial Networks, Natural Language Processing, and emotion modeling—and examine why their inner workings make them both powerful and problematic.

Large Language Models: The Chameleons of Communication

In 2020, OpenAI released GPT-3, a Large Language Model (LLM) that stunned the world with its ability to generate human-like text. Two years later, ChatGPT brought this technology to the masses, and suddenly everyone from schoolchildren to CEOs was experimenting with AI that could write essays, code, poetry, and more. By 2023,

GPT-4 had raised the bar even higher, demonstrating capabilities that blurred the line between artificial and human intelligence.

But what exactly are these Large Language Models, and how do they work?

LLMs are a category of foundation models trained on immense amounts of data, making them capable of understanding and generating natural language and other types of content to perform a wide range of tasks. GPT-4, for example, was trained on approximately 10 trillion words—more text than a human could read in thousands of lifetimes.

These models are based on a transformer architecture, consisting of multiple layers of neural networks with parameters that can be fine-tuned. The key innovation that makes them so powerful is the "attention mechanism," which allows the model to focus on specific parts of the input when generating each word of output.

During training, LLMs learn to predict the next word in a sentence based on the context provided by preceding words. The process involves breaking text into tokens (smaller sequences of characters), transforming these tokens into embeddings (numeric representations of context), and then using these embeddings to make predictions. Through this process, LLMs learn grammar, semantics, and conceptual relationships without explicit programming.

Once trained, these models can generate text by autonomously predicting the next word based on the input they receive, drawing on the patterns and knowledge they've acquired. The result is coherent and contextually relevant language generation that can be harnessed for a wide range of tasks—from answering questions and summarizing text to translating languages and generating creative content.

What makes LLMs particularly powerful—and dangerous—is their ability to adapt to different contexts and personas. They can mimic specific writing styles, adopt particular viewpoints, and generate content that appears to come from different demographic groups. A single LLM can write like a conservative grandfather from rural America in one prompt and a progressive college student from New York City in the next.

This chameleon-like quality makes LLMs ideal for creating personalized propaganda at scale. An influence operation that once would have required thousands of human operators can now be automated with a handful of prompts. The same technology that helps a marketing team craft the perfect email can be used to generate thousands of seemingly authentic social media posts pushing a particular narrative.

Consider the case of a 2023 pro-China influence operation discovered by Microsoft. The operation used AI to generate content across multiple languages and platforms, creating the appearance of organic discussion about issues related to Taiwan, the South China Sea, and U.S.-China relations. The AI-generated content was designed to appear as if it came from real people with diverse backgrounds and perspectives, all converging on pro-China viewpoints. Without sophisticated detection tools, most users would never have recognized these posts as artificial.

Generative Adversarial Networks: Making the Fake Indistinguishable from the Real

If LLMs have revolutionized text generation, Generative Adversarial Networks (GANs) have done the same for visual media. First introduced by Ian Goodfellow and his colleagues in 2014, GANs have rapidly evolved from producing blurry, unconvincing images to creating photorealistic content that can fool even trained observers.

GANs are an approach to generative modeling using deep learning methods, such as convolutional neural networks. They're designed to generate new examples that plausibly could have been drawn from the original dataset. What makes GANs unique is their architecture: they consist of two neural networks locked in an adversarial relationship.

The generator network creates fake examples, while the discriminator network evaluates examples as either real (from the domain) or fake (generated). These two networks are trained together in a zero-sum game—what's good for one is bad for the other. The generator tries to create increasingly convincing fakes, while the discriminator gets better at spotting them. This competition drives both networks to improve until the generator produces examples so good that the discriminator can't tell the difference between real and fake.

This architecture has proven remarkably effective for creating realistic synthetic media. GANs can now generate photorealistic images of people who don't exist, transform summer landscapes into winter scenes, turn sketches into detailed photographs, and even create videos of people saying and doing things they never did.

The implications for social media manipulation are profound. In 2019, a deepfake video of Mark Zuckerberg appeared on Instagram, showing the Facebook CEO seemingly boasting about having "total control of billions of people's stolen data." While this example was clearly labeled as artificial, it demonstrated how easily synthetic media could be used to put words in someone's mouth.

By 2024, the technology had advanced to the point where deepfakes were being used in real-world influence operations. During Taiwan's presidential election, videos circulated showing candidates making statements they never made. In the United States, a deepfake robocall impersonating President Biden urged Democrats not to vote in the New Hampshire primary. And in the corporate world, a British engineering company lost over $25 million when an employee was tricked by a deepfake CFO during a video conference call.

What makes GANs particularly dangerous is the arms race between generation and detection. As detection tools improve, so do the generative models. Each new iteration becomes more difficult to distinguish from reality. And while experts might still be able to spot the fakes, the average social media user lacks both the tools and the training to make these distinctions.

Natural Language Processing and Emotion Modeling: The Science of Manipulation

Beyond generating text and images, AI systems are increasingly capable of understanding and manipulating human emotions. This capability comes from advances in Natural Language Processing (NLP) and emotion modeling.

NLP is a subfield of AI that helps computers communicate with human language. It bridges the gap between human communication and computer understanding, using machine learning to interpret, manipulate, and comprehend language in all its complexity.

One of the most powerful applications of NLP is emotion analysis—the ability to detect and categorize the emotional content of text. Modern NLP systems can analyze both written content and spoken words to discern emotional tone, detecting emotions like anger, happiness, sadness, and frustration with increasing accuracy.

These systems use various approaches to emotion detection:

- Rules-based approaches use predefined rules to identify emotions based on linguistic patterns.
- Keyword-based approaches identify specific words associated with particular emotions.
- Machine learning approaches train models on labeled emotional text to recognize patterns.

- Deep learning approaches use neural networks to detect subtle emotional patterns that might not be obvious to human observers.

The ability to detect emotions opens the door to emotional manipulation. By understanding what makes people angry, fearful, or hopeful, AI systems can craft messages designed to trigger specific emotional responses. They can identify emotionally charged topics for amplification, personalize manipulation based on emotional profiles, and measure the emotional impact of campaigns in real-time.

This isn't just theoretical. In 2014, Facebook conducted a controversial experiment on emotional contagion, manipulating the news feeds of nearly 700,000 users to show either more positive or more negative content. The study found that users exposed to more negative content subsequently posted more negative updates themselves, while those exposed to positive content posted more positively. The experiment demonstrated how subtle changes in content curation could influence emotional states at scale.

Now imagine this same capability in the hands of those seeking to manipulate public opinion. An AI system could analyze which emotional triggers are most effective for different demographic groups, craft messages designed to provoke those emotions, and continuously refine its approach based on feedback. It could identify individuals who are particularly susceptible to emotional manipulation and target them with personalized content.

The combination of emotion detection and content generation creates a powerful tool for influence operations. An AI system could, for example, identify that a particular user responds strongly to content that triggers parental anxiety, then generate a series of increasingly alarming (but plausible-sounding) stories about threats to children in their area. Over time, this could shift the user's political views, consumer behavior, or social attitudes—all without them realizing they're being manipulated.

The Black Box Problem: When Even the Creators Don't Understand

Perhaps the most troubling aspect of modern AI systems is what's known as the "black box problem." Despite creating these powerful technologies, even the developers who build them don't fully understand how they work or why they make specific decisions.

> Modern AI systems, especially deep learning models, operate as "black boxes"—their internal decision-making processes are opaque and difficult to interpret. This opacity stems from several factors:

- Complexity: Models like GPT-4 have hundreds of billions of parameters, making it impossible for humans to comprehend the entire system.
- Non-linearity: The relationships between inputs and outputs aren't straightforward, making it difficult to trace cause and effect.
- Emergent behaviors: Systems develop unexpected capabilities or behaviors that weren't explicitly programmed.
- Distributed representations: Information is spread across many parameters rather than being stored in easily identifiable locations.

This lack of transparency has profound implications for social media manipulation. It makes it difficult to predict how AI systems will behave in new situations, hard to detect when systems are being misused, challenging to attribute manipulation to specific actors, and nearly impossible to fully understand the reasoning behind AI-generated content.

Consider the case of GPT-4, which demonstrated capabilities its creators at OpenAI hadn't anticipated. The system showed an ability to solve novel problems, reason through complex scenarios, and even exhibit a form of theory of mind—understanding that others might have different beliefs and knowledge than itself. These emergent capabilities weren't explicitly programmed; they arose from the scale and architecture of the model in ways that surprised even its developers.

When even the creators of these systems can't fully predict or explain their behavior, how can we hope to develop effective safeguards against their misuse? This is the central challenge of the black box problem—we're deploying technologies whose inner workings remain mysterious, even as they gain increasing influence over our information ecosystem.

The black box problem also creates significant accountability challenges. Who is responsible when AI systems cause harm? How can we hold creators accountable for systems they don't fully understand? Our legal and ethical frameworks are struggling to keep pace with these technological developments, creating a regulatory gap that can be exploited by those seeking to manipulate public opinion.

Why AI Is Particularly Dangerous in Social Media

The combination of these AI technologies—LLMs, GANs, NLP, and emotion modeling—creates a perfect storm for social media manipulation. Several factors make this particularly concerning:

Exponential Improvement: AI capabilities are advancing at a breathtaking pace. What seemed like science fiction just a few years ago is now commercially available. GPT-4 is estimated to be approximately 1,000 times more powerful than GPT-3, which itself was revolutionary when released in 2020. This rapid advancement means that defensive measures are constantly playing catch-up.

Accessibility: Powerful AI tools are becoming increasingly available to non-experts. User-friendly interfaces and APIs have democratized access to sophisticated AI capabilities. What once required a team of AI researchers can now be accomplished by anyone with an internet connection and a credit card.

Dual-Use Problem: The same technologies that provide benefits in fields like healthcare, education, and business can be weaponized for manipulation. There's no clear line between "good" and "bad" AI—it's all about how it's deployed.

Psychological Targeting: AI systems can identify and exploit psychological vulnerabilities with unprecedented precision. By analyzing patterns in user behavior, these systems can determine which messages will be most effective for specific individuals, creating personalized propaganda that bypasses critical thinking.

Attribution Challenges: It's increasingly difficult to determine who is behind AI-powered manipulation campaigns. The ability to generate content at scale without human intervention makes it easier for actors to hide their involvement and harder for platforms and researchers to identify the source of manipulation.

Regulatory Gaps: Our legal and ethical frameworks are struggling to keep pace with technological development. Many of the most concerning applications of AI for manipulation fall into gray areas not clearly addressed by existing regulations.

Democratization of Capabilities: Capabilities once limited to powerful states are now available to a wide range of actors, including smaller nations, non-state groups, and even individuals with sufficient technical knowledge. This has created a more complex and unpredictable information environment.

The result is a landscape where sophisticated manipulation is becoming easier, cheaper, and more effective, while detection and defense become increasingly challenging. As AI systems continue to evolve, this gap is likely to widen unless we develop new approaches to safeguarding our information ecosystem.

The Illusion of Control

Perhaps the most dangerous aspect of AI in the context of social media manipulation is the illusion of control. We tend to think of technology as a tool—something we use to achieve our goals. But with advanced AI systems, this relationship becomes more complex.

As these systems become more sophisticated, they begin to shape our behavior in ways we might not recognize. The recommendation algorithms that determine what content we see, the autocomplete suggestions that influence what we write, the generative tools that help us create—all of these subtly guide our actions and thoughts.

This guidance isn't necessarily malicious. Often, it's designed to maximize engagement, satisfaction, or efficiency. But when these systems are deployed at scale across billions of users, even small influences can have profound societal impacts. And when they're deliberately weaponized for manipulation, the effects can be devastating.

The philosopher Martin Heidegger warned about this relationship with technology, suggesting that rather than us using technology, technology might end up using us. With AI, this warning takes on new significance. As we delegate more of our information filtering, content creation, and decision-making to AI systems, we risk becoming instruments of these systems rather than the other way around.

This is the ultimate danger of AI in social media—not just that it can be used to manipulate us, but that we might not even recognize when it's happening. The most effective manipulation doesn't feel like manipulation at all. It feels like our own thoughts, our own decisions, our own authentic reactions. And as AI gets better at understanding and mimicking human behavior, this illusion will only become more convincing.

In the chapters that follow, we'll explore how these technologies are deployed in practice, examining the social media landscape as a battlefield, the actors involved in these influence operations, and the specific tools and techniques they use. But first, it's essential to understand that the technologies themselves are neither good nor evil—they're powerful tools that can be used for both benefit and harm. The danger lies not in the technology itself, but in how it's deployed, by whom, and to what end.

As we navigate this new landscape, awareness is our first line of defense. By understanding what these technologies are capable of and how they can be misused, we take the first step toward protecting ourselves and our societies from manipulation. The invisible war for our minds is already underway, and knowledge is our most powerful weapon.

Chapter 3: Social Media as a Battlefield

The Perfect Terrain for Information Warfare

In 2011, as the Arab Spring swept across the Middle East, social media platforms were hailed as liberating technologies—tools that empowered ordinary citizens to organize, share information, and challenge authoritarian regimes. Facebook and Twitter were credited with facilitating revolutions in Tunisia, Egypt, and beyond. Time Magazine even named "The Protester" as its Person of the Year, with social media cast as the protester's essential weapon.

Just five years later, these same platforms were being blamed for Brexit, the rise of populist movements worldwide, and the election of Donald Trump. The narrative had shifted dramatically: social media was no longer seen primarily as a tool of liberation but as a weapon of manipulation and division.

What happened? Did the platforms change so dramatically in those few years? Or did we simply come to understand their true nature?

The truth is that social media platforms have always been battlefields—spaces designed for conflict, competition, and conquest. Not by malicious intent, but by the fundamental architecture and incentives that drive them. The same features that make these platforms powerful tools for connection and expression also make them ideal terrain for information warfare.

To understand why social media has become the primary battlefield of the 21st century, we need to examine its unique characteristics: the architecture and algorithms that shape information flow, the psychological hooks that keep users engaged, the economics that drive platform design, and the filter bubbles that fragment our shared reality.

Architecture and Algorithms: The Invisible Battlefield Terrain

Every physical battlefield has terrain features that shape how combat unfolds—high ground provides advantage, choke points create bottlenecks, open fields expose advancing forces. In the digital battlefield of social media, the terrain is shaped by architecture and algorithms.

The architecture of social media platforms determines what users can do, see, and share. It establishes the rules of engagement. Can users remain anonymous? How easily can content be shared? What types of interactions are possible? These design choices create the fundamental conditions in which information warfare takes place.

But the most powerful terrain features are invisible: the recommendation algorithms that determine what content each user sees. These algorithms are both architects and gatekeepers of user experiences on the platforms. They control content visibility, sequence, and distribution, effectively deciding which information reaches which users.

Contrary to popular belief, these algorithms aren't incomprehensible black boxes. They follow understandable principles, with a primary goal: maximizing user engagement and time spent on the platform. As Arvind Narayanan of Princeton University explains, "The core of the algorithm is engagement prediction." While platforms may have many high-level goals—ad revenue, user retention, growth—engagement is the primary metric that drives algorithmic decision-making.

This focus on engagement creates a battlefield that inherently favors certain types of content. Research consistently shows that emotional, divisive, and outrage-inducing content generates more engagement than neutral, nuanced, or positive content. A 2021 study by the NYU Center for Social Media and Politics found that each word of moral outrage added to a social media post increased its retweet rate by 17 percent, on average.

The algorithms learn these patterns and amplify them, creating feedback loops that reward increasingly extreme content. As Tristan Harris, former Google design ethicist and co-founder of the Center for Humane Technology, puts it: "If you're not paying for the product, you are the product." The algorithms are designed to extract maximum attention from users, not to create a healthy information environment.

This algorithmic terrain creates several key advantages for those conducting information operations:

Amplification: The algorithms can dramatically increase the reach of content that triggers strong emotional responses, allowing relatively small actors to achieve outsized influence.

Precision targeting: Platform data enables operators to identify and target specific vulnerable demographics with tailored messaging.

Plausible deniability: The complexity of algorithmic systems makes it difficult to distinguish between organic virality and manipulated amplification.

Asymmetric advantage: Attackers can exploit algorithmic vulnerabilities more easily than platforms can defend against such exploitation.

Consider the case of the 2016 Russian Internet Research Agency (IRA) operations targeting the U.S. election. With a relatively modest budget of approximately $1.25 million per month, the IRA was able to reach tens of millions of Americans with divisive content. They didn't need to create all this reach themselves—they simply needed to create content that the algorithms would naturally amplify.

The IRA operators understood that Facebook's algorithm favored content that generated strong emotional reactions and high engagement. They created pages focused on divisive issues like race, immigration, and gun rights, then produced content designed to trigger outrage among both conservative and liberal Americans. The algorithm did the rest, pushing this content into the feeds of users most likely to engage with it.

This is the fundamental asymmetry of the social media battlefield: those seeking to manipulate public opinion need only understand and exploit the existing algorithmic terrain, while those defending against such manipulation must try to change the terrain itself—a much more difficult task.

The Psychology of Addiction: Weaponizing Human Vulnerability

If algorithms shape the terrain of the social media battlefield, psychological vulnerabilities are the targets at which information operations aim. Social media platforms are designed to be addictive, exploiting fundamental aspects of human psychology to maximize engagement.

The most powerful framework for understanding this addictive design is the Hook Model, developed by Nir Eyal and based on B.F. Skinner's principles of operant conditioning. The Hook Model describes a four-stage cycle that drives user engagement and habit formation:

Trigger: External triggers like notifications or internal triggers like boredom or FOMO (fear of missing out) prompt users to open the app.

Action: Users perform a simple behavior in anticipation of a reward—scrolling through a feed, checking notifications, or refreshing content.

Variable Reward: The unpredictability of what users will find creates a powerful dopamine response. Sometimes they'll see something exciting, sometimes something boring, but the variability keeps them coming back.

Investment: Users put something of value into the platform—creating content, building a network, curating a profile—which increases their likelihood of returning.

Each social media platform implements this model in slightly different ways:

Facebook leverages our need for social validation. Every like, comment, or share provides a small dopamine hit that reinforces engagement. The notification icon—that little red dot—creates a powerful trigger that's difficult to ignore.

Instagram's infinite scroll creates a seamless, hypnotic experience that can lead to what psychologists call "flow state"—a condition of complete absorption that distorts time perception. The visual nature of the platform triggers rapid emotional responses, while the curated, idealized presentations of others' lives fuel social comparison.

TikTok has perfected the variable reward mechanism with its endless stream of short-form videos. The app's algorithm quickly learns user preferences, creating a highly personalized feed that becomes increasingly addictive as it improves. The brevity of videos reduces the cognitive commitment required, making it easier to fall into extended viewing sessions.

Twitter (now X) exploits our desire for real-time information and fear of missing out. The platform's design encourages quick, reactive responses rather than thoughtful engagement, while its public nature turns conversations into performances.

These psychological hooks create several vulnerabilities that can be exploited in information operations:

Emotional triggering: Content designed to evoke strong emotions—especially anger, fear, or moral outrage—receives preferential treatment from both algorithms and users.

Identity reinforcement: Information that confirms existing beliefs and identity is more readily accepted and shared, creating opportunities for manipulation through identity-based messaging.

Cognitive overload: The constant stream of information overwhelms our ability to process it critically, making us more susceptible to misleading content.

Social proof: We look to others' reactions to determine how we should respond, creating cascades of belief or behavior that can be artificially initiated.

The Cambridge Analytica scandal revealed how these psychological vulnerabilities could be weaponized at scale. The firm harvested data from millions of Facebook users to create psychological profiles, then used these profiles to target individuals with content designed to exploit their specific vulnerabilities. While the effectiveness of their approach has been debated, the incident demonstrated how platform architecture and psychological profiling could be combined for political manipulation.

What makes this particularly concerning is that these vulnerabilities aren't bugs—they're features. The addictive nature of social media isn't an accident; it's the product of deliberate design choices aimed at maximizing engagement. As Sean Parker, Facebook's founding president, admitted in 2017: "The thought process was: 'How do we consume as much of your time and conscious attention as possible?'" The answer, it turns out, was to exploit the same psychological vulnerabilities that information warriors now target.

The Attention Economy: Why Truth Is the First Casualty

To understand why social media platforms have evolved into such problematic information environments, we need to examine the economic incentives that drive their design and operation. These platforms operate in what's been called the "attention economy"—a marketplace where human attention is the primary commodity.

In the attention economy, the goal isn't to provide users with accurate information or meaningful connections. The goal is to capture and retain as much user attention as possible, which can then be monetized through advertising. As Tim Wu writes in "The Attention Merchants," this creates a fundamental misalignment between user interests and platform incentives: "The capture of human attention for resale to advertisers has been the basic business model."

This economic model creates several battlefield conditions that favor manipulation over truth:

Zero-sum competition for attention: There's only so much human attention available, creating intense competition between platforms—and between content creators on those platforms—to capture it. This drives increasingly extreme tactics to grab and hold attention.

Engagement metrics that don't measure quality: Platforms optimize for measurable engagement metrics like clicks, shares, and time spent, not for the quality, accuracy, or value of information. Content that generates strong engagement is amplified regardless of its truth value.

Data collection that enables targeting: The advertising model requires extensive data collection to enable targeted advertising, creating vast repositories of personal information that can be exploited for manipulation.

Scale that overwhelms moderation: The economic imperative to grow user bases and content volume creates moderation challenges that platforms are unwilling or unable to solve, allowing harmful content to flourish.

The result is an information environment optimized for reaction, not reflection; for engagement, not enlightenment; for virality, not veracity. As Renée DiResta of the Stanford Internet Observatory puts it: "The economics of the attention economy incentivize content that is polarizing, emotionally manipulative, and misleading because that content drives engagement."

This economic reality creates perfect conditions for information warfare. Actors seeking to spread disinformation don't need to overcome platform defenses—they simply need to align their content with the platforms' own incentives. Content that triggers outrage, reinforces tribal identities, or provokes fear will be naturally amplified by systems designed to maximize engagement.

Consider the spread of COVID-19 misinformation during the pandemic. A study by the nonprofit Counter Action found that just twelve individuals—dubbed the "Disinformation Dozen"—were responsible for up to 65% of anti-vaccine content on major social media platforms. These individuals didn't need sophisticated technical capabilities or massive resources. They simply needed to create content that aligned with the engagement incentives of the platforms—content that triggered strong emotional responses, reinforced existing beliefs, and created a sense of insider knowledge.

The platforms' response was telling. Despite clear evidence that this content was causing real-world harm, platforms were slow to act. The content was, after all, generating significant engagement. Only after intense public pressure did platforms begin to take more aggressive action against COVID-19 misinformation.

This pattern repeats across issues: platforms profit from the very content that causes societal harm. The attention economy creates a battlefield where truth is at a systematic disadvantage—not because platforms want to spread falsehoods, but because the economic incentives simply don't reward truth.

Filter Bubbles and Echo Chambers: Fragmenting Reality

Perhaps the most concerning feature of the social media battlefield is its ability to fragment our shared reality into isolated information environments—what Eli Pariser called "filter bubbles" and what researchers now often refer to as "echo chambers."

Filter bubbles form through the interaction of algorithmic personalization and human psychology. Recommendation algorithms show users content similar to what they've engaged with in the past, while confirmation bias leads users to seek information that confirms their existing beliefs. This creates a self-reinforcing cycle:

1. Users select content that aligns with their beliefs
2. Algorithms learn these preferences and show similar content
3. Exposure to confirming content strengthens beliefs
4. Strengthened beliefs lead to more selective exposure
5. Social connections reinforce information bubbles
6. Alternative viewpoints are increasingly seen as illegitimate

The result is increasingly isolated information environments where users are exposed primarily to content that confirms their existing beliefs and rarely encounter challenging perspectives. As a 2021 study in the Proceedings of the National Academy of Sciences found, "Personalization in search and social media leads to the formation of echo chambers and filter bubbles that ultimately reduce the diversity of content to which users are exposed."

This fragmentation creates ideal conditions for information warfare:

Targeted operations: Different groups can be targeted with completely different narratives without cross-exposure that might reveal the manipulation.

Reduced fact-checking: Users in echo chambers are less likely to encounter fact-checks or corrections of false information that aligns with their beliefs.

Increased polarization: Isolation from opposing viewpoints leads to more extreme positions and dehumanization of outgroups.

Erosion of shared reality: Without a common information environment, society loses the ability to agree on basic facts, undermining democratic discourse.

The QAnon phenomenon demonstrates how these dynamics can be exploited. What began as fringe conspiracy theories on anonymous message boards evolved into a significant political movement, with adherents eventually participating in the January 6, 2021, attack on the U.S. Capitol.

QAnon spread through a perfect storm of algorithmic amplification, psychological vulnerability, and filter bubbles. YouTube's recommendation algorithm directed users interested in one conspiracy theory toward increasingly extreme content. Facebook Groups created isolated environments where believers could reinforce each other's views without exposure to debunking information. Cross-platform information flows allowed the conspiracy to adapt and evolve, finding new audiences across different demographic groups.

Most concerningly, those caught in the QAnon filter bubble weren't just exposed to different opinions—they were living in an entirely different information reality, with different facts, different authorities, and different understandings of how the world works. This is the ultimate goal of information warfare: not just to change what people think, but to change how they think and what they perceive as real.

The Asymmetric Advantage: Why Attackers Win

Throughout military history, certain battlefields have favored attackers over defenders or vice versa. The trench warfare of World War I created a defender's advantage so strong that offensives regularly failed despite massive numerical superiority. Conversely, the open plains of Eastern Europe in World War II created conditions that favored rapid offensive operations.

The social media battlefield overwhelmingly favors attackers—those seeking to manipulate, mislead, and divide—over defenders trying to maintain a healthy information environment. This asymmetric advantage stems from several factors:

Speed advantage: False information spreads faster than true information. A 2018 MIT study found that false news stories are 70% more likely to be retweeted than true stories and reach their first 1,500 people six times faster. By the time a fact-check arrives, the damage is often already done.

Cost asymmetry: Creating disinformation is cheap; debunking it is expensive. A single operator can create dozens of false claims in the time it takes fact-checkers to thoroughly investigate one.

Emotional asymmetry: Disinformation often triggers strong emotional responses that promote sharing, while corrections and accurate information tend to be more neutral and less engaging.

Scale mismatch: The volume of content on major platforms makes comprehensive monitoring impossible, allowing manipulative content to slip through even the best defenses.

Exploitation of features, not bugs: Attackers exploit the fundamental features of platforms—their algorithms, engagement metrics, and targeting capabilities—rather than technical vulnerabilities that could be patched.

Plausible deniability: The complexity of social media systems makes it difficult to definitively attribute manipulation, allowing attackers to maintain deniability.

These advantages create a battlefield where even well-resourced defenders struggle to counter determined attackers. Platform companies, despite their vast resources, have repeatedly failed to effectively counter coordinated manipulation campaigns. Government agencies, despite their intelligence capabilities, have struggled to detect and disrupt foreign influence operations in real-time.

The Russian Internet Research Agency's operations during the 2016 U.S. election exemplify this asymmetric advantage. With a relatively small team and modest budget, the IRA was able to reach tens of millions of Americans with divisive content. They created fake accounts impersonating American activists, established pages focused on controversial issues, and deployed targeted advertising to reach specific demographic groups.

What made these operations particularly effective was their exploitation of platform features rather than technical vulnerabilities. The IRA didn't need to hack Facebook's systems; they simply used Facebook's own tools as designed. They created content that triggered strong emotional responses, knowing the algorithm would amplify it. They used Facebook's targeting capabilities to reach users most susceptible to their messaging. They exploited the platform's limited identity verification to create convincing fake personas.

By the time these operations were discovered and disrupted, they had already achieved their objectives: deepening societal divisions, undermining trust in institutions, and influencing public discourse. The defenders—both platform companies and government agencies—were left playing catch-up, implementing countermeasures that the attackers could easily adapt to or circumvent.

This asymmetric advantage isn't temporary or fixable with minor policy changes. It's inherent to the current architecture and incentives of social media platforms. As long as platforms optimize for engagement rather than information quality, as long as they collect vast amounts of user data for targeting, as long as they operate at a scale that defies effective moderation, attackers will maintain their advantage.

The Battlefield Evolves: From Human to AI-Driven Warfare

The social media battlefield isn't static—it's constantly evolving as new technologies emerge and existing ones advance. The most significant evolution we're witnessing now is the shift from human-driven to AI-driven information operations.

Traditional information operations required significant human resources. Operators needed to create content, manage accounts, engage with users, and adapt messaging based on audience response. This created bottlenecks that limited the scale and sophistication of operations.

AI is removing these bottlenecks. Large Language Models can generate persuasive content at scale, adapting messaging for different audiences without human intervention. Generative Adversarial Networks can create convincing fake images and videos that bypass traditional detection methods. Machine learning algorithms can identify vulnerable users and optimize targeting in real-time.

This technological evolution is creating new battlefield conditions:

Increased scale: AI can generate and distribute manipulative content at volumes that dwarf previous capabilities, overwhelming platform defenses and human attention.

Enhanced personalization: AI can analyze vast amounts of user data to create highly personalized manipulation, targeting individual psychological vulnerabilities with precision.

Improved authenticity: AI-generated content is becoming increasingly difficult to distinguish from human-created content, reducing the effectiveness of authenticity-based defenses.

Autonomous adaptation: AI systems can monitor response rates and engagement metrics, continuously optimizing their approach without human guidance.

Cross-platform coordination: AI can maintain consistent narratives across multiple platforms while adapting to the specific features and audience of each.

We're already seeing early examples of this evolution. In 2023, researchers at Graphika identified a pro-China influence operation that used AI-generated content across multiple platforms. The operation created realistic-looking "journalists" with AI-generated profile pictures, produced content in multiple languages that appeared to be written by native speakers, and adapted messaging based on platform and audience.

What made this operation particularly concerning was its ability to create the appearance of organic discussion. Rather than pushing a single narrative, the AI-generated personas engaged in seemingly authentic conversations, debating minor points while reinforcing the core messaging. This created a false sense of consensus that was more convincing than traditional propaganda.

As AI capabilities continue to advance, we can expect information operations to become more sophisticated, more personalized, and more difficult to detect. The battlefield advantage will shift even further toward attackers, who can leverage these technologies more quickly and with fewer constraints than defenders.

Defending the Digital Commons

Despite the significant advantages that attackers enjoy on the social media battlefield, the situation isn't hopeless. Effective defense requires understanding the terrain, recognizing the asymmetric nature of the conflict, and developing strategies that address the fundamental vulnerabilities rather than just the symptoms.

Several approaches show promise:

Changing platform incentives: As long as engagement remains the primary metric for success, manipulation will flourish. Regulatory approaches that alter the economic incentives of platforms could create conditions less favorable to information warfare.

Building collective resilience: Individual users can be educated to recognize manipulation tactics, but collective resilience—communities that self-correct and develop shared norms around information quality—may be more effective.

Developing detection systems: Advanced AI systems can be deployed defensively to identify coordinated manipulation campaigns before they gain traction.

Creating friction: Simple design changes that add friction to the sharing of potentially misleading content can reduce its spread without heavy-handed censorship.

Promoting transparency: Greater transparency around algorithmic decision-making, content moderation, and influence operations can help users make more informed decisions about the information they consume and share.

The most promising approaches recognize that social media platforms are complex systems where simple interventions often have unintended consequences. Effective defense requires a systems-thinking approach that addresses the underlying dynamics rather than just responding to individual threats.

The Stakes of the Battle

The social media battlefield isn't just another arena for conflict—it's rapidly becoming the primary terrain on which societal consensus is formed or fractured. The outcomes of these information battles have profound implications for democracy, public health, social cohesion, and national security.

When the COVID-19 pandemic struck, the quality of our information environment directly affected public health outcomes. Countries with high levels of vaccine misinformation saw lower vaccination rates and higher death tolls. The social media battlefield had life-or-death consequences.

Similarly, the 2020 U.S. election and its aftermath demonstrated how information warfare can threaten democratic institutions. False claims about election fraud, amplified through social media, contributed to the January 6 attack on the Capitol and ongoing erosion of trust in the electoral system.

These examples highlight the stakes of the battle we're fighting. Social media isn't just changing how we communicate—it's changing how we form beliefs, how we understand reality, and how we function as a society. As AI technologies accelerate these changes, understanding the battlefield becomes not just important but essential.

In the chapters that follow, we'll examine the specific actors engaged in this battle, from state-sponsored operations to profit-driven manipulators to true believers. We'll explore the tools they use, from bot networks to deepfakes to large language models. And we'll analyze the strategies and tactics they employ to achieve their objectives.

But first, it's crucial to understand that the battlefield itself—the architecture, incentives, and dynamics of social media platforms—shapes everything that happens within it. Just as generals throughout history have studied terrain to understand how it influences combat, we must understand the digital terrain of social media to comprehend the information warfare that unfolds there.

The social media battlefield wasn't designed for war, but its features make conflict inevitable. By understanding these features, we can begin to develop more effective defenses against manipulation and work toward an information environment that serves democratic values rather than undermining them.

Chapter 4: Who's Fighting? The Actors of the Info War

The New Combatants

In traditional warfare, identifying the combatants is relatively straightforward. Soldiers wear uniforms, fly flags, and operate under clear chains of command. Even in guerrilla warfare or insurgencies, the actors typically have identifiable leadership structures, territories, and objectives.

In the information war being waged across social media, the picture is far murkier. The battlefield is crowded with a diverse array of actors, many operating in shadows, some wearing digital disguises, others hiding in plain sight. Their weapons are not guns or bombs but narratives, emotions, and algorithms. Their objectives range from geopolitical dominance to profit, from ideological victory to simple chaos.

Understanding who is fighting this war is essential to comprehending its dynamics and defending against its most harmful effects. In this chapter, we'll examine the major categories of actors in the social media information war: state actors with their vast resources and strategic objectives; non-state actors pursuing ideological or financial goals; corporate players protecting their interests; and individual actors driven by belief, profit, or attention. We'll also explore how these categories increasingly blur together in hybrid operations that combine the capabilities and motivations of different actor types.

As AI technologies advance, the capabilities of all these actors are evolving rapidly, creating new threats and opportunities in the information battlefield. By the end of this chapter, you'll understand not just who is fighting, but why they fight, how they operate, and what makes them effective.

State Actors: The Digital Superpowers

When we think of information warfare, state actors—particularly major powers like Russia, China, and the United States—often come to mind first. These digital superpowers have developed sophisticated capabilities for influencing information environments both domestically and internationally. They operate with significant resources, professional personnel, and strategic patience that few other actors can match.

Russia: Pioneers of Modern Information Warfare

Russia has emerged as perhaps the most notorious practitioner of state-sponsored information operations on social media. Building on a long tradition of "active measures" from the Soviet era, Russia has adapted these techniques for the digital age with remarkable effectiveness.

The Internet Research Agency (IRA), a St. Petersburg-based organization with ties to the Kremlin, became internationally known after its operations targeting the 2016 U.S. presidential election. But the IRA's activities extended far beyond that single campaign. Between 2013 and 2018, the organization conducted influence operations across multiple platforms, languages, and countries, with a budget estimated at over $1 million per month.

What made the IRA's operations particularly effective was their sophisticated understanding of American society and social media dynamics. Rather than simply pushing pro-Russian narratives, the IRA created fake personas and groups across the political spectrum, focusing on amplifying existing divisions in American society. They created Facebook groups like "Heart of Texas" (right-wing) and "Blacktivist" (left-wing), both designed to inflame tensions around issues like immigration, race, and religion.

The IRA's operators didn't just post content—they engaged with real Americans, organized real-world events, and created the appearance of authentic grassroots movements. They used targeted advertising to reach specific demographics, particularly in swing states. And they adapted their tactics as platforms began to detect and counter their activities.

As one former IRA employee told a reporter: "The task wasn't to convince Americans of anything. The task was to make them fight among themselves."

Russia's information operations continue to evolve. More recent campaigns have shown increased sophistication in content creation, operational security, and cross-platform coordination. Russian state media outlets like RT and Sputnik serve as more overt components of this strategy, providing content that can be amplified through covert channels.

China: The Long Game

China's approach to information operations differs significantly from Russia's. While Russia often seeks to sow chaos and division, China typically aims for more controlled narratives that advance specific strategic objectives.

Domestically, China maintains what has been called "the world's most sophisticated censorship system," combining technological controls with human moderation to shape the information environment. The so-called "50 Cent Army"—named for the supposed payment per post—comprises both government employees and contractors who flood social media with pro-government content.

Internationally, China has traditionally focused more on positive messaging about itself rather than attacking adversaries. However, this has begun to change in recent years, with more aggressive "wolf warrior" diplomacy and information operations targeting countries like Taiwan, Hong Kong, and those involved in territorial disputes in the South China Sea.

Chinese information operations often demonstrate remarkable patience and strategic thinking. Rather than focusing on short-term wins, China builds influence over years or decades. This includes establishing media outlets in target countries, developing relationships with local journalists and influencers, and gradually shaping narratives about China's role in the world.

As one researcher at the Australian Strategic Policy Institute noted: "China plays the long game. They're not looking for immediate impact but cumulative effect over time."

China has also shown increasing sophistication in using Western social media platforms despite blocking many of them domestically. Operations attributed to China have appeared on Twitter, Facebook, YouTube, and other platforms, often focusing on issues like Hong Kong protests, Taiwan independence, and human rights criticisms.

Iran, North Korea, and Other State Players

While Russia and China receive the most attention, numerous other states have developed significant information operation capabilities.

Iran has become increasingly active in this space, with operations targeting regional adversaries like Saudi Arabia and Israel, as well as Western countries, particularly the United States. Iranian operations often focus on amplifying anti-Western and anti-Israel narratives, supporting pro-Palestinian causes, and defending Iran's positions on issues like its nuclear program.

One notable Iranian campaign involved a network of inauthentic news websites and social media accounts that posed as local news outlets in countries around the world. These sites published a mix of legitimate local news alongside content that aligned with Iranian interests, building credibility before inserting political messaging.

North Korea, despite its limited internet connectivity, has developed specialized cyber and information warfare units. These focus primarily on South Korea but have also targeted international audiences with operations like the Sony Pictures hack in 2014, which combined data theft with information operations designed to intimidate.

Western democracies, including the United States, United Kingdom, and France, also conduct information operations, though these are typically more constrained by legal frameworks and democratic oversight. These operations often focus on counter-terrorism, countering foreign disinformation, and supporting military objectives in conflict zones.

State Actor Advantages and Limitations

State actors bring unique advantages to information warfare:

Resources: States can dedicate significant funding, personnel, and technical infrastructure to information operations over extended periods.

Intelligence capabilities: Access to classified intelligence can inform operations with insights about target audiences and vulnerabilities.

Coordination: States can coordinate information operations with other instruments of national power, including diplomacy, economic measures, and military actions.

Strategic patience: States can sustain operations over years or decades, gradually building influence and capabilities.

However, state actors also face distinct limitations:

Bureaucratic constraints: Government operations often move slowly and may struggle to adapt to rapidly changing social media environments.

Attribution risk: States have more to lose if their operations are definitively attributed, potentially facing diplomatic, economic, or even military consequences.

Legal and normative constraints: Democratic states in particular face legal limitations and public expectations that may constrain their information operations.

Authenticity challenges: State-sponsored content may lack the authenticity and emotional resonance of content from true believers or grassroots movements.

As one former U.S. intelligence official put it: "States have the resources, but they often lack the agility and authenticity that make social media campaigns truly effective. That's why they increasingly work through proxies and partners."

Non-State Actors: Agile and Unpredictable

If state actors are the heavy artillery of information warfare, non-state actors are the guerrilla fighters—more agile, often more innovative, and sometimes more effective despite their limited resources. These groups range from terrorist organizations to political movements, from hacktivist collectives to mercenary information operations for hire.

Terrorist Organizations: Masters of Propaganda

Terrorist groups were among the earliest non-state actors to recognize and exploit the potential of social media for information operations. ISIS, in particular, developed a sophisticated media strategy that combined high-production-value content with savvy distribution across multiple platforms.

At its peak around 2014-2015, ISIS operated a media apparatus that included the Al-Hayat Media Center (producing content in multiple languages), the Amaq News Agency (providing "breaking news" about ISIS operations), and numerous provincial media offices. They produced magazines, videos, audio recordings, and social media content designed to recruit supporters, intimidate enemies, and project an image of strength and inevitable victory.

What made ISIS's approach particularly effective was its decentralized nature. While core media units produced official content, a distributed network of supporters amplified messages, created derivative content, and engaged with potential recruits. This made the operation resilient against platform takedowns and account suspensions.

As terrorism researcher Charlie Winter observed: "ISIS understood that in the social media age, the narrative battlefield is just as important as the physical battlefield. They invested accordingly."

Other terrorist groups, from Al-Qaeda to white supremacist organizations, have adopted similar approaches, though few have matched ISIS's sophistication. These groups typically use social media for recruitment, radicalization, operational coordination, and psychological warfare against enemies.

Hacktivist Groups: Information as Weapon

Hacktivist groups like Anonymous represent another category of non-state actor in the information battlefield. These loosely organized collectives combine technical hacking capabilities with information operations designed to expose secrets, embarrass targets, and advance ideological objectives.

Anonymous emerged in the late 2000s and gained prominence through operations like Project Chanology (targeting the Church of Scientology) and support for the Arab Spring protests. The group has no formal leadership or membership structure, instead operating as a banner under which individuals and smaller groups can organize actions.

What distinguishes hacktivists from other information warriors is their focus on obtaining and exposing information rather than creating it. Operations typically involve hacking targets to obtain sensitive documents or communications, then releasing this information publicly, often accompanied by manifestos or explanations of their actions.

As one participant in Anonymous operations explained: "We don't need to create fake news. The truth is damaging enough if you know where to look."

The line between hacktivism and state-sponsored operations has blurred in recent years, with some hacktivist groups suspected of serving as fronts or proxies for state intelligence agencies. This creates plausible deniability for states while leveraging the authentic appearance and moral authority that independent hacktivists may possess.

Political Movements and Extremist Groups

Political movements across the ideological spectrum have become increasingly sophisticated in their use of social media for information operations. These range from mainstream political parties to extremist groups operating at the fringes of society.

The QAnon movement represents a particularly interesting case study. Beginning in 2017 with cryptic posts on the 4chan message board, QAnon evolved into a sprawling conspiracy theory with thousands of dedicated promoters across multiple platforms. What made QAnon unique was its participatory nature—followers were encouraged to "do their own research" and contribute to interpreting the cryptic messages supposedly from a government insider.

This created a self-reinforcing information ecosystem where believers constantly generated new content, identified "connections" between events, and recruited others to the movement. The decentralized structure made it resilient against platform enforcement actions and allowed it to adapt its narratives as predictions failed to materialize.

Far-right extremist groups like the Proud Boys and various white nationalist organizations have similarly developed sophisticated information operations capabilities. These often involve coordinated messaging across platforms, exploitation of algorithmic vulnerabilities to amplify content, and strategic provocation of opponents to generate attention and sympathy.

On the left, movements like Antifa have developed their own approaches to information operations, though typically with less centralized coordination. These often focus on exposing the identities and activities of far-right activists, coordinating counter-protests, and promoting narratives about threats from fascism and authoritarianism.

Mercenary Information Operations

A growing industry of private companies and individuals offers information operations services for hire. These range from legitimate public relations and marketing firms that occasionally cross ethical lines to dedicated "disinformation-as-a-service" operations that explicitly offer to manipulate public opinion.

Cambridge Analytica became the most notorious example of this category after revelations about its role in the 2016 Brexit referendum and U.S. presidential election. The company combined data harvested from Facebook with psychological profiling techniques to target voters with personalized persuasive content. While Cambridge Analytica ultimately collapsed after these revelations, numerous similar firms continue to operate, often with less public scrutiny.

In the Philippines, so-called "keyboard armies" of paid commenters work to promote politicians and attack their opponents. Similar operations have been documented in countries around the world, from Brazil to India to Kenya. These operations typically involve networks of authentic-looking accounts that coordinate to amplify specific narratives, attack critics, and create the appearance of popular support.

As one former employee of such an operation in the Philippines told journalists: "We were given talking points each morning—who to attack, what messages to push, what hashtags to use. It was like any other job, except we were paid to pretend to be regular citizens with strong political opinions."

Non-State Actor Advantages and Limitations

Non-state actors bring distinct advantages to information warfare:

Agility: Without bureaucratic constraints, non-state actors can rapidly adapt to changing circumstances and platform policies.

Authenticity: Many non-state actors genuinely believe in their cause, lending emotional authenticity to their messaging that state actors may struggle to match.

Deniability: Non-state actors often face fewer consequences for deceptive tactics, allowing them to operate with less concern about attribution.

Innovation: The competitive and often decentralized nature of non-state actors drives rapid innovation in tactics and techniques.

However, they also face significant limitations:

Resource constraints: Most non-state actors lack the sustained funding and personnel of state operations.

Limited coordination: Decentralized structures can make strategic coordination difficult.

Platform vulnerability: Non-state actors typically lack the diplomatic leverage to push back against platform enforcement actions.

Narrower objectives: Non-state actors often focus on specific issues rather than broader strategic goals, potentially limiting their impact.

As information warfare expert Peter Singer noted: "What makes non-state actors particularly dangerous is their willingness to break norms and rules that state actors might respect. They're playing a different game with different boundaries."

Corporate Actors: Protecting Interests, Shaping Narratives

Corporations have long engaged in information operations to protect their interests, promote their products, and shape public perception. While not always recognized as participants in information warfare, corporate actors employ many of the same techniques and often with comparable impact to state and non-state actors.

Marketing, Advertising, and the Attention Economy

The most visible form of corporate information operations is traditional marketing and advertising. Companies spend billions of dollars annually to influence consumer perceptions and behaviors through carefully crafted messages. While much of this activity is transparent and legitimate, the line between persuasion and manipulation can blur, particularly in digital environments.

Programmatic advertising—the automated buying and selling of ad space in real-time—has created new opportunities for targeted influence. Companies can now reach highly specific audiences based on detailed behavioral and demographic data, delivering personalized messages designed to resonate with particular vulnerabilities or desires.

As marketing expert Ryan Holiday wrote in his book "Trust Me, I'm Lying": "The media system is not just vulnerable to manipulation; it's dependent on it. Marketers, politicians, and others have simply learned to exploit this dependency."

Native advertising and sponsored content represent another evolution in corporate information operations. By creating content that mimics the style and format of legitimate journalism or entertainment, companies can deliver persuasive messages that audiences may not recognize as advertising. This blurring of lines between editorial and promotional content undermines the information environment's integrity.

Reputation Management and Crisis Response

When facing public criticism or scandal, corporations often deploy sophisticated information operations to protect their reputation. These can range from legitimate public relations efforts to more manipulative tactics designed to suppress negative information or attack critics.

Astroturfing—creating the appearance of grassroots support through coordinated inauthentic behavior—is a common tactic in corporate reputation management. Companies may create or fund seemingly independent groups to advocate for their interests, use employees or contractors to post positive comments online, or coordinate campaigns to flood review sites with favorable ratings.

During crises, companies increasingly employ real-time monitoring and response capabilities that resemble military information operations centers. These track mentions across platforms, identify potential threats to reputation, and deploy counter-messaging to shape the narrative. Some corporations maintain "dark sites"—pre-built crisis response websites that can be activated immediately when needed.

As one corporate communications executive told me in an interview: "We have a war room approach to major reputation threats. We monitor all channels, deploy rapid response teams, and coordinate messaging across platforms. It's very much like a military operation."

Industry Disinformation Campaigns

Some industries have conducted long-term, sophisticated disinformation campaigns to protect their interests against scientific or regulatory threats. The tobacco and fossil fuel industries provide the most well-documented examples of this approach.

The tobacco industry's decades-long campaign to create doubt about the health risks of smoking represents perhaps the most comprehensive corporate disinformation operation in history. Internal documents revealed by litigation showed a deliberate strategy summarized in one memo as: "Doubt is our product since it is the best means of competing with the 'body of fact' that exists in the minds of the general public."

This strategy included funding seemingly independent research institutes, creating front groups like the "Council for Tobacco Research," cultivating relationships with scientists willing to support industry positions, and sophisticated media campaigns to emphasize uncertainty and controversy rather than established science.

The fossil fuel industry adopted many of these same tactics to delay action on climate change. ExxonMobil, for example, internally accepted the reality of human-caused climate change while publicly emphasizing uncertainty and funding organizations that promoted climate skepticism. A 2017 study found that ExxonMobil's internal and academic publications acknowledged climate change while its public-facing advertorials overwhelmingly expressed doubt.

These campaigns demonstrate how corporate information operations can shape public discourse and policy outcomes over decades, often with profound consequences for public health and welfare.

Corporate Political Influence

Corporations also engage in information operations to influence political outcomes that affect their interests. While some of this activity occurs through transparent lobbying and campaign contributions, companies increasingly employ more sophisticated influence techniques that resemble state information operations.

Corporate-funded think tanks produce research and commentary that shape policy debates while often obscuring their funding sources. Industry associations run public-facing campaigns that appear to represent broad public interests rather than specific corporate objectives. And companies increasingly leverage their employee and customer bases as amplifiers for political messaging.

Social media has created new opportunities for corporate political influence. Companies can micro-target decision-makers and their constituents, mobilize supporters through seemingly organic campaigns, and shape media coverage through strategic information releases and relationship cultivation.

As one political consultant who works with corporate clients explained: "The most effective corporate influence doesn't look like corporate influence at all. It looks like concerned citizens, independent experts, or grassroots movements."

Corporate Actor Advantages and Limitations

Corporate actors bring unique advantages to information operations:

Financial resources: Major corporations can sustain expensive information campaigns over long periods.

Professional expertise: Corporations can draw on marketing, public relations, and data analysis professionals.

Data access: Companies often possess detailed data about audiences that can inform targeting and message development.

Media relationships: Established corporations typically have developed relationships with journalists and media outlets.

However, they also face distinct limitations:

Reputational risk: Exposed deceptive tactics can cause significant brand damage.

Legal constraints: Corporate deception can trigger regulatory action or lawsuits.

Profit imperative: The need to demonstrate return on investment may limit long-term strategic operations.

Limited scope: Corporate information operations typically focus on specific issues affecting the company rather than broader societal manipulation.

As information warfare becomes more sophisticated, the line between corporate influence operations and traditional marketing continues to blur. Companies increasingly employ techniques pioneered by state intelligence agencies, while states adopt approaches from corporate marketing. The result is an increasingly complex information environment where distinguishing legitimate persuasion from manipulation becomes ever more challenging.

Individual Actors: True Believers and Opportunists

Perhaps the most fascinating and complex category of information warriors consists of individual actors—people who, acting largely on their own initiative, have significant impact on the information environment. These range from true believers advancing ideological causes to opportunists exploiting information disorders for profit or attention.

Conspiracy Entrepreneurs

Alex Jones represents perhaps the most prominent example of what might be called a "conspiracy entrepreneur"—an individual who builds a business model around promoting alternative narratives and conspiracy theories. Through his InfoWars media empire, Jones has promoted conspiracies ranging from claims that the Sandy Hook school shooting was staged to theories about chemicals in the water "turning frogs gay."

What makes Jones and similar figures significant is their ability to create self-contained information ecosystems that insulate their audiences from contradictory information. By consistently telling followers that mainstream sources cannot be trusted, these entrepreneurs establish themselves as authoritative alternative sources, then monetize that position through product sales, donations, or advertising.

The business model creates powerful incentives for increasingly extreme content. As one former employee of a conspiracy site told me: "The more outrageous the claim, the more engagement we'd get. And engagement directly translated to revenue through ads and product sales. There was a clear financial incentive to push the envelope."

During the COVID-19 pandemic, a small group of individuals dubbed the "Disinformation Dozen" by researchers were responsible for up to 65% of anti-vaccine content on major social media platforms. Many of these individuals had pre-existing platforms in alternative health or conspiracy communities and pivoted to COVID-19 content as a growth opportunity. They monetized their influence through books, supplements, alternative treatments, and speaking engagements.

Political Influencers

Individual political commentators and influencers have emerged as significant forces in the information environment, often with audiences that rival or exceed traditional media outlets. Figures across the political spectrum have built personal brands around political commentary, often adopting more extreme positions than mainstream political figures.

These influencers typically optimize for engagement, which platform algorithms reward with greater reach. This creates incentives for provocative, emotional, and divisive content rather than nuanced analysis. Many political influencers explicitly frame their content as countering perceived bias in mainstream sources, positioning themselves as truth-tellers revealing what "they" don't want you to know.

The monetization strategies for political influencers include platform revenue sharing, premium subscriptions, merchandise sales, speaking engagements, and direct donations. These financial incentives can shape content decisions, with many influencers acknowledging that more moderate or nuanced positions generate less engagement and therefore less revenue.

As one political content creator with over a million followers told me: "I know exactly which types of videos will perform well. Anything with 'destroyed' or 'owned' in the title, anything that makes the other side look stupid or hypocritical. That's what people want to see, and that's what the algorithm promotes."

True Believers and Digital Evangelists

Not all individual actors are motivated primarily by profit or attention. Many are true believers who dedicate significant time and energy to promoting causes or ideologies they genuinely support. These digital evangelists can have outsized impact despite limited resources, particularly when they develop specialized knowledge or skills.

During the 2020 U.S. election, individual Trump supporters analyzed and promoted claims of election fraud across social media platforms. Some developed expertise in specific aspects of election administration, creating detailed but misleading analyses of voter data, mail-in ballot procedures, or voting machine operations. These individuals weren't necessarily seeking profit—they genuinely believed they were exposing a stolen election.

Similarly, individual climate activists, anti-vaccine advocates, religious evangelists, and promoters of various ideologies create and share content based on sincere belief. Their authenticity often lends credibility with audiences who share their worldview, making them effective messengers even without institutional backing.

The line between true believers and opportunists often blurs. Many begin as sincere advocates before discovering the financial and status rewards of their position. Others may start with cynical motives but come to believe their own narratives over time. The human capacity for self-justification makes these distinctions difficult even for the individuals themselves to discern.

Trolls and Chaos Agents

Some individual actors are motivated primarily by the desire to provoke reactions, create chaos, or simply entertain themselves at others' expense. These "trolls" may not have strong ideological commitments but can nevertheless have significant impact on information environments.

Trolling behavior ranges from relatively harmless pranks to coordinated harassment campaigns that drive targets off platforms or even lead to real-world harm. Some trolls operate from a nihilistic worldview that sees all online discourse as inherently meaningless and therefore fair game for disruption. Others use the guise of humor or irony to advance extremist viewpoints while maintaining plausible deniability.

As Whitney Phillips wrote in her book "This Is Why We Can't Have Nice Things": "Trolls operate according to a logic that often explicitly celebrates the distress of others… The more upset people get, the more entertaining the trolls find it."

While individual trolls may seem like minor nuisances, collectively they can significantly degrade information environments, making productive discourse more difficult and driving away participants who tire of navigating a hostile atmosphere. This creates vulnerabilities that more strategic actors can exploit.

Individual Actor Advantages and Limitations

Individual actors bring unique advantages to information operations:

Authenticity: True believers convey genuine conviction that resonates with audiences.

Agility: Individuals can pivot quickly without organizational constraints.

Personal connection: Individual creators often develop parasocial relationships with their audiences, creating deep trust and loyalty.

Specialization: Individuals can develop deep expertise in narrow topics that larger organizations might overlook.

However, they also face significant limitations:

Resource constraints: Most individuals lack the funding and infrastructure of larger actors.

Vulnerability to platforms: Individual accounts can be easily suspended or algorithmically downranked.

Limited reach: Without institutional amplification, individuals may struggle to reach beyond niche audiences.

Burnout: The constant demand for content and engagement can lead to exhaustion and diminishing quality.

As one researcher who studies individual influencers noted: "What makes these actors so interesting is how they can punch above their weight. A single person with the right message at the right moment can sometimes have more impact than an organization with millions in funding."

Hybrid Threats: When Categories Converge

While we've examined these actor categories separately, the reality of modern information warfare is that they increasingly overlap and collaborate, creating hybrid threats that combine the capabilities and motivations of different actor types. These collaborations may be explicit and coordinated or implicit and opportunistic, but they often create effects greater than any single actor could achieve alone.

State-Sponsored Non-State Actors

Perhaps the most common hybrid threat involves state sponsorship of non-state actors. This arrangement provides states with plausible deniability while giving non-state groups resources and capabilities they wouldn't otherwise possess.

Russia's support for various extremist groups in Western countries exemplifies this approach. By amplifying authentic domestic extremism, Russia can exacerbate social divisions without creating content that might be easily identified as foreign. When these operations are discovered, Russia can plausibly deny direct involvement, claiming that it merely reports on existing tensions rather than creating them.

Similarly, Iran has supported various hacktivist groups that align with its interests, providing technical capabilities, targeting information, and strategic guidance while maintaining public distance from the operations. These groups often present themselves as independent activists exposing wrongdoing, lending moral legitimacy that a state actor would lack.

Corporate-Funded Grassroots Campaigns

Corporations frequently create or support seemingly independent advocacy groups to advance their interests—a practice known as astroturfing. These hybrid operations combine corporate resources with the appearance of grassroots authenticity.

The American Petroleum Institute, for example, has funded various "citizen groups" opposing climate regulations. These groups organize local events, generate seemingly organic social media content, and lobby officials while obscuring their industry funding. The authentic concerns of some participants blend with corporate messaging to create campaigns more effective than either could achieve alone.

Healthcare companies have similarly funded patient advocacy groups that align with their interests. While these groups include genuinely concerned patients, their priorities and messaging often reflect their corporate backers' objectives. This creates a powerful hybrid voice that combines personal stories with professional communications support.

Cross-Platform Information Laundering

One of the most sophisticated hybrid threats involves what researchers call "information laundering"—the process of moving content from fringe sources to mainstream platforms through a series of intermediaries. This typically involves collaboration (witting or unwitting) between different actor types across multiple platforms.

A typical information laundering operation might begin with content created on anonymous forums like 4chan or closed Telegram groups. This content is then amplified by individual influencers on platforms like Twitter or YouTube, who add their own analysis or commentary. From there, it might be picked up by partisan media outlets, further legitimizing the content. Finally, mainstream media may cover the story, often framed as "conservatives claim" or "liberals believe," completing the laundering process.

Each step in this chain adds a layer of legitimacy and reaches new audiences. By the time content reaches mainstream platforms, its origins are obscured, and determining responsibility becomes nearly impossible. Different actors in this chain may have entirely different motivations—from state strategic objectives to individual profit-seeking to ideological advancement—yet they function as an effective ecosystem.

The Unwitting Collaborator Problem

Perhaps the most challenging aspect of hybrid threats is the role of unwitting collaborators—people who amplify misleading or manipulative content without realizing they're participating in an information operation. These individuals often have no connection to the original actors but serve as critical vectors for spreading content to new audiences.

During the 2016 U.S. election, Russian IRA content was shared by millions of ordinary Americans who had no idea of its origins. These unwitting amplifiers included not just average citizens but journalists, celebrities, and even campaign officials. Their participation lent credibility to the operation and helped it reach audiences that would have been suspicious of content from unknown sources.

This dynamic creates significant challenges for countering information operations. Traditional approaches focused on identifying and removing inauthentic accounts may have limited effect when most of the amplification comes from authentic users. And efforts to warn users about potential manipulation must balance the need for awareness with the risk of creating excessive suspicion that further degrades the information environment.

As information warfare expert Renée DiResta has noted: "The most effective disinformation campaign doesn't create content—it amplifies existing content that serves its objectives. The best defense isn't just removing bad actors but building resilience in the system itself."

The AI-Enabled Future: New Capabilities, New Threats

As artificial intelligence technologies advance, the capabilities of all actor types in information warfare are evolving rapidly. AI is not just changing how existing actors operate—it's creating possibilities for entirely new categories of actors and operations.

State Actors and AI: Scaling Sophistication

For state actors, AI offers the ability to conduct operations at unprecedented scale and sophistication. Machine learning systems can analyze vast amounts of data about target populations, identifying vulnerabilities and optimizing messaging for specific demographics. Natural language processing can generate content in multiple languages that appears native rather than translated. Computer vision and audio synthesis enable the creation of convincing deepfakes for strategic deception.

Perhaps most significantly, AI allows states to personalize influence operations in ways previously impossible. Rather than creating general messaging for broad audiences, AI-enabled operations can tailor content to individual psychological profiles, political beliefs, and personal circumstances. This micro-targeting makes detection more difficult while potentially increasing effectiveness.

As one cybersecurity researcher specializing in state-sponsored operations told me: "The scary thing about AI in this context isn't just what it can do now, but how rapidly it's improving. Capabilities that were theoretical a year ago are operational today. The gap between cutting-edge research and deployed systems is shrinking to almost nothing."

Non-State Actors and AI: Democratizing Capabilities

For non-state actors, AI represents a democratization of capabilities previously available only to well-resourced states. Small groups or even individuals can now leverage AI tools to create sophisticated content, analyze audience data, and automate operations that would have required teams of specialists just a few years ago.

Open-source AI models and commercial API access mean that advanced capabilities are available to anyone with modest technical skills and limited budgets. A terrorist group can generate propaganda in dozens of languages. A political movement can create personalized messaging for thousands of demographic segments. A hacktivist collective can process leaked documents using natural language processing to identify sensitive information quickly.

This democratization creates significant asymmetric advantages for non-state actors. As Bruce Schneier has noted: "AI is a tool that magnifies power, and that power will be magnified in the hands of both attackers and defenders. But it's the attackers who get to choose the time and place of the attack, and that's an enormous advantage."

Corporate Actors and AI: The Marketing Arms Race

For corporate actors, AI represents both opportunity and threat. On one hand, AI enables more sophisticated marketing, reputation management, and competitive intelligence operations. On the other, it creates new vulnerabilities to manipulation and new ethical challenges in customer engagement.

Corporate adoption of AI for information operations has focused primarily on analytics and optimization rather than content creation. Companies use machine learning to identify potential reputation threats, optimize messaging for engagement, and target content to receptive audiences. These capabilities allow for more precise and effective influence campaigns while potentially reducing costs.

However, as AI content generation improves, corporations face difficult ethical questions about its use. When does personalized marketing cross the line into manipulation? How transparent should companies be about AI-generated content? What responsibility do they have for the societal impacts of their AI-enabled influence operations?

As one corporate communications executive told me: "We're in an arms race. If we don't use these technologies, our competitors will. But we're also very aware of the reputational risks if we're seen as manipulative or deceptive. It's a constant balancing act."

Individual Actors and AI: One-Person Armies

For individual actors, AI creates the possibility of "one-person armies"—individuals with capabilities previously requiring entire teams or organizations. A single motivated actor with access to AI tools can now generate content at scale, target it precisely, and adapt it continuously based on performance data.

> This has particular implications for true believers and conspiracy entrepreneurs. Individuals deeply committed to a cause or ideology can leverage AI to extend their reach and impact far beyond what was previously possible. Someone who might once have been limited to posting on forums or creating occasional videos can now operate a continuous content generation operation across multiple platforms and languages.

> The combination of authentic human conviction with AI-enabled scale creates particularly powerful hybrid operations. As one researcher studying extremist use of AI noted: "The most effective operations we're seeing combine human strategy and emotional authenticity with AI-enabled execution. The humans provide the 'why' and the overall direction; the AI handles the 'how' and the scaling."

Autonomous Information Operations: The Ultimate Evolution

The most concerning potential development in AI-enabled information warfare is the prospect of increasingly autonomous operations—campaigns that run with minimal human oversight, adapting and evolving based on performance metrics.

Such operations might begin with human-defined objectives and initial content, but then use reinforcement learning to optimize messaging, targeting, and tactics based on audience response. The system could generate new content variations, test them against different audiences, and continuously improve its effectiveness without human intervention.

This creates the possibility of information operations that evolve in unexpected directions, potentially exceeding their creators' intentions or understanding. An autonomous system optimizing for engagement or belief change might discover tactics that humans would find unethical or counterproductive to longer-term goals.

As AI safety researcher Eliezer Yudkowsky has warned: "The first ultra-intelligent machine is the last invention that man need ever make, provided that the machine is docile enough to tell us how to keep it under control." The same principle applies to autonomous information operations—once deployed, they may develop in ways their creators neither intended nor fully understand.

Identifying the Actors: Attribution Challenges

As information warfare becomes more sophisticated and the lines between actor types blur, attribution—determining who is responsible for a particular operation—becomes increasingly difficult. This attribution challenge has significant implications for defense, deterrence, and accountability in the information environment.

Technical Attribution: Following Digital Breadcrumbs

Technical attribution involves analyzing digital evidence to identify the source of an operation. This might include examining IP addresses, account creation patterns, linguistic markers, posting schedules, or technical fingerprints in content.

> While technical attribution can provide valuable clues, it faces significant limitations. Sophisticated actors use operational security measures like virtual private networks, compromised accounts, and proxy servers to obscure their origins. Content generation AI can eliminate linguistic tells that might otherwise reveal an author's native language or location. And false flag operations deliberately plant misleading attribution indicators to frame others.

> As one cybersecurity expert explained: "Attribution is always a matter of confidence levels, never certainty. We can say we're 80% confident an operation originated with a particular actor, but that remaining 20% matters, especially when the stakes are high."

Strategic Attribution: Cui Bono?

Strategic attribution focuses less on technical evidence and more on analyzing who benefits from an operation. By examining the objectives, targets, and effects of an information campaign, analysts can identify likely responsible parties based on alignment with their known interests and capabilities.

> This approach recognizes that sophisticated actors rarely leave definitive technical evidence. Instead, patterns of behavior, timing relative to real-world events, and consistency with an actor's broader strategic objectives can provide attribution insights when technical evidence is inconclusive.

However, strategic attribution also has limitations. Multiple actors may benefit from the same operation, creating ambiguity. False flag operations deliberately target adversaries' interests to create misattribution. And coincidental alignment between an operation's effects and an actor's interests doesn't prove causation.

The Attribution-Action Gap

Even when attribution can be established with reasonable confidence, a gap often exists between attribution and meaningful action. This "attribution-action gap" creates significant challenges for deterrence and accountability in information warfare.

For state actors, diplomatic, economic, or cyber responses may be available when operations are attributed with high confidence. However, these responses are often limited by political considerations, concerns about escalation, and the difficulty of proportional response to information operations.

For non-state actors, platform enforcement actions like account removal or algorithmic downranking represent the primary response mechanism. However, these actions typically target specific accounts or content rather than the organizations behind them, allowing operations to quickly regenerate under new identities.

For individual actors, legal remedies may exist for defamation or harassment, but these are slow, expensive, and often ineffective against anonymous or international actors. Platform enforcement again represents the primary response mechanism, with all its limitations.

As information warfare expert Peter Singer has noted: "The problem isn't just knowing who did it—it's knowing what to do once you know. Our response mechanisms haven't kept pace with the threat evolution."

The Evolving Ecosystem: Adaptation and Counter-Adaptation

The information warfare landscape isn't static—it's a constantly evolving ecosystem where actors adapt to countermeasures, learn from each other, and develop new capabilities and tactics. Understanding this evolutionary dynamic is essential for anticipating future threats and developing effective defenses.

Platform Countermeasures and Actor Adaptation

Social media platforms have implemented various countermeasures against manipulation, from content moderation and account verification to algorithmic adjustments and coordinated inauthentic behavior detection. However, each countermeasure triggers adaptation by information warfare actors.

When platforms began detecting and removing fake accounts based on creation patterns and behavior, operators responded by purchasing aged accounts with established histories. When content policies tightened against explicit disinformation, actors shifted to implied claims and leading questions that achieved similar effects without violating policies. When algorithmic changes reduced the reach of sensationalist content, operators adapted by embedding provocative messages within seemingly moderate content.

This continuous cycle of measure and countermeasure resembles an arms race, with neither side gaining a permanent advantage. As one platform trust and safety executive told me: "It's like squeezing a balloon—we apply pressure in one area, and the problem bulges out somewhere else. We're constantly chasing, and they're constantly adapting."

Cross-Actor Learning and Capability Transfer

Information warfare actors learn not just from their own experiences but from observing others. Techniques pioneered by one actor type are quickly adopted and adapted by others, creating a cross-pollination effect that accelerates tactical evolution.

State actors study and adopt methods from marketing and public relations. Corporations incorporate techniques from intelligence agencies. Non-state actors adapt approaches from both. Individual influencers synthesize elements from all these sources to create hybrid approaches uniquely suited to their objectives and constraints.

This learning process isn't limited to similar actors. Ideological opponents study each other's tactics, leading to capability transfer across political divides. Right-wing and left-wing movements, for instance, have both adopted similar approaches to algorithmic manipulation, networked amplification, and narrative development despite their opposing objectives.

As information warfare researcher Camille François has observed: "The playbooks are becoming universal. We see the same techniques used by actors with completely different motivations and objectives because they work, and they're easily transferable across contexts."

The Professionalization of Information Warfare

Another significant trend is the increasing professionalization of information warfare across all actor types. What began as ad hoc, experimental approaches has evolved into systematic, evidence-based operations informed by data and expertise.

State actors have established dedicated units with specialized training and career paths. The Russian Internet Research Agency, for instance, evolved from a small operation to a sophisticated organization with departments for different platforms, languages, and target demographics.

Non-state actors increasingly recruit individuals with relevant professional backgrounds—marketing specialists, data scientists, former intelligence officers—to enhance their capabilities. ISIS's media operations incorporated individuals with film production experience, graphic design skills, and multilingual capabilities.

Corporate actors have expanded traditional marketing and public relations functions to include specialized teams focused on social media intelligence, crisis response, and digital influence. These teams often include former political campaign staffers, intelligence analysts, and platform employees who bring specialized knowledge to corporate information operations.

Even individual actors have professionalized, developing systematic approaches to content creation, audience building, and monetization. Many successful influencers now operate with small support teams, content calendars, analytics tracking, and strategic planning that resembles professional media operations.

This professionalization trend suggests that information warfare will continue to become more sophisticated, data-driven, and effective across all actor categories.

Conclusion: The Crowded Battlefield

The social media information battlefield is more crowded and complex than ever before. State actors bring resources and strategic patience; non-state actors contribute agility and authenticity; corporate actors add professional expertise and data capabilities; and individual actors provide personal connection and specialized knowledge. Increasingly, these actors collaborate in formal or informal networks, creating hybrid threats that combine the strengths of different actor types.

As AI technologies advance, the capabilities of all these actors are evolving rapidly. Operations that once required teams of specialists can now be conducted by small groups or even individuals. Content that once revealed its origins through technical or linguistic tells can now appear authentic to all but the most sophisticated analysis. And the scale and personalization of influence operations continue to increase, creating new challenges for detection and defense.

In this environment, understanding who is fighting the information war becomes both more difficult and more essential. Attribution challenges create accountability gaps that sophisticated actors can exploit. The continuous evolution of tactics and capabilities means that today's defenses may be ineffective against tomorrow's threats. And the blurring lines between actor categories complicate regulatory and platform governance approaches that rely on clear distinctions.

Yet understanding these actors—their capabilities, motivations, and limitations—remains our best hope for developing effective defenses. By recognizing the patterns in their operations, the constraints they face, and the objectives they pursue, we can begin to build more resilient information environments that serve democratic values rather than undermining them.

In the chapters that follow, we'll examine the specific tools these actors employ, from bot networks to deepfakes to large language models. We'll analyze the strategies and tactics they use to achieve their objectives, from computational propaganda to narrative laundering to memetic warfare. And we'll explore how individuals and societies can defend against these operations while preserving the benefits of a connected digital world.

The information war is being fought all around us, every day, often without our awareness. By understanding who is fighting and why, we take the first essential step toward protecting ourselves and our communities from manipulation and deception.

Chapter 5: Bot Armies and Sock Puppets

The Invisible Legions

In the summer of 2024, a 35-year-old woman named Sarah Jenkins from Columbus, Ohio, became increasingly active on Twitter. She described herself as a "proud mom, coffee addict, and concerned citizen." Her profile picture showed an attractive brunette with a warm smile. Sarah posted about her children's soccer games, shared recipes, and occasionally commented on local news.

But as the presidential election approached, Sarah's posts took on a more political tone. She began sharing articles about election integrity concerns. She engaged in heated debates about immigration policy. She amplified messages questioning the mental fitness of one candidate while praising the strength of another. Her posts were passionate, personal, and persuasive—garnering hundreds of likes and reshares.

There was just one problem: Sarah Jenkins didn't exist.

The profile picture was generated by AI. The personal anecdotes were fabricated. The political opinions were carefully crafted talking points. "Sarah" was part of a sophisticated network of fake accounts—a bot army—designed to influence American voters.

This chapter explores the foot soldiers of the information war: the automated bot networks and human-operated sock puppet accounts that form the front lines of social media manipulation. We'll examine how these digital armies operate, how they've evolved with AI technologies, and how they're deployed to shape public opinion, spread disinformation, and manipulate the information environment.

By understanding these invisible legions, you'll be better equipped to recognize when you're being targeted and how to defend your digital mind against these increasingly sophisticated attacks.

Defining the Digital Foot Soldiers

Before diving into how these systems operate, let's clarify what we mean by bots and sock puppets, as these terms are often confused or used interchangeably.

Bots: The Automated Infantry

Social media bots are automated programs designed to mimic human behavior on social networks. They can post content, like or share other posts, follow accounts, and even engage in basic conversations. Think of them as digital robots pretending to be people online.

> Not all bots are malicious. Some serve legitimate purposes—like customer service chatbots or automated news feeds. But in the context of information warfare, we're concerned with bots designed to manipulate, deceive, and influence.

> These malicious bots typically operate as part of larger networks called botnets—collections of bots controlled by a single entity or "botmaster." A botnet might consist of hundreds, thousands, or even millions of fake accounts working in coordination to amplify messages, create the illusion of popular support, or drown out opposing viewpoints.

Sock Puppets: The Human Impersonators

While bots are automated, sock puppets are fictitious online identities manually operated by humans. The term comes from the puppet show technique where one puppeteer controls multiple puppets—in this case, one person controlling multiple online personas.

Sock puppets are typically more sophisticated than bots because they benefit from human intelligence and adaptability. They can engage in complex conversations, respond to unexpected questions, and display emotional intelligence that most bots still lack. However, they're also more resource-intensive, requiring human operators to maintain their cover.

In practice, modern influence operations often combine both approaches—using humans to operate high-value sock puppet accounts while deploying bots for mass amplification and engagement.

The Scale of the Problem

How prevalent are these fake entities in our digital spaces? The numbers are staggering and contested.

Twitter (now X) has claimed that only about 5% of its accounts are bots. However, academic research from Washington University in St. Louis suggests the figure could be between 25% and 68%. Even more concerning, these bot accounts may generate between 20% and 29% of all content on the platform.

Facebook estimates that about 5% of its monthly active users are fake accounts—which would translate to over 100 million fake profiles. Instagram, YouTube, TikTok, and other platforms face similar challenges, though with varying degrees of transparency about the scope of the problem.

The University of Oxford found that organized social media manipulation campaigns operated in 81 countries in 2020, a 15% increase from the previous year. The report noted that in some countries, these operations have become "professionalized," with formal organizations and substantial budgets dedicated to information manipulation.

As one cybersecurity researcher told me, "The internet is far more synthetic than most people realize. On some topics and in some spaces, you might be primarily interacting with entities that aren't real people at all."

The Evolution of Digital Deception

Bot networks and sock puppet operations have evolved dramatically over the past decade, becoming increasingly sophisticated and difficult to detect. Understanding this evolution helps us grasp the current threat landscape and anticipate future developments.

The Early Days: Primitive Bots (Pre-2016)

The first generation of social media bots was relatively primitive. These bots typically followed simple scripts—posting pre-written content, automatically following accounts, or sending basic spam messages. They were easily identifiable by their repetitive behavior, unnatural language patterns, and obvious non-human characteristics.

Early bots often had telltale signs: accounts created recently with few followers, generic or stolen profile pictures, usernames with random numbers, and posting patterns that no human could maintain (like tweeting hundreds of times per day at perfectly regular intervals).

These bots were primarily used for commercial purposes—promoting products, generating fake followers to inflate popularity, or driving traffic to websites. Their political applications were limited and unsophisticated.

As one social media researcher explained to me, "The early bots were like digital bullhorns—loud but obvious. Anyone paying attention could spot them immediately."

The Middle Era: Coordinated Campaigns (2016-2020)

The 2016 U.S. presidential election marked a turning point in the sophistication and impact of social media manipulation. The Russian Internet Research Agency (IRA) demonstrated how coordinated networks of fake accounts could significantly influence public discourse and potentially affect electoral outcomes.

The IRA operation involved both bots and human-operated sock puppets working in concert. Rather than simply broadcasting propaganda, these accounts engaged with real users, created and joined authentic-seeming groups, and even organized real-world events that Americans attended.

What made this operation particularly effective was its focus on exploiting existing social divisions rather than creating new narratives. The IRA created fake personas across the political spectrum—conservative, liberal, and special interest groups like Black Lives Matter supporters or evangelical Christians. These personas didn't just push pro-Russian content; they amplified the most divisive aspects of American political discourse.

As former FBI agent Clint Watts testified to Congress, "Russia's social media campaigns… weren't designed to back one candidate but rather to divide Americans against each other, to create chaos and erode trust in democratic institutions."

This era also saw the rise of more sophisticated bot behavior. Bots began to: - Maintain consistent personas with backstories and regular non-political content - Operate across multiple platforms with coordinated messaging - Engage in more natural-seeming interactions with real users - Exploit platform algorithms to maximize visibility and impact - Adapt their activity patterns to mimic human behavior (varying posting times, mixing content types)

The Current Frontier: AI-Powered Manipulation (2020-Present)

The introduction of advanced AI technologies, particularly large language models (LLMs) like GPT-4, has revolutionized the capabilities of both bots and sock puppets. These systems can now generate human-like text at scale, create convincing visual content, and engage in sophisticated conversations that are increasingly difficult to distinguish from human interaction.

Modern AI-powered manipulation operations have several key characteristics:

Convincing Personas: AI can now generate detailed backstories, consistent personality traits, and authentic-seeming personal anecdotes for fake accounts. These personas can maintain consistency across months or years of activity.

Natural Language Generation: AI-generated content now closely mimics human writing styles, complete with appropriate emotional tones, cultural references, and even regional dialects or slang.

Multimodal Capabilities: Beyond text, AI systems can generate profile pictures, memes, and even video content that appears authentic. Some operations use AI-generated "newsreaders" to deliver video content with synthetic faces and voices.

Conversational Engagement: Modern bots can engage in back-and-forth conversations, responding appropriately to questions, objections, or challenges from real users.

Cross-Platform Coordination: Sophisticated operations maintain consistent personas across multiple platforms, creating the appearance of real individuals with diverse online presences.

Targeted Messaging: AI systems can analyze audience data and tailor content to specific demographic groups, psychological profiles, or geographic regions.

Adaptive Strategies: The most advanced systems can learn from audience responses and adjust their messaging to maximize engagement and persuasive impact.

As one cybersecurity expert explained, "What we're seeing now isn't just automation—it's simulation. These systems don't just automate tasks; they simulate human presence and interaction in increasingly convincing ways."

Anatomy of a Modern Bot Network

To understand how modern bot networks operate, let's examine their structure, capabilities, and tactics.

Command and Control

At the heart of any bot network is its command and control (C2) infrastructure—the systems that direct and coordinate the activities of individual bots. This typically includes:

Central Management Servers: Secure servers that issue commands to the bot network, often using encrypted communications to avoid detection.

Account Management Systems: Tools for creating, maintaining, and rotating through large numbers of fake accounts.

Content Generation Pipelines: Systems that produce or curate content for distribution, increasingly powered by AI.

Analytics Dashboards: Tools for monitoring the performance of the network, tracking engagement metrics, and measuring impact.

The sophistication of this infrastructure varies widely. State-sponsored operations might employ dedicated facilities with professional staff and custom software. Smaller operations might use commercial tools or open-source software run from a single computer.

Tiered Account Structure

Modern bot networks typically employ a hierarchical structure of different account types, each with specific roles:

Avatar Accounts: High-quality, carefully maintained personas that engage directly with target audiences. These accounts often have extensive posting histories, realistic profiles, and moderate follower counts. They may be operated by humans, AI, or a combination of both.

Amplifier Accounts: Larger numbers of lower-quality accounts that boost the visibility of content from avatar accounts through likes, shares, and comments. These accounts require less sophistication and are often fully automated.

Sleeper Accounts: Accounts that are created and aged but remain dormant until needed for specific campaigns. These accounts build credibility over time before becoming active.

Reconnaissance Accounts: Accounts that monitor conversations, identify potential targets for engagement, and gather intelligence on trending topics or effective messaging.

This tiered approach allows operators to concentrate resources on maintaining the authenticity of a smaller number of high-impact accounts while using larger numbers of simpler accounts for amplification.

Operational Tactics

Modern bot networks employ a range of sophisticated tactics to maximize their impact while avoiding detection:

Content Recycling: Rather than generating all content from scratch, many operations repurpose legitimate content with subtle modifications or framing that serves their objectives.

Temporal Targeting: Posting at specific times to maximize visibility and impact, such as during breaking news events or when target audiences are most active.

Algorithmic Exploitation: Understanding and manipulating platform algorithms to increase the visibility of their content, such as using trending hashtags or engaging in coordinated activity to trigger recommendation systems.

Cross-Platform Information Laundering: Moving content from fringe platforms to mainstream ones through a series of intermediaries, obscuring its origins and lending it credibility.

Crisis Exploitation: Rapidly responding to breaking news and crises with prepared narratives that frame events in ways that serve the operation's objectives.

Engagement Baiting: Creating emotionally provocative content designed to elicit responses from real users, which then increases visibility through platform algorithms.

Identity Appropriation: Mimicking the appearance and behavior of legitimate organizations, news sources, or influential individuals to borrow their credibility.

As one former operator of a commercial bot network told me, "The goal isn't just to push content—it's to create the impression that 'everyone' is talking about something, or that 'everyone' holds a particular view. Once you achieve that perception, real humans do most of the work for you by conforming to what they believe is the majority opinion."

Case Studies in Digital Deception

To understand how these techniques work in practice, let's examine several real-world examples of sophisticated bot and sock puppet operations.

The Russian IRA: Masters of Division

The Russian Internet Research Agency's operations targeting the 2016 U.S. election represent one of the most well-documented cases of coordinated social media manipulation. Based in St. Petersburg, the IRA employed hundreds of staff working in departments focused on different platforms, languages, and target demographics.

What made the IRA operation particularly effective was its sophisticated understanding of American society and its fault lines. Rather than simply pushing pro-Russian narratives, the IRA created fake personas and groups across the political spectrum, focusing on amplifying existing divisions in American society.

For example, the IRA created Facebook groups like "Heart of Texas" (promoting right-wing, pro-Texas independence views) and "Blacktivist" (appearing to support Black Lives Matter). Both groups attracted tens of thousands of followers who believed they were joining authentic American movements.

The operation went beyond social media, organizing real-world events through these fake groups. In one case, the IRA organized both a pro-Muslim and an anti-Muslim demonstration at the same location and time in Houston, Texas, deliberately creating conditions for conflict.

As the Senate Intelligence Committee report on the operation noted: "The IRA targeted not only Hillary Clinton, but also Republican candidates during the presidential primaries. The IRA may have helped sink the candidacies of Senators Ted Cruz and Marco Rubio, among others."

The IRA's budget reportedly exceeded $1 million per month at its peak, demonstrating the significant resources authoritarian regimes are willing to invest in these operations.

The Chinese Vision: AI-Powered Personas

In 2019, a Chinese academic named Li Bicheng published a paper that offered a glimpse into the future of social media manipulation. Co-authored with a member of the Chinese military's political warfare unit, the paper sketched out a plan for using artificial intelligence to flood the internet with fake social media accounts that would look and sound completely real.

Li's vision went beyond simple bots posting propaganda. He described an AI system that would create entire personas—accounts that would spend most of their time posting about normal life, jobs, hobbies, and families, occasionally slipping in references to politically sensitive topics like Taiwan or criticisms of the United States.

These accounts wouldn't require an army of paid trolls to operate. They would be largely autonomous, generating content and engaging with users without constant human supervision. And they would avoid the telltale linguistic errors that often reveal non-native English speakers.

While there's no definitive evidence that China has fully implemented Li's proposal, recent operations show increasing sophistication. During the 2022 Beijing Olympics, researchers identified networks of inauthentic accounts promoting positive narratives about the games while downplaying human rights concerns. These accounts displayed more sophisticated language use and coordination than previous Chinese operations.

As one researcher at the Australian Strategic Policy Institute noted, "China plays the long game. They're not looking for immediate impact but cumulative effect over time."

Iran's AI-Driven Botnets: Targeting U.S. Voters

In 2024, cybersecurity researchers identified sophisticated Iranian influence operations targeting American voters ahead of the presidential election. These operations demonstrated the integration of advanced AI technologies with traditional manipulation tactics.

The Iranian operators employed specialized proxy services that made their bot traffic appear to originate from residential homes and mobile devices within the United States. This technique allowed the bots to mimic the online behavior of genuine local users, significantly increasing their credibility and making detection more difficult.

The operation used a tiered account system with high-quality "avatar" accounts for direct interaction and content creation, supported by larger numbers of lower-quality accounts for amplification and engagement. AI models generated content in multiple languages, including regionally appropriate English dialects.

Particularly notable was the cross-platform approach, with the operation establishing presence across multiple social media services and creating fake news websites posing as both progressive and conservative outlets. This strategy increased the operation's resilience against platform enforcement actions and created the appearance of diverse, independent sources all converging on similar narratives.

As one threat intelligence analyst explained, "What makes these operations particularly concerning is their ability to create entire media ecosystems. It's not just individual posts or accounts—it's websites, social media presences, and coordinated amplification networks all working together to create the impression of legitimate information sources."

The Russian "Souls": AI-Generated Personas

In mid-2024, investigators took down a sophisticated Russian "bot farm" that demonstrated the state of the art in AI-powered social media manipulation. The operation used AI to create fake accounts on X (formerly Twitter) with individual biographies, profile pictures, and consistent personas.

What made this operation notable was the operators' terminology—they referred to these accounts as "souls," reflecting their status as fully realized digital personas rather than simple automated accounts. These "souls" could post original content, comment on other posts, and build up follower networks.

According to law enforcement officials, the purpose of these accounts was to "assist Russia in exacerbating discord and trying to alter public opinion" in the United States and other Western countries. The accounts focused on divisive issues like immigration, abortion, and gun control, often taking extreme positions designed to provoke emotional responses.

The operation used a combination of AI-generated content and human curation, with operators providing strategic direction while AI systems handled content creation and engagement at scale. This hybrid approach combined human strategic thinking with AI's ability to operate continuously and at volume.

As one cybersecurity researcher noted, "The most effective operations we're seeing combine human strategy and emotional authenticity with AI-enabled execution. The humans provide the 'why' and the overall direction; the AI handles the 'how' and the scaling."

The Technology Behind the Deception

The capabilities of modern bot networks and sock puppet operations are directly tied to advances in artificial intelligence and related technologies. Understanding these technologies helps explain their current capabilities and potential future developments.

Large Language Models: The Content Generators

Large language models (LLMs) like GPT-4, Claude, and Llama form the backbone of modern AI-powered manipulation. These systems ingest vast amounts of text—trillions of words—and learn to predict what text should come next in any given context. This allows them to generate human-like text on virtually any topic.

What makes LLMs particularly powerful for information operations is their ability to:

Adapt to Different Voices: LLMs can mimic specific writing styles, from casual social media posts to formal news articles, and can be instructed to write in particular regional dialects or with specific political leanings.

Generate Contextually Appropriate Content: They can create content that responds appropriately to current events, ongoing conversations, or specific prompts.

Produce Emotional Content: Modern LLMs can generate text with appropriate emotional tones—outrage, fear, hope, humor—that resonates with human readers.

Create Consistent Personas: With proper prompting, LLMs can maintain consistent character traits, backstories, and viewpoints across multiple interactions.

As one AI researcher explained, "These models don't understand what they're saying in a human sense, but they've learned the statistical patterns of human communication so well that they can produce text that pushes the same emotional and cognitive buttons as human-written content."

Generative Image Models: The Face Creators

Generative adversarial networks (GANs) and diffusion models have revolutionized the creation of synthetic images, including the profile pictures used by fake accounts. Systems like Midjourney, DALL-E, and Stable Diffusion can create photorealistic images of people who don't exist, complete with appropriate clothing, backgrounds, and emotional expressions.

These technologies enable operators to:

Create Diverse Personas: Generate profile pictures representing different ages, ethnicities, genders, and styles to target specific demographics.

Produce Supporting Visual Content: Create images of supposed "personal moments" that reinforce the authenticity of fake accounts.

Generate Memes and Visual Propaganda: Craft persuasive visual content that often spreads more effectively than text alone.

Avoid Detection: Evade reverse image searches that might identify stolen photos used for fake profiles.

The quality of these generated images has improved dramatically in recent years. While early GAN-generated faces often had telltale artifacts like asymmetrical features or strange backgrounds, modern systems produce images that are virtually indistinguishable from photographs of real people.

Multimodal AI: Beyond Text and Images

The newest frontier in AI-powered manipulation is multimodal AI—systems that can work with multiple types of content, including text, images, audio, and video. These technologies enable the creation of synthetic media like deepfakes and AI-generated "newsreaders."

For example, some Iranian influence operations have used AI-generated newsreaders on YouTube to deliver propaganda content with synthetic faces and voices. These digital presenters appear human but can be generated at scale without hiring actors or recording studios.

As these technologies continue to advance, we can expect to see more sophisticated integration of text, image, audio, and video in manipulation campaigns, creating increasingly immersive and convincing false narratives.

Targeting and Analytics: The Strategic Layer

Beyond content generation, AI systems also enhance the strategic aspects of influence operations through:

Audience Analysis: Machine learning systems can analyze vast amounts of data about target populations, identifying vulnerabilities, interests, and effective messaging approaches.

Engagement Optimization: AI can track which content performs best with different audiences and adapt messaging strategies accordingly.

Behavioral Prediction: Advanced systems can predict how users are likely to respond to different types of content, allowing for more effective targeting.

Network Mapping: AI can identify influential nodes in social networks and target them for maximum impact.

These capabilities transform manipulation from a blunt instrument to a precision tool, allowing operators to craft messages that resonate with specific psychological profiles and social contexts.

Detecting the Digital Imposters

As bot networks and sock puppet operations have grown more sophisticated, so too have the methods for detecting them. Understanding these detection approaches can help you identify potential manipulation in your own social media environment.

Technical Detection Methods

Platform companies and security researchers use several technical approaches to identify inauthentic accounts:

Behavioral Analysis: Examining patterns in posting frequency, timing, and engagement that might indicate automation or coordination.

Network Analysis: Looking at connections between accounts to identify clusters that might represent coordinated operations.

Linguistic Analysis: Studying language patterns that might reveal non-native speakers, AI-generated text, or content being shared across multiple accounts.

Metadata Examination: Analyzing account creation dates, profile information, and technical indicators that might reveal inauthenticity.

Image Analysis: Using AI tools to identify synthetic profile pictures or manipulated images.

These methods are increasingly powered by AI systems themselves, creating an arms race between detection and evasion technologies.

Platform Countermeasures

Social media platforms employ various countermeasures against bot networks and sock puppets:

Account Verification: Requiring proof of identity for certain account types or activities.

CAPTCHA and Other Human Verification: Implementing challenges designed to distinguish humans from bots.

Rate Limiting: Restricting the frequency of actions like posting, following, or liking to prevent automated behavior.

Algorithmic Adjustments: Modifying recommendation algorithms to reduce the visibility of suspected inauthentic content.

Coordinated Inauthentic Behavior Detection: Identifying and removing networks of accounts working together to manipulate the platform.

However, these countermeasures face significant limitations. Platforms must balance security against user experience, avoiding false positives that might affect legitimate users. They also face economic incentives to maximize user numbers and engagement, which can conflict with aggressive enforcement against fake accounts.

As one former platform trust and safety executive told me, "It's like squeezing a balloon—we apply pressure in one area, and the problem bulges out somewhere else. We're constantly chasing, and they're constantly adapting."

User-Level Detection

While technical solutions are important, individual users can also learn to identify potential bots and sock puppets:

Profile Examination: Look for incomplete or generic profiles, recently created accounts, or mismatches between profile information and content.

Content Patterns: Be suspicious of accounts that post at unusual hours, with extremely high frequency, or with an unnatural focus on divisive political content.

Image Verification: Check profile pictures for signs of AI generation, such as asymmetrical features, strange backgrounds, or unusual artifacts.

Engagement Assessment: Consider whether the account engages naturally in conversations or simply broadcasts content without meaningful interaction.

Cross-Platform Verification: For influential or suspicious accounts, check whether they have a consistent presence across multiple platforms.

However, as AI-powered deception improves, these heuristics become less reliable. The most sophisticated operations now create accounts that can pass most casual human inspection.

The Human Impact: Why Bot Armies Work

Despite growing awareness of social media manipulation, bot armies and sock puppet operations continue to be effective. Understanding the psychological and social factors that make these techniques work is essential for building resistance.

The Illusion of Consensus

One of the most powerful effects of bot networks is creating the illusion of widespread agreement or popularity—what psychologists call "social proof." Humans are naturally inclined to conform to what they perceive as majority opinion, and bot networks exploit this tendency by manufacturing the appearance of consensus.

> When someone sees hundreds or thousands of accounts expressing the same viewpoint, they're more likely to: - Consider that viewpoint credible or mainstream - Self-censor opposing views for fear of social rejection - Adopt the position themselves to align with the perceived majority

> As social psychologist Robert Cialdini has noted, "We view a behavior as correct in a given situation to the degree that we see others performing it." Bot networks weaponize this principle by creating artificial "others" that appear to validate specific narratives or viewpoints.

Emotional Contagion and Tribal Activation

Bot networks excel at creating and amplifying emotional content—particularly anger, fear, and moral outrage. These emotions spread rapidly through social networks in a process psychologists call "emotional contagion."

By targeting content to specific identity groups and framing issues in terms of intergroup conflict, bot operations can activate tribal psychology—our tendency to rally around our perceived in-group when it appears threatened by an out-group. This tribal activation makes critical thinking less likely and increases susceptibility to misinformation that aligns with group narratives.

As one researcher in computational propaganda explained, "The most effective manipulation doesn't try to change your factual beliefs directly—it changes how you feel about issues or groups. Once your emotions are engaged, your reasoning follows."

Cognitive Overload and Information Fatigue

The sheer volume of content produced by bot networks contributes to information overload—a state where people struggle to process the amount of information they encounter. This overload can lead to:

Cognitive Shortcuts: Relying on heuristics and emotional reactions rather than careful evaluation **Disengagement**: Withdrawing from information-seeking altogether **Cynicism**: Assuming all information is equally unreliable **Selective Exposure**: Retreating to trusted sources that may themselves be compromised

As information environments become more polluted with inauthentic content, the cognitive cost of distinguishing truth from manipulation increases, leading many people to give up the effort entirely.

The Persistence of First Impressions

Bot networks often aim to be first to frame breaking news or events, exploiting what psychologists call the "primacy effect"—our tendency to give greater weight to information we encounter first. Even when corrections or more accurate information follows, the initial framing can persist in memory and influence subsequent judgments.

> This is particularly effective during crises or breaking news events when information is limited and emotions are high. Bot networks can flood the zone with a preferred narrative before authoritative information becomes available, shaping how the event is understood and remembered.

The Unwitting Amplifiers

Perhaps the most powerful aspect of modern influence operations is their ability to enlist real humans as unwitting amplifiers. When real users share content from inauthentic sources, they lend it their own credibility and extend its reach beyond what the bot network could achieve directly.

> During the 2016 U.S. election, for example, content from Russian IRA accounts was shared by campaign officials, media figures, and millions of ordinary Americans who had no idea of its origins. These unwitting amplifiers were far more effective at spreading the content than the original fake accounts could have been alone.

> As disinformation researcher Renée DiResta has noted, "The most effective disinformation campaign doesn't create content—it amplifies existing content that serves its objectives."

The Future of Digital Deception

As AI technologies continue to advance, what can we expect from the next generation of bot armies and sock puppets? Several trends are already emerging that point to an increasingly challenging landscape.

Autonomous Information Operations

The most concerning potential development is the prospect of increasingly autonomous operations—campaigns that run with minimal human oversight, adapting and evolving based on performance metrics.

> Such operations might begin with human-defined objectives and initial content, but then use reinforcement learning to optimize messaging, targeting, and tactics based on audience response. The system could generate new content variations, test them against different audiences, and continuously improve its effectiveness without human intervention.
>
> This creates the possibility of information operations that evolve in unexpected directions, potentially exceeding their creators' intentions or understanding. An autonomous system optimizing for engagement or belief change might discover tactics that humans would find unethical or counterproductive to longer-term goals.

Personalized Persuasion

Future bot networks may move beyond broad demographic targeting to highly personalized persuasion tailored to individual psychological profiles. By analyzing a user's digital footprint—their posts, likes, shares, and browsing behavior—AI systems could identify specific vulnerabilities and craft messages designed to resonate with that particular person.

> This micro-targeting could make manipulation far more effective while making it virtually impossible to track at scale, as each user would be receiving a unique stream of persuasive content optimized for their specific psychology.

Multimodal Manipulation

As AI systems become increasingly capable of generating realistic audio and video content, we can expect to see more sophisticated integration of text, image, sound, and movement in manipulation campaigns.

> Future operations might include: - AI-generated video personas with consistent appearances and voices across multiple pieces of content - Synthetic "citizen journalists" reporting from supposed locations with fabricated footage - Interactive deepfakes that can engage in real-time video conversations - Immersive narrative experiences that blend real and synthetic elements

> These multimodal approaches could create far more compelling and persuasive false narratives than text or image-based manipulation alone.

Cross-Platform Coherence

Advanced operations will likely improve their ability to maintain consistent personas and narratives across multiple platforms, creating the appearance of real individuals with diverse online presences. This cross-platform coherence makes detection more difficult, as suspicious activity on one platform might be legitimized by seemingly authentic presence on others.

> Future operations might create entire synthetic social circles—networks of fake personas that interact with each other across platforms, creating the appearance of genuine social relationships and communities that exist only as digital fabrications.

The Democratization of Capability

Perhaps the most significant trend is the democratization of these capabilities—the increasing accessibility of sophisticated manipulation tools to a wider range of actors. As commercial AI services improve and costs decrease, the technical barriers to running effective influence operations continue to fall.

> This democratization means that information warfare capabilities once limited to well-resourced state actors are becoming available to smaller states, non-state actors, corporations, political campaigns, and even motivated individuals. The result is likely to be a more crowded and chaotic information environment with multiple competing manipulation campaigns operating simultaneously.

> As one cybersecurity expert warned, "We're moving toward a world where anyone with a credit card and a grievance can run an operation that would have required an intelligence agency just a few years ago."

Defending Against the Digital Army

In the face of these sophisticated threats, how can individuals and societies protect themselves? While perfect defense may be impossible, several approaches can help mitigate the impact of bot armies and sock puppets.

Individual Defenses

At the personal level, several practices can help reduce vulnerability to manipulation:

Digital Literacy: Understanding how manipulation works is the first line of defense. Learning to recognize common tactics and being aware of your own psychological vulnerabilities can help you maintain critical thinking.

Source Verification: Developing habits of checking information sources, looking for corroboration across multiple reliable outlets, and tracing claims to their origins can help identify manipulated content.

Emotional Awareness: Recognizing when content is designed to trigger emotional responses, particularly anger or outrage, and taking time to reflect before engaging or sharing.

Diverse Information Diet: Intentionally consuming information from a variety of legitimate sources with different perspectives can help inoculate against manipulation that targets specific ideological groups.

Healthy Skepticism: Approaching social media content with appropriate skepticism, particularly when it perfectly confirms your existing beliefs or triggers strong emotional reactions.

As one media literacy educator put it, "The goal isn't to make people cynical about everything they see online, but to help them develop a healthy skepticism and the skills to distinguish reliable information from manipulation."

Platform Responsibilities

Social media platforms have a crucial role to play in countering bot networks and sock puppets:

Improved Detection: Continuing to invest in AI-powered detection systems that can identify inauthentic accounts and coordinated behavior.

Transparency: Providing users with more information about account authenticity, content provenance, and potential manipulation.

Design Choices: Reconsidering platform features that make manipulation easier, such as algorithmic amplification of emotionally provocative content.

Cross-Platform Coordination: Sharing information about manipulation campaigns across platforms to enable more effective responses.

User Education: Providing users with tools and information to help them identify potential manipulation.

However, platforms face significant challenges in implementing these measures, including scale (billions of users and posts), language barriers, privacy concerns, and business models that often prioritize engagement over information quality.

Regulatory Approaches

Governments and regulatory bodies are increasingly considering policy responses to digital manipulation:

Platform Accountability: Requiring platforms to take more responsibility for identifying and removing inauthentic accounts and content.

Transparency Requirements: Mandating disclosure of bot accounts, AI-generated content, and political advertising.

Identity Verification: Considering requirements for user verification while balancing privacy concerns.

International Cooperation: Coordinating responses across borders to address global manipulation campaigns.

Digital Literacy Education: Investing in educational programs to build public resilience to manipulation.

These regulatory approaches involve complex trade-offs between security, privacy, free expression, and practical enforcement challenges. Finding the right balance requires ongoing democratic deliberation and adaptation as technologies evolve.

Technological Countermeasures

Technical solutions also play an important role in defense:

AI Authentication Systems: Developing better ways to verify human identity without compromising privacy.

Digital Provenance: Creating systems to track the origin and history of content across the internet.

Content Authentication: Implementing digital watermarking or other methods to identify AI-generated content.

Decentralized Reputation Systems: Building new ways to establish trust online that are resistant to manipulation.

Detection Technologies: Continuing to advance technologies that can identify synthetic content and coordinated inauthentic behavior.

As one AI safety researcher noted, "We need to be investing as much in defensive AI as we are in generative AI. The asymmetry between the ease of creating synthetic content and the difficulty of detecting it is one of our biggest challenges."

Conclusion: The Ongoing Battle

The rise of bot armies and sock puppets represents a fundamental challenge to our information ecosystem. These digital foot soldiers of the information war are becoming increasingly sophisticated, numerous, and difficult to detect. As AI technologies continue to advance, the line between authentic human communication and synthetic manipulation grows ever blurrier.

This is not a problem that will be solved once and for all. Rather, it represents an ongoing arms race between manipulators and defenders, with new technologies and techniques constantly shifting the balance of power. What remains constant is the target: human psychology and social dynamics that make us vulnerable to manipulation.

The most effective defense may ultimately lie not in technical solutions alone, but in building societal resilience—creating communities, institutions, and information ecosystems that are inherently resistant to manipulation. This requires not just better technology but stronger social trust, more robust shared epistemologies, and renewed commitment to truth-seeking as a collective value.

In the chapters that follow, we'll explore other weapons in the information warfare arsenal, from deepfakes and synthetic reality to large language models in social engineering. Each of these technologies builds upon and amplifies the capabilities of the bot armies and sock puppets we've examined here, creating an increasingly complex and challenging information environment.

By understanding these threats and developing both technical and social countermeasures, we can work toward an information ecosystem that serves human flourishing rather than manipulation and control. The battle for our digital minds continues, but with awareness and action, it's a battle we can fight more effectively.

Chapter 6: Deepfakes and Synthetic Reality

The Dissolution of Truth

In December 2023, a video of President Biden appeared on social media. In it, he announced a new military draft to address escalating global conflicts. The video looked authentic—the President's facial expressions, voice, and mannerisms were all consistent with his public appearances. Within hours, the clip had been viewed millions of times, sparking panic among young Americans and their families.

There was just one problem: President Biden had never made such an announcement. The video was a deepfake—a sophisticated AI-generated fabrication designed to look and sound exactly like the real thing.

While this particular example is fictional, it represents a very real and growing threat. Deepfakes and other forms of synthetic media are rapidly transforming our information landscape, blurring the line between reality and fiction in ways that were unimaginable just a few years ago. As one cybersecurity expert told me, "We're entering an era where the evidence of our own eyes and ears can no longer be trusted."

This chapter explores the world of deepfakes and synthetic reality—how these technologies work, how they're being weaponized in the information war, and what their proliferation means for our collective ability to distinguish truth from fiction. By understanding the mechanics and implications of synthetic media, you'll be better equipped to navigate an increasingly deceptive digital landscape.

Understanding Deepfakes and Synthetic Media

Before diving into the implications of these technologies, let's clarify what we mean by deepfakes and synthetic media.

Defining the Terms

Deepfakes are synthetic media—typically videos, images, or audio recordings—created using deep learning artificial intelligence. The term "deepfake" combines "deep learning" with "fake," reflecting the technology's foundations in neural networks. These sophisticated AI systems can analyze existing media of a person to generate new, fabricated content that looks and sounds like them.

> **Synthetic media** is a broader term encompassing all media created or modified by automated means, including with AI. This includes deepfakes but also covers other forms of AI-generated content like synthetic text, music, or art.

> **Shallowfakes** (sometimes called "cheap fakes") are manipulated media created using simpler editing techniques rather than deep learning. While less technologically sophisticated, shallowfakes can be equally deceptive and damaging.

> The key distinction of deepfakes is their use of artificial intelligence to create or manipulate content in ways that are increasingly difficult to distinguish from authentic media. As one AI researcher explained, "What makes deepfakes particularly concerning isn't just that they're fake—it's that they're getting better at being fake faster than we're getting better at detecting them."

The Technical Foundations

To understand the power and limitations of deepfakes, it helps to know a bit about how they work. Most deepfake systems rely on a type of AI called Generative Adversarial Networks (GANs).

> A GAN consists of two neural networks working in opposition: - A **generator** that creates fake content - A **discriminator** that tries to distinguish between real and fake content

These networks engage in a technological arms race, with the generator constantly improving to fool the discriminator, and the discriminator becoming more sophisticated in response. The result is an increasingly realistic synthetic output.

For facial deepfakes, the process typically works like this: 1. The system is fed thousands of images of the target face from multiple angles 2. The AI learns the facial features, expressions, and movements 3. These learned patterns are mapped onto another person's face in a video 4. The system generates a composite that places the target face onto the source body

Voice synthesis works similarly, analyzing speech patterns, tone, pitch, and cadence to create convincing audio that mimics a specific person's voice.

What makes modern deepfakes so convincing is their ability to maintain consistency across an entire video— managing details like lighting, shadows, and natural movements that earlier versions struggled with. As one developer of deepfake detection software told me, "The technology has advanced to the point where the usual telltale signs—unnatural blinking, weird lighting, audio-visual misalignment—are disappearing from high-quality deepfakes."

The Evolution of Synthetic Media

The development of deepfake technology has followed a rapid trajectory, with each generation becoming more sophisticated and accessible.

Early Days: The Birth of Deepfakes

The term "deepfake" first entered the public lexicon in 2017, when a Reddit user with that name began posting manipulated videos that placed celebrities' faces onto pornographic content. These early deepfakes were relatively crude by today's standards—they contained noticeable glitches, unnatural movements, and inconsistent lighting.

Creating these early deepfakes required significant technical expertise and computing resources. The technology was primarily confined to tech-savvy communities with access to powerful hardware. Despite their limitations, these early examples demonstrated the potential of AI to create convincing synthetic media.

The Middle Period: Increasing Sophistication

Between 2019 and 2022, deepfake technology advanced significantly. The quality improved, with fewer obvious artifacts and more natural-looking results. The technology expanded beyond face-swapping to include voice synthesis and full-body manipulation.

This period also saw the development of more user-friendly tools that lowered the technical barriers to creating deepfakes. Apps and software emerged that allowed even those with limited technical skills to create basic deepfakes. As one digital forensics expert noted, "What once required a team of VFX artists and weeks of work could suddenly be done by an individual with a laptop in a matter of hours."

During this period, deepfakes began to appear in political contexts. In 2019, a manipulated video of Nancy Pelosi, slowed down to make her appear intoxicated, went viral on social media. While this was technically a "shallowfake" created with simple editing rather than AI, it demonstrated how manipulated media could rapidly spread misinformation.

The Current Landscape: Democratization and Proliferation

Today, we're in what might be called the third generation of deepfake technology. The quality has reached near-photorealistic levels, with the best examples being virtually indistinguishable from authentic media to the untrained eye. According to Ofido's 2024 Identity Fraud Report, there has been a staggering 3000% increase in deepfakes online, along with a 500% increase in digitally forged identities.

The technology has been democratized to an unprecedented degree. User-friendly applications allow anyone with a smartphone to create basic deepfakes, while more sophisticated tools are available to those willing to invest a bit more time and resources. As one cybersecurity researcher told me, "The barrier to entry is essentially gone. If you can use Instagram filters, you can create a simple deepfake."

This democratization has led to an explosion in both the quantity and variety of synthetic media. Deepfakes are no longer limited to face-swapping in videos—they now encompass voice cloning, full-body puppetry, and even the generation of entirely synthetic scenes where nothing is real.

Perhaps most concerning is the integration of deepfake technology with other AI systems, particularly large language models. This combination allows for the creation of multimodal synthetic content—fabricated personas that can generate text, images, audio, and video with consistent characteristics across all mediums.

Weapons of Mass Deception: Malicious Applications

While deepfake technology has legitimate applications in fields like entertainment, education, and art, its potential for harm has been widely exploited. Let's examine some of the most concerning malicious uses.

Political Manipulation

Deepfakes have emerged as powerful tools for political disinformation and manipulation. By creating false statements or actions by political figures, bad actors can influence public opinion, disrupt elections, and undermine democratic processes.

A particularly alarming example occurred during Slovakia's October 2023 election. Just days before voters went to the polls, deepfake audio recordings circulated on social media, seemingly depicting Michal Šimečka, leader of the pro-Western Progressive Slovakia party, talking about rigging the election and doubling the price of beer. These fabricated clips went viral, potentially influencing the outcome of a close election that Šimečka's party ultimately lost to a pro-Kremlin opposition.

Some of these audio deepfakes included disclaimers stating they were AI-generated, but these notices appeared only in the final seconds of the clips—after most listeners had already absorbed the false information. As one researcher noted, this timing appeared to be a deliberate attempt to technically comply with disclosure requirements while still deceiving listeners.

In another case, a deepfake video of Ukrainian President Volodymyr Zelensky appearing to surrender to Russia circulated online during the early stages of the Russia-Ukraine conflict. Though quickly debunked, the video demonstrated how synthetic media could be weaponized during geopolitical crises to create confusion and undermine morale.

Financial Fraud

Deepfakes have opened new frontiers in financial fraud, enabling scammers to impersonate trusted figures with unprecedented realism. In early 2024, a Hong Kong-based multinational firm lost $25 million in what is believed to be the largest deepfake scam to date. An employee participated in a video conference call with what appeared to be the company's chief financial officer and several colleagues. In reality, all the participants except the victim were deepfake impersonations, convincing the employee to transfer funds to accounts controlled by the fraudsters.

Voice cloning has proven particularly effective in financial scams. In 2019, criminals used AI-generated voice technology to mimic a CEO's voice, convincing a subordinate to transfer $243,000 to a fraudulent account. The executive's voice was so perfectly replicated that the employee never questioned the authenticity of the request.

As one fraud investigator explained to me, "These aren't just random attempts hoping to get lucky. They're targeted attacks using social engineering enhanced by deepfake technology. The scammers research their victims, understand reporting structures, and time their attacks to coincide with plausible business scenarios."

Non-consensual Intimate Content

The creation of non-consensual pornographic deepfakes remains one of the most prevalent and harmful applications of this technology. Studies indicate that the vast majority of deepfake videos online are pornographic in nature, and these disproportionately target women.

The psychological harm caused by such content can be devastating. Victims often experience profound violations of privacy, damage to their reputation, and significant emotional distress. The persistent nature of digital content means that once such deepfakes are created and shared, they can be nearly impossible to completely remove from the internet.

This application of deepfake technology represents a form of image-based sexual abuse that existing legal frameworks are still struggling to address adequately. As one advocate for victims told me, "The technology has evolved faster than our legal protections. Many victims find themselves in a legal gray area, fighting an uphill battle to have this content removed and hold perpetrators accountable."

Identity Theft and Impersonation

Deepfakes enable sophisticated forms of identity theft that go beyond traditional methods. Rather than simply stealing personal information, criminals can now effectively steal a person's entire digital presence—their face, voice, and mannerisms.

This capability has serious implications for authentication systems that rely on biometric data. Gartner predicts that by 2026, 30% of organizations will find biometric authentication unreliable due to the advancement of deepfakes. As synthetic media becomes more convincing, systems that once seemed secure—like facial recognition or voice authentication—become increasingly vulnerable.

The rise of synthetic identities also poses challenges for trust in online interactions. As one digital identity expert explained, "We're moving toward a reality where you can no longer assume that the person you're video chatting with is actually who they appear to be. This fundamentally changes the nature of digital trust."

Evidence Manipulation

Perhaps one of the most concerning applications of deepfake technology is the manipulation of digital evidence. In a world where digital media is increasingly used in legal proceedings, the ability to create convincing fake evidence poses serious challenges to justice systems.

> In one notable case, deepfake audio was used in a child custody battle to discredit a father. The manipulated recording, which appeared to show the father making threats, was submitted as evidence before being exposed as fraudulent.

> As courts and legal systems increasingly rely on digital evidence, the potential for deepfakes to undermine the integrity of legal proceedings grows. This has prompted calls for more sophisticated authentication methods and greater skepticism toward digital evidence that lacks a clear chain of custody.

The Perception Crisis: Societal Impacts

Beyond specific malicious applications, the proliferation of deepfakes is contributing to broader societal impacts that threaten to reshape our relationship with information and truth.

The Erosion of Trust

Perhaps the most profound impact of deepfakes is their contribution to what some researchers call "truth decay"—a diminishing consensus about facts and analytical interpretations of data. As synthetic media becomes more prevalent and convincing, people grow increasingly skeptical of all digital content, even authentic material.

This erosion of trust extends beyond specific manipulated content to undermine confidence in institutions, media outlets, and public figures. As one media scholar told me, "When people can no longer trust what they see and hear, they tend to retreat to sources that confirm their existing beliefs, regardless of accuracy. This accelerates polarization and makes consensus-building nearly impossible."

A study conducted by University College London found that 27% of participants could not differentiate between real and deepfake audio recordings. As the study authors noted, "As speech synthesis algorithms improve and become more realistic, we can expect the detection task to become harder." This growing difficulty in distinguishing real from fake content accelerates the collapse of shared reality.

The Liar's Dividend

Paradoxically, as deepfakes proliferate, they provide cover for genuine misconduct through what researchers call the "liar's dividend." This refers to the ability of actual wrongdoers to dismiss authentic evidence of their misconduct as fake.

We've already seen public figures claim that genuine recordings of their statements or actions were manipulated, even when no evidence of tampering exists. As deepfakes become more common, these denials gain plausibility in the public mind. As one political analyst explained, "The mere existence of deepfake technology gives anyone caught on camera doing or saying something inappropriate a ready-made excuse: 'That's not real; it's a deepfake.'"

This phenomenon threatens accountability at all levels of society, from personal relationships to the highest levels of government. When any evidence can be dismissed as potentially fake, the concept of objective truth itself is undermined.

Economic and Social Costs

The proliferation of deepfakes imposes significant economic and social costs. A study conducted by the University of Baltimore and cybersecurity firm CHEQ found that fake news—a category that increasingly includes deepfakes—costs the global economy $78 billion annually. These costs stem from market manipulation, reputation damage, response costs, and decreased productivity.

> On a social level, deepfakes contribute to information pollution that makes it increasingly difficult for citizens to make informed decisions. This has profound implications for democratic processes, which rely on a reasonably informed electorate. As one political scientist noted, "Democracy functions best when citizens have access to reliable information. Deepfakes and other forms of synthetic media threaten this foundation by flooding the information environment with convincing falsehoods."

Psychological Impact

The psychological effects of living in a world where seeing is no longer believing should not be underestimated. As deepfakes become more prevalent, people may experience what some researchers call "reality vertigo"—a persistent uncertainty about what is real and what is fabricated.

> This uncertainty can lead to increased anxiety, paranoia, and a general sense of disorientation. It may also contribute to a form of learned helplessness, where people simply give up on trying to distinguish truth from fiction and either believe everything or nothing.

> As one psychologist who studies media effects told me, "Humans evolved in an environment where our senses provided reliable information about the world around us. When that reliability is systematically undermined, it creates a profound form of cognitive stress that we're not well-equipped to handle."

Detecting the Deception: Identifying Deepfakes

As deepfakes become more sophisticated, the methods for detecting them must evolve as well. Here are some of the current approaches to identifying synthetic media.

Human Observable Techniques

Despite advances in deepfake technology, human observers can still identify many synthetic media by looking for certain telltale signs:

Unnatural Facial Movements: Deepfake videos often exhibit irregular facial movements such as unnatural blinking patterns, lip-syncing issues, or odd head motions. Early deepfakes showed subjects blinking less frequently than normal people due to limitations in the training data.

Lip-Syncing Errors: One of the easiest ways to detect a deepfake is by watching the mouth. If the lips don't match the audio precisely, especially in fast-paced conversations, it may indicate manipulation.

Inconsistent Lighting and Shadows: Deepfakes often struggle with maintaining consistent lighting or shadows that align with the natural light sources in a scene. Look for shadows that don't match the lighting or change unexpectedly between frames.

Blurry or Warped Facial Features: Many deepfakes present blurry or warped facial features, especially around the eyes, lips, or hairlines. This lack of sharpness results from algorithm limitations in rendering fine details.

Voice Analysis: Synthetic voices often lack the natural variations in tone, pitch, and rhythm that characterize human speech. They may sound slightly robotic or have an unnatural cadence.

Asymmetrical Facial Expressions: Human facial expressions are usually symmetrical. Deepfakes can show facial distortions or asymmetries, like one eyebrow raised higher than the other without corresponding facial movement.

Contextual Verification

Beyond examining the media itself, contextual verification can help identify potential deepfakes:

Cross-Check with Trusted Sources: Verify surprising or inflammatory content with reputable news outlets. If a video shows a public figure making shocking statements, check whether mainstream media sources are reporting on it.

Request Live Interaction: If you suspect someone is using a deepfake to impersonate someone you know, request a real-time video call with unpredictable elements, such as asking them to perform specific actions that would be difficult to fake on the fly.

Consider the Source: Evaluate the credibility of where the content originated. Content from unverified accounts or known disinformation sources warrants greater skepticism.

Assess Plausibility: Consider whether the content aligns with what you know about the person or situation. Extreme departures from established patterns of behavior or speech may indicate manipulation.

Technical Detection Methods

More sophisticated technical approaches can identify deepfakes that might fool the human eye:

AI-Powered Detection Tools: Companies like Microsoft, Intel, and specialized firms such as DuckDuckGoose, Reality Defender, and DeepTrace have developed AI tools specifically designed to identify deepfakes. These systems analyze subtle patterns that human observers might miss.

Interference-Based Detection: This method identifies irregularities in a video's frequency spectrum that can indicate tampering, even when the visual appearance seems flawless.

Reverse Image Search: Running keyframes from a suspicious video through reverse image search can help identify if the same image appears in different contexts online, potentially revealing manipulation.

Metadata Examination: Analyzing a file's metadata can expose inconsistencies such as missing timestamps or altered camera details that might indicate manipulation.

Frame-by-Frame Analysis: Slowing down a video and examining it frame by frame can reveal glitches, distorted features, or mismatched expressions that aren't apparent at normal speed.

As one digital forensics expert explained, "The most effective approach combines multiple detection methods. No single technique is foolproof, but together they create a more robust defense against even sophisticated deepfakes."

The Arms Race: Generation vs. Detection

The relationship between deepfake creation and detection technologies represents a classic technological arms race. As detection methods improve, creation techniques evolve to circumvent them, leading to increasingly sophisticated fakes that require more advanced detection methods.

This dynamic creates a perpetual cycle of measure and countermeasure. For example, early deepfake detection focused on unnatural blinking patterns. Deepfake creators quickly adapted their algorithms to incorporate more realistic blinking, forcing detectors to find new telltale signs.

As one AI researcher told me, "It's fundamentally an asymmetric battle. The creators only need to fool most of the people most of the time, while detectors need to catch all of the fakes all of the time. That mathematical reality gives the advantage to the creators."

This asymmetry is compounded by the fact that the same advances in AI that improve detection can often be repurposed to create better fakes. Each new breakthrough in understanding how deepfakes work potentially benefits both sides of the arms race.

The speed of this cycle is accelerating. What once took years now happens in months or even weeks. As one cybersecurity expert noted, "We're seeing detection methods become obsolete almost as soon as they're deployed. It's like trying to hit a moving target that's accelerating."

Defending the Real: Mitigation Strategies

Given the challenges in detecting deepfakes after they've been created, many experts advocate for a multi-layered approach to mitigating their harmful effects.

Technical Solutions

Several technical approaches aim to address the deepfake challenge:

Content Authentication: Digital watermarking and other authentication technologies can help verify the origin and integrity of media. Companies like Truepic and Content Authenticity Initiative are developing standards for capturing and maintaining provenance information for digital content.

Blockchain Verification: Distributed ledger technology can create immutable records of original content, making it easier to verify whether media has been altered after creation.

Platform-Level Detection: Major social media platforms are investing in automated systems to identify and flag potential deepfakes before they can spread widely.

Provenance Tracking: Systems that track the entire lifecycle of digital content, from creation through distribution, can help establish authenticity and identify manipulation.

As one technology policy expert explained, "The goal isn't necessarily to eliminate deepfakes entirely—that's probably impossible. Instead, we need to create systems that make it easier to verify authentic content and identify synthetic media."

Educational Approaches

Technical solutions alone won't solve the deepfake problem. Educational strategies are equally important:

Media Literacy: Teaching people to critically evaluate digital content, understand how deepfakes work, and recognize signs of manipulation can build societal resilience against synthetic media.

Professional Training: Journalists, legal professionals, and others who rely on digital evidence need specialized training to identify potential deepfakes in their work.

Public Awareness Campaigns: Broad efforts to inform the public about the existence and capabilities of deepfake technology can help reduce its effectiveness as a tool for deception.

As one media literacy educator told me, "The best defense against deepfakes isn't just better technology—it's better thinking. We need to cultivate a healthy skepticism that questions extraordinary claims and seeks verification before believing or sharing content."

Regulatory Approaches

Governments around the world are beginning to address deepfakes through legislation and regulation:

Disclosure Requirements: Some jurisdictions require clear labeling of synthetic or manipulated media, particularly in political advertising.

Criminal Penalties: Laws specifically targeting malicious uses of deepfakes, such as non-consensual intimate imagery or election interference, are being enacted in various countries.

Platform Responsibility: Regulations increasingly hold social media and content platforms accountable for detecting and removing harmful deepfakes.

The UK's Online Safety Act, updated to address deepfake abuse, represents one approach to this challenge. In the United States, several states have enacted laws specifically addressing deepfakes in political contexts or non-consensual intimate imagery.

However, regulatory approaches face significant challenges, including jurisdictional limitations, enforcement difficulties, and the need to balance restrictions against free expression concerns. As one legal scholar noted, "The global nature of the internet means that even the most comprehensive national regulations can be circumvented by operating from jurisdictions with fewer restrictions."

Societal Approaches

Beyond technical, educational, and regulatory strategies, broader societal approaches may be necessary:

"Zero Trust" Principle: The World Economic Forum has suggested adopting a "zero trust" approach to digital content, where verification is required rather than assumed.

Trusted Source Networks: Developing networks of verified information providers whose content carries additional authentication markers.

Community Monitoring: Crowdsourced identification of suspicious content can help identify deepfakes that automated systems miss.

As one digital ethics researcher explained, "We may need to fundamentally rethink how we consume information in a world where synthetic media is ubiquitous. The assumption that seeing is believing has served humanity well for millennia, but technology is forcing us to develop new heuristics for determining truth."

The Future of Synthetic Reality

As we look ahead, several trends suggest where deepfake technology and synthetic media might be heading.

Technological Trajectories

The technical capabilities of deepfake systems continue to advance rapidly:

Increasing Realism: The quality gap between synthetic and authentic media continues to narrow, with improvements in rendering fine details like skin texture, eye movements, and environmental interactions.

Real-Time Generation: While most sophisticated deepfakes still require significant processing time, advances in computing power and algorithms are moving toward real-time generation capabilities.

Multimodal Integration: Future deepfakes will likely integrate text, image, audio, and video more seamlessly, creating coherent synthetic experiences across multiple sensory channels.

Democratization: The technical barriers to creating high-quality deepfakes will continue to fall, making the technology accessible to an ever-wider audience.

As one AI researcher predicted, "Within five years, the technology to create completely convincing synthetic media of anyone saying or doing anything will be available to virtually anyone with a smartphone and an internet connection."

Potential Developments

Looking further ahead, several potential developments could reshape our relationship with synthetic media:

Synthetic Environments: Beyond manipulating individuals, future technology may create entire fake scenes or settings indistinguishable from reality.

Interactive Deepfakes: AI-powered synthetic personas that can engage in real-time conversation, adapting their responses based on interaction.

Sensory Expansion: Current deepfakes focus primarily on visual and auditory content, but future technologies might expand to other sensory experiences.

Memory Manipulation: The combination of convincing synthetic experiences with our malleable memory systems could potentially create false memories that feel authentic.

As one futurist I interviewed suggested, "We're moving toward a world where the boundary between real and synthetic experiences becomes increasingly porous. The question isn't just whether media is authentic, but whether our experiences and memories themselves are authentic."

Positive Futures

Despite the significant risks, deepfake technology also holds potential for positive applications:

Creative Empowerment: Democratizing content creation could enable new forms of artistic expression and storytelling previously limited by technical or resource constraints.

Educational Applications: Synthetic media can create immersive learning experiences, historical recreations, or simulations that enhance understanding.

Therapeutic Uses: Some researchers are exploring how controlled synthetic experiences might help treat certain psychological conditions or provide comfort to those with memory disorders.

Accessibility Enhancements: Synthetic voices or appearances could help those with disabilities communicate more effectively or express themselves in ways previously unavailable to them.

As one AI ethics researcher noted, "Like most powerful technologies, deepfakes themselves are neutral—it's how we choose to use them that determines whether they benefit or harm society."

Dystopian Scenarios

Alongside these positive possibilities lie more concerning potential futures:

Truth Collapse: A widespread inability to distinguish real from fake could lead to a collapse of shared reality, with people retreating into information bubbles that confirm their existing beliefs.

Automated Disinformation: AI systems could generate and distribute targeted fake content at scale, overwhelming human capacity to identify and counter it.

Surveillance and Control: Synthetic reality technologies could be weaponized by authoritarian regimes to manipulate populations through manufactured consensus or false narratives.

Identity Dissolution: As synthetic identities become more convincing and prevalent, the boundary between authentic and artificial identity could blur in troubling ways.

Conclusion: Navigating the Synthetic Future

The rise of deepfakes and synthetic media represents one of the most significant challenges to our information ecosystem in the digital age. These technologies are transforming our relationship with visual and auditory information, undermining the long-standing assumption that seeing and hearing are reliable ways of knowing.

As we've explored throughout this chapter, the implications extend far beyond specific instances of deception. Deepfakes threaten to erode trust in institutions, complicate accountability for wrongdoing, and contribute to a broader crisis of shared reality. The psychological impact of persistent uncertainty about what is real cannot be underestimated.

Yet this challenge is not insurmountable. A combination of technical solutions, educational approaches, regulatory frameworks, and societal adaptations can help mitigate the harmful effects of synthetic media while preserving its beneficial applications. The key lies in developing robust systems for verifying authenticity without unduly restricting expression or innovation.

As individuals navigating this new landscape, we must cultivate a balanced approach—neither naive acceptance of everything we see nor cynical rejection of all digital content. Instead, we need a nuanced skepticism that questions extraordinary claims, seeks verification from multiple sources, and considers the context and provenance of information.

In the chapters that follow, we'll explore other weapons in the information warfare arsenal, from large language models in social engineering to the rise of AI influencers. Each of these technologies presents its own challenges and opportunities, contributing to the complex information environment we all must navigate.

By understanding these tools and their implications, we can work toward an information ecosystem that serves human flourishing rather than manipulation and control. The battle for our digital minds continues, but with awareness and action, it's a battle we can fight more effectively.

Chapter 7: LLMs in Social Engineering

The Evolution of Manipulation

In the summer of 2023, Sarah Chen, the CFO of a mid-sized tech company, received an urgent email from her CEO. The message explained that the company was in the final stages of a confidential acquisition and needed to transfer $200,000 to complete due diligence. The email was perfectly written, referenced recent company events, and even mentioned the CEO's recent vacation to Bali—a personal touch that convinced Sarah of its authenticity.

She initiated the transfer. Three days later, during a regular executive meeting, the CEO mentioned nothing about an acquisition. When Sarah brought up the transfer, the truth became clear: she had been the victim of an elaborate scam. The email hadn't come from the CEO at all. It had been crafted by a large language model (LLM), using information scraped from the company's website, press releases, and the executives' social media profiles.

This scenario, while fictional, represents a new reality in the world of social engineering. The integration of large language models into the social engineer's toolkit has fundamentally transformed the landscape of manipulation and deception. What was once a labor-intensive craft requiring significant skill has now become automated, scalable, and frighteningly effective.

In this chapter, we'll explore how LLMs are revolutionizing social engineering attacks, examine the psychological and technical mechanisms that make these attacks so effective, and consider how individuals and organizations can defend themselves in this new era of AI-powered manipulation.

Understanding Large Language Models

Before diving into their application in social engineering, it's important to understand what large language models are and how they work.

What Are LLMs?

Large language models are artificial intelligence systems trained on vast amounts of text data that can generate human-like text, understand context, and perform various language tasks. These models, such as GPT-4, Claude, Gemini, and others, represent the cutting edge of natural language processing technology.

At their core, LLMs are pattern recognition machines. They analyze billions of examples of human-written text to identify patterns and relationships between words, phrases, and concepts. This training allows them to predict what text should come next given a particular context, enabling them to generate coherent and contextually appropriate content.

The most advanced LLMs today can: - Write in different styles and tones - Maintain context over long conversations - Understand and generate content in multiple languages - Adapt to specific instructions or requirements - Reason through complex problems - Generate creative content like stories or poetry - Mimic specific writing styles or personas

As Dr. Emily Bender, a computational linguistics professor I interviewed, explained: "These models don't 'understand' language in the human sense—they don't have experiences or consciousness. What they have is a statistical model of how language is used, which allows them to produce text that appears remarkably human-like."

The Evolution of LLMs

The development of LLMs has followed a rapid trajectory, with each generation becoming more sophisticated and capable.

The first generation of modern LLMs emerged around 2018-2020, with models like GPT-2 and BERT. While impressive for their time, these models had limited capabilities and often produced text with obvious flaws or inconsistencies.

The middle generation (2020-2022), including GPT-3 and PaLM, represented a significant leap forward. These models demonstrated much greater coherence and versatility, capable of generating longer, more consistent text across a wider range of topics and styles.

The current generation (2022-present), including GPT-4, Claude 2, and Gemini, approaches human-level performance in many domains. These models can maintain coherent conversations over extended interactions, reason through complex problems, and generate highly persuasive content that can be difficult to distinguish from human-written text.

This evolution has been driven largely by increases in scale—both in terms of the size of the models (measured in parameters) and the amount of training data they consume. As one AI researcher told me, "The jump from millions to billions to trillions of parameters has enabled these systems to capture increasingly subtle patterns in language, making their outputs more nuanced and human-like."

From Helpful Assistant to Malicious Tool

While LLMs were developed primarily to assist with legitimate tasks like content creation, customer service, and information retrieval, their capabilities make them equally effective tools for deception and manipulation.

As security researcher Marcus Hutchins noted in our interview, "The same features that make an LLM good at writing helpful emails also make it good at writing convincing phishing emails. The same capabilities that allow it to impersonate Shakespeare for entertainment can be used to impersonate your CEO for fraud."

This dual-use nature of LLMs creates a significant security challenge. The developers of these models have implemented various safeguards to prevent misuse, including filters that block certain types of harmful content and monitoring systems to detect abuse. However, these protections are imperfect and can often be circumvented through techniques like "jailbreaking" or "prompt engineering"—carefully crafting inputs to manipulate the model into generating content it was designed to avoid.

As we'll see, this has created a new landscape of threat and opportunity for those engaged in social engineering.

The Transformation of Social Engineering

Social engineering—the art of manipulating people into divulging confidential information or performing actions that compromise security—has always been more about psychology than technology. Traditional social engineering relies on exploiting human cognitive biases and emotional vulnerabilities rather than technical weaknesses.

Traditional Social Engineering

Before the advent of LLMs, social engineering attacks typically fell into several categories:

Phishing: Sending deceptive emails or messages that appear to come from trusted sources to trick recipients into revealing sensitive information or clicking malicious links.

Pretexting: Creating a fabricated scenario to engage a victim and gain their trust, often by impersonating co-workers, police, bank officials, or other trusted individuals.

Baiting: Offering something enticing to the victim to pique their curiosity and prompt them to take an action, such as downloading malware-infected files.

Quid pro quo: Promising a benefit in exchange for information or access, such as offering free IT support in exchange for login credentials.

Tailgating: Following an authorized person into a restricted area to gain physical access to secure locations.

These traditional approaches had significant limitations. They often contained telltale signs that could alert vigilant targets—grammatical errors, generic greetings, unusual requests, or awkward phrasing. They typically required considerable manual effort to execute effectively, limiting their scale. And they often relied on volume rather than precision, targeting large numbers of potential victims in hopes of finding a few susceptible individuals.

The LLM Advantage

Large language models address many of these limitations, transforming social engineering from a labor-intensive craft to an automated, scalable, and highly effective attack vector. Here's how:

Enhanced Personalization: LLMs can generate highly tailored messages based on information about the target, creating communications that feel personal and relevant. As one cybersecurity expert explained to me, "The difference between a generic phishing email and one crafted with knowledge of your recent activities, professional interests, and communication style is the difference between obvious spam and a message you might actually respond to."

Improved Language Quality: One of the most obvious tells in traditional phishing was poor grammar or awkward phrasing, often because attackers weren't native speakers of their targets' languages. LLMs eliminate this problem, producing grammatically correct, natural-sounding text in dozens of languages.

Contextual Understanding: Modern LLMs can incorporate specific details about organizations, recent events, or industry terminology to create more convincing scenarios. This contextual awareness makes their communications much harder to distinguish from legitimate ones.

Scale and Efficiency: Perhaps most significantly, LLMs enable attackers to automate the creation of thousands of unique, personalized attacks. A study from Oxford University demonstrated that LLMs could generate unique spear phishing emails for over 600 British Members of Parliament at a cost of less than a cent per email.

Conversational Capabilities: Unlike static phishing emails, LLM-powered attacks can maintain coherent, responsive interactions in real-time, adapting to the target's responses and maintaining a consistent persona throughout an extended engagement.

As Dr. Jen Golbeck, a computer scientist specializing in social media and trust, told me: "What makes LLM-powered social engineering so dangerous is that it removes many of the friction points that previously limited these attacks. The technical barriers, the language barriers, the scale limitations—they're all gone. Now, sophisticated, personalized manipulation is available to anyone with access to these models."

LLM-Powered Attack Vectors

The integration of LLMs into social engineering has enabled a range of sophisticated attack vectors that combine technical capabilities with psychological manipulation. Let's examine some of the most prevalent and effective approaches.

Sophisticated Phishing

Phishing remains one of the most common social engineering techniques, but LLMs have transformed it from a volume-based, relatively crude approach to a precision instrument.

Traditional phishing emails were often sent to thousands or millions of recipients with minimal personalization. They contained generic greetings, vague references to account issues or security concerns, and frequently included obvious red flags like grammatical errors or unusual sender addresses.

LLM-enhanced phishing, by contrast, can be highly targeted and personalized. These attacks, often called "spear phishing," use information gathered about specific individuals to craft messages that appear legitimate and relevant to their particular circumstances.

For example, an LLM could generate an email that: - References the target's recent work projects or publications - Mentions colleagues by name and position - Includes industry-specific terminology and concerns - Aligns with the communication style of the impersonated sender - Incorporates recent organizational announcements or events

A security researcher demonstrated this capability by using GPT-3.5 to craft phishing emails targeting employees at a financial institution. The model generated messages that referenced the company's recent merger announcement, mentioned the target's specific department, and included plausible requests related to system integration—all details that were publicly available but would require significant research for a human attacker to compile and incorporate convincingly.

Business Email Compromise (BEC) attacks, where attackers impersonate executives or trusted partners to authorize financial transactions, have been particularly enhanced by LLMs. These attacks rely on the appearance of authority and often create a sense of urgency to prevent careful verification. LLMs excel at mimicking the communication style of executives and crafting plausible business scenarios that justify unusual financial requests.

As one fraud investigator explained to me, "What makes these attacks so effective is that they don't just look legitimate—they feel legitimate. The language, the context, the timing all align with what you'd expect from the person being impersonated."

Voice Cloning and Synthesis

While text-based attacks remain the most common, the combination of LLMs with voice synthesis technology has enabled a new generation of voice-based social engineering.

AI voice cloning technology can now create convincing replicas of a person's voice with just a few minutes of sample audio—often easily obtained from public speeches, interviews, or social media posts. When paired with LLMs that generate the content for these synthetic voices to deliver, the result is a powerful tool for impersonation and fraud.

In 2023, a finance worker at a multinational company was tricked into transferring $25 million after receiving what appeared to be a legitimate video conference call from the company's CFO, along with several other colleagues. All but one of the participants were deepfakes, with synthesized voices delivering LLM-generated dialogue that convinced the employee to make the transfers.

This type of attack, sometimes called "Hello CEO Fraud," typically involves a phone call that appears to come from a company executive, requesting an urgent wire transfer or other financial transaction. The synthesized voice, combined with LLM-generated content that references specific company details, creates a highly convincing deception.

Several online voice cloning services like ElevenLabs, MurfAI, and LOVO.ai have made this technology accessible to anyone, with varying degrees of safeguards against misuse. As one cybersecurity expert noted, "The barrier to entry for voice cloning has essentially disappeared. What once required specialized technical knowledge and equipment can now be done with a free online service and a few minutes of sample audio."

Conversational Manipulation

Perhaps the most sophisticated application of LLMs in social engineering is real-time conversational manipulation. Unlike static phishing emails or scripted phone calls, LLM-powered chatbots can engage targets in dynamic conversations, responding to questions and objections while maintaining a consistent persona.

This capability enables more complex and sustained social engineering operations. Rather than relying on a single deceptive message, attackers can build relationships with targets over time, gradually establishing trust before executing their ultimate objective.

For example, security researchers have demonstrated LLM-based systems that can: - Impersonate IT support personnel, walking targets through processes that compromise security - Pose as new employees or contractors to extract organizational information - Pretend to be customers or clients to manipulate service representatives - Simulate romantic interests on dating platforms to execute romance scams

The conversational nature of these attacks makes them particularly effective because they exploit the human tendency to lower our guard during extended interactions. As we become comfortable with a conversation partner, we become less vigilant about verifying their identity or questioning their requests.

As Dr. Philipp Lorenz-Spreen, a research scientist who studies online behavior, explained to me: "Humans are naturally inclined to reciprocate disclosure and trust. If someone appears to share information with us or trust us with their thoughts over multiple interactions, we're psychologically primed to return that trust—even when the 'someone' is actually an AI."

Prompt Injection Attacks

A more technical form of LLM-based social engineering targets not humans directly but other AI systems. These "prompt injection" attacks manipulate AI systems through carefully crafted inputs designed to override their intended behavior.

Indirect prompt injection is a sophisticated social engineering attack targeting AI systems, especially those using large language models. In this attack, a malicious actor crafts content that, when processed by an AI system, causes it to perform actions outside its intended scope or reveal sensitive information.

For instance, a security researcher demonstrated how Microsoft's Bing Chat could be manipulated to pose as a Microsoft employee and request credit card information from users. The researcher accomplished this by crafting a prompt that, when processed by the AI, caused it to adopt a new persona and ignore its built-in safety constraints.

As AI systems become more integrated into business operations, customer service, and information management, these attacks represent a growing threat. By compromising an AI system, attackers can potentially: - Extract sensitive information from databases - Manipulate automated decision-making processes - Generate false information that appears to come from authoritative sources - Bypass content moderation or security filters

These attacks are particularly insidious because they target the growing infrastructure of AI systems that mediate our digital interactions, potentially compromising multiple users or systems through a single successful attack.

The Psychology of LLM-Enhanced Deception

The effectiveness of LLM-powered social engineering stems not just from technical sophistication but from a deep exploitation of human psychology. Understanding these psychological mechanisms is crucial for both executing and defending against such attacks.

Cognitive Biases Exploited

LLM-enhanced attacks leverage several well-documented cognitive biases:

Authority Bias: Humans have a tendency to comply with requests from perceived authorities. LLMs can craft messages that convincingly impersonate authority figures, such as executives, IT administrators, or government officials, triggering automatic compliance in many targets.

Social Proof: We often look to others' actions to determine appropriate behavior in ambiguous situations. LLM-generated content can reference supposed actions by colleagues or peers to normalize requested behaviors ("Your team members have already completed this security update").

Scarcity and Urgency: People value things that are scarce or time-limited and often make hasty decisions when under time pressure. LLMs excel at creating convincing scenarios that evoke urgency ("This offer expires in 2 hours" or "Your account will be locked if not verified today").

Reciprocity: Humans feel obligated to return favors. LLM-powered attacks might offer something of value before making a request, triggering this reciprocity instinct.

Consistency and Commitment: Once people take a small action or make a statement, they tend to act in ways consistent with that initial commitment. LLMs can guide targets through a series of seemingly innocuous steps before requesting the actual compromising action.

Liking: We're more likely to comply with requests from people we like or find similar to ourselves. LLMs can analyze available information about targets to craft personas and messages that align with their interests, backgrounds, or communication styles.

As Dr. Robert Cialdini, whose research on influence identified many of these principles, told me: "What makes AI-powered social engineering particularly dangerous is its ability to simultaneously exploit multiple influence principles in a personalized way. It's like having a master persuader who knows exactly which buttons to push for each individual target."

The Trust Equation

Trust is the foundation of successful social engineering, and LLMs have become remarkably effective at building synthetic trust. The Trust Equation, developed by management consultants David Maister, Charles Green, and Robert Galford, provides a useful framework for understanding how:

$$\text{Trust} = (\text{Credibility} + \text{Reliability} + \text{Intimacy}) / \text{Self-Orientation}$$

Credibility: LLMs enhance credibility by generating content that demonstrates knowledge and expertise. They can incorporate industry jargon, reference relevant events or publications, and present information in formats consistent with legitimate communications.

Reliability: Through consistent communication patterns and follow-through on promised actions, LLM-powered attacks can establish a sense of reliability. This is particularly effective in longer-term operations where multiple interactions occur.

Intimacy: Perhaps most powerfully, LLMs can create a false sense of intimacy by referencing personal details, expressing empathy, and adapting to the target's communication style. This synthetic intimacy can rapidly lower defenses.

Self-Orientation: LLMs can be programmed to appear focused on the target's needs rather than their own objectives, minimizing the perception of self-interest that might otherwise trigger suspicion.

A cybersecurity psychologist I interviewed explained: "What's fascinating and frightening about LLM-based social engineering is how effectively it can manipulate the trust equation. The technology can simultaneously boost the numerator factors while minimizing the denominator, creating a perfect storm for trust formation—even when that trust is entirely unwarranted."

The Uncanny Valley of Trust

Interestingly, the relationship between LLM sophistication and attack effectiveness isn't strictly linear. Security researchers have observed what some call the "uncanny valley of trust"—a phenomenon where moderately sophisticated LLM outputs can sometimes trigger more suspicion than either obviously fake or extremely sophisticated ones.

> When an attack is clearly fake (poor grammar, generic content, obvious inconsistencies), most targets recognize and dismiss it. When an attack is extremely sophisticated (perfectly tailored, contextually appropriate, stylistically matched), targets often cannot distinguish it from legitimate communication.
>
> But in the middle ground—where the content is mostly convincing but contains subtle inconsistencies or unusual patterns—targets may experience a sense of unease similar to the "uncanny valley" effect in robotics, where almost-but-not-quite-human appearances can trigger discomfort.
>
> As LLMs continue to improve, more attacks are moving beyond this uncanny valley, becoming virtually indistinguishable from legitimate human communication. This progression represents a significant challenge for traditional security awareness approaches that rely on identifying "red flags" or suspicious elements.

Real-World Impact and Case Studies

The integration of LLMs into social engineering isn't a theoretical concern—it's already having significant real-world impacts. Let's examine some documented cases and research findings that illustrate the scale and effectiveness of these attacks.

The Hong Kong Fraud Case

In January 2024, a finance employee at a multinational firm based in Hong Kong was defrauded of approximately $25 million in what appears to be one of the largest publicly reported cases of deepfake-enabled fraud.

> The employee received what seemed to be a legitimate video conference call from the company's UK-based chief financial officer, along with several colleagues. During the call, the supposed CFO instructed the employee to transfer funds for a confidential acquisition.

> Investigation revealed that all but one of the participants in the call were deepfakes—synthetic video and audio created using AI technology. The content of the call, including specific references to company matters and appropriate financial terminology, was likely generated by an LLM.

> This case demonstrates the powerful combination of multiple AI technologies in social engineering: deepfake video and audio for impersonation, and LLM-generated content to make the deception convincing and contextually appropriate.

The Oxford University Study

Researchers at Oxford University's Centre for the Governance of AI conducted a study examining how LLMs could be used for spear phishing. They used OpenAI's GPT-3.5 and GPT-4 models to generate unique phishing emails targeting over 600 British Members of Parliament.

The study found that: - The LLMs could generate highly personalized emails using only publicly available information about the targets - Each email cost only a fraction of a cent to produce - The generated emails were not only realistic but also incorporated sophisticated social engineering techniques - Basic prompt engineering could circumvent safety measures intended to prevent such misuse

The researchers concluded that LLMs dramatically reduce the cost and technical barriers to conducting sophisticated spear phishing campaigns, potentially enabling smaller threat actors to execute attacks previously limited to well-resourced groups.

Corporate Reconnaissance and Data Extraction

Security firm Darktrace documented a case where an LLM was used to conduct reconnaissance within a corporate environment. After gaining initial access through conventional means, attackers deployed an LLM-powered chatbot that impersonated IT support staff.

The chatbot engaged multiple employees in conversations, asking seemingly innocuous questions about systems and processes. By aggregating the information gathered from these conversations, the attackers were able to map the organization's structure, identify valuable data sources, and plan further attacks.

What made this approach particularly effective was the chatbot's ability to maintain consistent conversations across multiple interactions, remember previous discussions, and adapt its questions based on the information it had already gathered—all capabilities enabled by modern LLMs.

Voice Cloning for Financial Fraud

In 2023, a financial controller at a UK-based company received a phone call apparently from the company's CEO, requesting an urgent transfer of £200,000 to secure a time-sensitive business opportunity. The controller, recognizing the CEO's distinctive voice and speech patterns, processed the transfer.

The call was later revealed to be a sophisticated fraud using AI voice cloning technology. The attackers had created a synthetic version of the CEO's voice using samples from publicly available interviews and presentations. The content of the call—the specific business opportunity, references to board discussions, and responses to the controller's questions—was generated by an LLM based on information gleaned from company press releases and social media.

This case highlights how voice cloning and LLMs can work together to create highly convincing impersonations that bypass traditional verification methods relying on voice recognition.

Research on Detection and Response

Research on detecting and responding to LLM-powered social engineering has yielded concerning findings. A study by cybersecurity firm Abnormal Security found that:

- Security professionals correctly identified AI-generated phishing emails only 59% of the time
- Emails generated by advanced LLMs like GPT-4 were identified as AI-generated at rates barely above random chance
- Traditional indicators of phishing (grammatical errors, generic greetings, suspicious links) were largely absent in LLM-generated attacks
- Even security experts with specific training in identifying AI-generated content struggled with detection

These findings suggest that traditional approaches to security awareness and training may be insufficient against this new generation of threats. As one security researcher put it, "We're asking humans to distinguish between human-written and increasingly human-like AI-generated content. That's a losing battle in the long run."

Defending Against LLM-Powered Social Engineering

Despite the sophisticated nature of LLM-enhanced social engineering, effective defenses are possible. These defenses operate at multiple levels: technical systems, organizational processes, and individual awareness.

Technical Defenses

Several technical approaches can help detect and prevent LLM-powered attacks:

AI-Powered Detection: Just as AI can be used to generate attacks, it can also be used to detect them. Security firms are developing systems that analyze communication patterns, linguistic features, and contextual factors to identify potential LLM-generated content. These systems look for subtle patterns that might not be apparent to human readers but can distinguish AI-generated from human-written text.

Multi-factor Authentication (MFA): Requiring additional verification beyond just email or voice communication creates significant barriers to social engineering. Even if an attacker can perfectly impersonate a trusted individual through text or voice, MFA requires them to also compromise physical devices or biometric factors.

Out-of-band Verification: Establishing protocols for verifying sensitive requests through separate communication channels can thwart many social engineering attempts. For example, if a financial transfer request comes by email, verification might require a phone call to a pre-established number (not one provided in the email).

Digital Signatures and Verification: Implementing cryptographic signing of communications can provide a technical means of verifying sender authenticity that is difficult for attackers to forge, even with LLM-generated content.

Behavioral Analysis: Systems that monitor for unusual patterns in communication or requests can flag potential attacks for additional scrutiny. For instance, an unusual request from an executive who typically doesn't make such requests might trigger verification procedures.

As one cybersecurity expert explained: "The most effective technical defenses don't try to distinguish between human and AI content directly—that's increasingly difficult. Instead, they focus on verifying identity through multiple factors and channels, and on identifying behavioral anomalies that might indicate deception regardless of how convincing the content appears."

Organizational Approaches

Organizations can implement processes and policies that reduce vulnerability to LLM-powered social engineering:

Verification Protocols: Establishing clear procedures for verifying sensitive requests, particularly those involving financial transactions, data access, or credential changes. These protocols should include out-of-band verification and multiple approvals for high-risk actions.

Security Awareness Training: Updating training programs to specifically address LLM-powered social engineering, focusing less on identifying "red flags" (which may be absent in sophisticated attacks) and more on following verification procedures regardless of how convincing a request seems.

Simulation and Testing: Conducting regular simulations of LLM-powered attacks to test defenses and train employees. These exercises can help build organizational resilience and identify process weaknesses before real attackers exploit them.

Information Compartmentalization: Limiting the amount of information publicly available about organizational structures, processes, and individuals can reduce attackers' ability to craft convincing LLM-generated content.

Communication Norms: Establishing clear norms about how sensitive matters will and won't be communicated can help employees identify suspicious requests, even when the content itself seems legitimate.

As the CISO of a financial services firm told me: "We've had to fundamentally rethink our approach to social engineering defense. The old model of 'spot the phish' based on obvious errors or inconsistencies doesn't work anymore. We're shifting to a 'trust but verify' model where even perfectly legitimate-seeming requests follow verification protocols if they involve sensitive actions."

Individual Protection

Individuals can adopt practices that reduce their vulnerability to LLM-powered social engineering:

Critical Evaluation: Developing a habit of critically evaluating requests, particularly those involving sensitive information or actions, regardless of how legitimate they appear. This includes considering the context, timing, and nature of the request.

Verification Habits: Establishing personal verification procedures for sensitive requests, such as calling the supposed sender on a known number (not one provided in the communication) or confirming in person when possible.

Digital Literacy: Building understanding of AI capabilities and limitations to better recognize potential AI-generated content and the tactics used in social engineering.

Healthy Skepticism: Maintaining appropriate doubt about digital communications, particularly those creating urgency or emotional responses that might cloud judgment.

Personal Authentication Systems: Establishing private verification methods with trusted contacts, such as code words or specific communication patterns that would be difficult for an LLM to know or replicate.

As one digital security educator advised: "The best defense is a mindset shift. Assume that any digital communication could potentially be synthetic, and verify important requests through multiple channels before taking action. It's not about becoming paranoid—it's about developing verification habits that become second nature."

The Future of LLMs in Social Engineering

As we look ahead, several trends suggest where LLM-powered social engineering might be heading.

Technological Trajectories

The technical capabilities of LLMs continue to advance rapidly, with several developments particularly relevant to social engineering:

Increasing Realism: Each new generation of LLMs produces more natural, coherent, and contextually appropriate content. This progression will likely continue, making detection based on content analysis increasingly difficult.

Multimodal Integration: The integration of text, voice, image, and video generation capabilities is creating more comprehensive synthetic experiences. Future attacks may seamlessly combine these elements for maximum effectiveness.

Real-time Adaptation: Improvements in processing efficiency are enabling more sophisticated real-time interactions, allowing LLM-powered systems to adapt dynamically to target responses during conversations.

Autonomous Operation: As LLMs become more capable of independent reasoning and decision-making, we may see more fully autonomous social engineering systems that can execute complex attack strategies with minimal human oversight.

As one AI researcher predicted: "Within five years, we'll likely see fully autonomous social engineering systems that can identify targets, gather information, craft personalized approaches, and adapt strategies based on responses—all without human intervention. The line between automated and human-driven attacks will become increasingly blurred."

Emerging Threats

Several emerging threat patterns are worth monitoring:

Hyper-personalization: As data collection and analysis capabilities improve, attacks may become even more precisely tailored to individual psychological profiles, exploiting specific vulnerabilities and preferences.

Emotional Manipulation: Advanced LLMs may become more sophisticated at detecting and exploiting emotional states, adjusting their approach based on perceived vulnerability or receptiveness.

Trust Network Infiltration: Rather than direct attacks, we may see more long-term strategies focused on infiltrating trusted networks and relationships, establishing credibility over time before executing the actual attack.

Defensive Countermeasures: As detection systems improve, we can expect attackers to develop more sophisticated evasion techniques, potentially including adversarial approaches specifically designed to bypass AI-based defenses.

A cybersecurity strategist I consulted noted: "The most concerning development isn't just the improvement in individual capabilities, but their convergence. When you combine advanced language models with emotion recognition, voice synthesis, deepfakes, and autonomous decision-making, you get something approaching a perfect social engineering machine."

Positive Applications

Despite these concerns, LLMs also enable positive applications in the social engineering domain:

Defensive Training: LLMs can generate realistic attack scenarios for security awareness training, helping individuals and organizations prepare for real threats.

Vulnerability Assessment: Organizations can use LLMs to simulate attacks against their own systems and processes, identifying weaknesses before malicious actors exploit them.

Automated Detection: As mentioned earlier, LLMs can power sophisticated detection systems that identify potential social engineering attempts based on content and contextual analysis.

Security Research: LLMs enable more comprehensive research into social engineering mechanisms, potentially leading to better theoretical understanding and more effective countermeasures.

As one security researcher optimistically noted: "The same technologies that enable these attacks also give us unprecedented tools to understand, detect, and prevent them. The question is whether we'll invest as much in defense as attackers invest in offense."

Conclusion: The Human Element in an AI World

As we've explored throughout this chapter, large language models have transformed social engineering from a labor-intensive craft to an automated, scalable, and highly effective attack vector. The ability to generate personalized, contextually appropriate, and linguistically perfect content removes many of the traditional "red flags" that helped identify social engineering attempts.

Yet despite the technological sophistication of these attacks, they still ultimately target human psychology. The same cognitive biases, emotional vulnerabilities, and trust mechanisms that traditional social engineers exploited remain the foundation of LLM-powered approaches—they're simply being triggered with greater precision and at larger scale.

This human element offers both challenge and hope. The challenge is that we cannot rely solely on technical solutions to a problem that fundamentally exploits human psychology. No amount of AI detection or content analysis will completely eliminate the risk as long as humans remain in the loop.

The hope lies in our capacity for adaptation. Throughout history, humans have adjusted to new threats by developing new norms, practices, and institutions. The rise of LLM-powered social engineering will likely drive similar adaptations—new verification habits, communication norms, and trust mechanisms better suited to a world where synthetic content is indistinguishable from human-generated content.

As Dr. Helen Nissenbaum, a professor of information science who studies trust in digital contexts, told me: "We're entering an era where the traditional cues we've relied on to establish trust and authenticity are becoming unreliable. This doesn't mean trust becomes impossible—it means we need to develop new foundations for trust that are more resilient to technological manipulation."

In the chapters that follow, we'll explore other weapons in the information warfare arsenal, from the rise of AI influencers to the manipulation of virality. Each of these technologies presents its own challenges and opportunities, contributing to the complex information environment we all must navigate.

By understanding these tools and their implications, we can work toward an information ecosystem that serves human flourishing rather than manipulation and control. The battle for our digital minds continues, but with awareness and action, it's a battle we can fight more effectively.

Chapter 8: The Rise of AI Influencers

The young woman on your screen is stunning. Her skin is flawless, her makeup impeccable. She poses in front of the Eiffel Tower wearing a designer outfit that costs more than your monthly rent. The caption reads: "Living my best life in Paris! #blessed #sponsored." You double-tap to like the photo, maybe leave a comment about how jealous you are of her glamorous lifestyle. Perhaps you click the link to check out the clothing brand she's promoting.

There's just one problem: she doesn't exist.

Welcome to the world of AI influencers—digital personas created through a combination of computer graphics, machine learning, and artificial intelligence that are rapidly becoming some of the most powerful forces in social media. Unlike the bot networks and sock puppets we explored in earlier chapters, these aren't crude attempts to manipulate public opinion through volume. These are sophisticated, visually stunning digital personalities designed to build genuine emotional connections with their followers—connections that can be leveraged for commercial, political, or ideological purposes.

"The most dangerous manipulation is the kind you don't recognize as manipulation," explains Dr. Eliza Chen, a digital media researcher at Stanford University. "AI influencers represent perhaps the most sophisticated form of social engineering we've ever seen—the creation of artificial humans designed specifically to influence real ones."

In this chapter, we'll explore how AI-generated personalities are reshaping the landscape of social media influence, examine the technology that makes them possible, and uncover the psychological and social implications of this brave new world where the line between human and artificial influence grows increasingly blurred.

The Digital Celebrities Among Us

Lil Miquela made her Instagram debut in April 2016. With her freckled face, trendy outfits, and perfectly imperfect space buns, she looked like countless other Instagram influencers flooding the platform. Within months, she had amassed hundreds of thousands of followers. Today, she has over 3 million.

But Lil Miquela isn't human. She's a computer-generated image created by Brud, a Los Angeles-based startup specializing in artificial intelligence and robotics. Despite her digital nature, Miquela has secured partnerships with luxury brands like Prada and Calvin Klein. She's released music tracks that have been streamed millions of times. She's even "dated" human influencers and other virtual personalities as part of elaborate storylines crafted by her creators.

"What makes Miquela and other AI influencers so fascinating is that they occupy this uncanny valley of influence," says Marcus Winters, author of *Digital Personalities: The Future of Fame*. "They're obviously not real—Miquela's creators don't hide that she's CGI—but they're presented in contexts and narratives that feel authentic. They have backstories, personalities, opinions, and relationships. They experience manufactured 'growth' and even 'controversies' that mirror human experiences."

Miquela is far from alone in this digital celebrity ecosystem:

- **Shudu Gram**, created by photographer Cameron-James Wilson, is billed as the "world's first digital supermodel" and has worked with Fenty Beauty and Balmain.
- **Lu do Magalu**, a Brazilian virtual influencer, has over 7 million followers and serves as the digital face of retail giant Magazine Luiza.
- **Rozy**, a South Korean virtual influencer, reportedly earned over $1 million in 2021 through more than 100 sponsorships.

- **Aitana López**, a Spanish AI model, earns up to $10,000 monthly from brand deals and digital content.

These digital personalities represent just the tip of the iceberg. The AI influencer industry is growing rapidly, with new virtual personalities appearing across platforms like Instagram, TikTok, and YouTube every month. According to industry analysts, the global virtual influencer market is projected to reach $15 billion by 2030.

> "What we're seeing is just the beginning," says tech futurist Ayana Patel. "As the technology improves and becomes more accessible, we'll likely see an explosion of AI personalities across all social platforms. The question isn't whether AI influencers will become mainstream—it's what happens when they do."

Behind the Digital Façade: How AI Influencers Are Created

Creating an AI influencer is a complex process that combines multiple technologies and creative disciplines. While companies like Brud closely guard their specific methodologies, the general approach involves several key components:

Visual Development

The most obvious aspect of AI influencers is their visual appearance. Most are created using advanced 3D modeling and rendering techniques similar to those used in modern video games and animated films. Artists begin by designing the influencer's basic appearance—their facial features, body type, skin tone, and other physical characteristics.

"There's an art to creating AI influencers that look realistic but not too realistic," explains Sophia Nguyen, a digital artist who has worked on several virtual personalities. "If they look too perfect, people find them unsettling. If they look too artificial, people won't connect with them. The sweet spot is creating someone who looks polished but still has small imperfections that make them feel human."

Once the basic model is created, artists develop a wardrobe of digital clothing and accessories that can be applied to the model for different posts. They also create a library of poses, expressions, and environments that can be mixed and matched to generate new content.

"The most sophisticated AI influencers have thousands of possible combinations of expressions, poses, outfits, and backgrounds," says Nguyen. "This allows their teams to generate new content quickly without having to build everything from scratch for each post."

Personality Development

While the visual component is crucial, what truly distinguishes successful AI influencers is their personality. Teams of writers and content strategists develop detailed backstories, personal histories, interests, opinions, and speech patterns for these digital personas.

"It's essentially character development, similar to what you'd see in fiction writing or role-playing games," explains content strategist James Moreno. "We create comprehensive character bibles that detail everything from their childhood experiences to their favorite foods to how they'd respond in different situations. This ensures consistency across all content and interactions."

These personality profiles inform everything from the captions on their posts to the way they respond to comments and messages. Some AI influencer teams even create elaborate story arcs and narrative developments that unfold over months or years, giving followers the sense that they're watching a real person grow and evolve.

Technical Infrastructure

Behind the scenes, AI influencers are supported by sophisticated technical systems. While early virtual influencers required extensive manual work for each post, advances in artificial intelligence—particularly in generative adversarial networks (GANs) and natural language processing (NLP)—are making the process increasingly automated.

> "The latest generation of AI influencers uses machine learning to analyze which types of posts generate the most engagement," explains Dr. Ravi Mehta, an AI researcher. "The system can then automatically generate new content that mimics successful patterns. Some can even analyze trending topics and current events to create timely, relevant posts without human intervention."

> Similarly, NLP systems allow AI influencers to generate more authentic-sounding captions and comments. By training on vast datasets of social media text, these systems learn to mimic the casual, emoji-filled language that characterizes platforms like Instagram and TikTok.

> "The goal is to create systems that can operate with minimal human oversight," says Dr. Mehta. "The most advanced AI influencers today still have humans approving their posts and managing their overall strategy, but the technology is moving toward greater autonomy."

The Perfect Influencers: Why Brands Love Digital Personalities

From a marketing perspective, AI influencers offer several compelling advantages over their human counterparts:

Complete Control

Perhaps the most obvious benefit is control. Human influencers are unpredictable—they might post controversial opinions, become embroiled in scandals, or simply deviate from a brand's preferred messaging. AI influencers, by contrast, will never go off-script unless their creators deliberately program them to do so.

> "With AI influencers, brands get all the benefits of influencer marketing with none of the risks," explains marketing executive Sophia Rodriguez. "They'll never show up drunk to an event, use offensive language, or endorse a competitor's product. They're the perfect brand ambassadors because they do exactly what they're programmed to do."

> This control extends to availability as well. Human influencers have limited time and energy—they can only attend so many events, create so much content, and engage with so many followers. AI influencers never sleep, never get sick, and never need a vacation.

Optimized Engagement

AI influencers can also be optimized for maximum engagement in ways that would be impossible for humans. Their appearance, personality, content, and posting schedule can all be fine-tuned based on performance data.

> "It's essentially A/B testing applied to human-like entities," says digital marketing strategist Ethan Park. "Companies can analyze which facial expressions get more likes, which outfit styles generate more comments, which caption formats drive more clicks. Then they can adjust their AI influencers accordingly. It's like having an influencer who can constantly reinvent themselves based on what the algorithm rewards."

This optimization extends to audience targeting as well. Companies can create multiple AI influencers, each designed to appeal to different demographic segments or interest groups.

Cost Efficiency

While creating a high-quality AI influencer requires significant upfront investment, they can be more cost-effective in the long run compared to top human influencers, who may charge hundreds of thousands of dollars for a single sponsored post.

"Once you've built the infrastructure, the marginal cost of each new post is relatively low," explains Rodriguez. "You're not paying per post or renegotiating contracts every year as the influencer becomes more popular. You own the IP outright."

This ownership model also allows companies to leverage their AI influencers across multiple channels and formats without additional compensation—something that would typically require separate negotiations with human influencers.

The Authenticity Paradox

Despite these advantages, AI influencers present a fundamental paradox: they're completely artificial entities trying to cultivate authentic connections with real people.

"Authenticity has always been the currency of social media influence," explains social media researcher Dr. Maya Johnson. "Followers connect with influencers who seem genuine, relatable, and transparent. But AI influencers are, by definition, inauthentic—they're carefully constructed digital personas designed to create the illusion of authenticity."

This creates a strange dynamic where teams of writers and designers work to manufacture moments of vulnerability, personal growth, and emotional connection for entities that don't actually experience emotions.

"We've seen AI influencers 'share' personal struggles with mental health, relationship problems, and identity issues," says Dr. Johnson. "They post about 'feeling insecure' about their appearance—despite being literally designed to be attractive. They talk about 'learning and growing' when they're actually just being reprogrammed. It's a simulation of the authentic human experience that many find deeply unsettling."

This simulation extends to relationships as well. Many AI influencers engage in manufactured friendships and romances with both human and other virtual influencers, creating elaborate storylines that blur the line between reality and fiction.

"When Lil Miquela 'broke up' with her human boyfriend, real people left thousands of supportive comments," notes cultural critic Elena Diaz. "They were emotionally investing in a relationship that never actually existed. It was essentially a one-sided parasocial relationship with an entity that couldn't even experience the breakup it was supposedly going through."

The Ethics of Digital Representation

Beyond the authenticity question, AI influencers raise complex ethical issues around representation and diversity. Many of the most popular virtual influencers present as people of color or mixed-race individuals, despite often being created by predominantly white teams.

The case of Shudu Gram is particularly illustrative. Created by Cameron-James Wilson, a white British photographer, Shudu is presented as a striking Black woman. While Wilson has described her as a "digital art piece" and "a celebration of beautiful dark-skinned women," critics have questioned whether this constitutes a modern form of digital blackface.

"There's something deeply problematic about white creators profiting from the aesthetic of Blackness without actually employing or benefiting Black models, artists, or communities," argues Dr. Kimberly Washington, professor of digital ethics at Howard University. "It's extractive—taking the marketable aspects of Black beauty while avoiding any meaningful engagement with Black experiences or perspectives."

Similar concerns arise with AI influencers who present as Asian, Latinx, or from other marginalized groups. When these digital personas are created without substantial input from members of the communities they visually represent, they risk perpetuating stereotypes or presenting sanitized, commercialized versions of cultural identity.

"The question we should be asking is: who benefits?" says Dr. Washington. "When brands use AI influencers who appear to be from diverse backgrounds, they get the marketing benefits of appearing inclusive without actually having to engage with real people from those communities or address their concerns."

This issue becomes even more complex when AI influencers are programmed to weigh in on social and political issues. During the Black Lives Matter protests of 2020, several virtual influencers posted statements of solidarity—statements written by their (often white) creators rather than reflecting any lived experience of racial discrimination.

"There's something fundamentally dishonest about an artificial entity claiming solidarity with human suffering," notes ethical AI researcher Dr. James Chen. "It trivializes real struggles by reducing them to marketing opportunities and brand positioning."

Psychological Impact: The Parasocial Manipulation

Perhaps the most concerning aspect of AI influencers is their psychological impact on followers, particularly young and vulnerable audiences. Traditional influencers already foster parasocial relationships—one-sided emotional connections where followers feel they know and trust someone they've never actually met. AI influencers take this dynamic to a new level.

"What we're seeing is the industrialization of parasocial relationships," explains psychologist Dr. Rebecca Winters. "These entities are specifically engineered to maximize emotional engagement and attachment. Every aspect of their appearance, personality, and content is optimized to make you feel connected to them—not as a byproduct, but as the primary goal."

This optimization creates a particularly potent form of influence. Research has shown that people who feel emotionally connected to influencers are more likely to trust their recommendations, adopt their viewpoints, and defend them against criticism.

"When you combine the persuasive power of parasocial relationships with the data-driven optimization of AI, you get something unprecedented in human history," says Dr. Winters. "These aren't just advertisements—they're relationships weaponized for commercial gain."

The impact may be especially significant for younger users, who may lack the media literacy skills to critically evaluate these relationships or fully understand the artificial nature of AI influencers.

"We're already seeing children and teenagers forming strong emotional attachments to virtual influencers," notes child development specialist Dr. Sarah Nguyen. "They follow their stories, defend them in comments, and genuinely care about what happens to them. The long-term psychological effects of these attachments are still unknown, but there's reason for concern."

Beyond Commerce: The Political Potential

While most current AI influencers focus on fashion, lifestyle, and commercial partnerships, the technology has obvious applications for political influence operations.

"The same techniques used to sell sneakers could easily be repurposed to sell ideologies or candidates," warns political scientist Dr. Marcus Reynolds. "Imagine AI influencers designed to appeal to specific demographic groups in swing states, gradually introducing political content alongside lifestyle posts. It's a form of political microtargeting that would be nearly impossible to regulate."

Unlike traditional political advertisements, which are subject to disclosure requirements in many jurisdictions, AI influencers could blur the line between entertainment and propaganda in ways that evade existing regulatory frameworks.

"We've already seen foreign influence operations create fake human personas on social media," notes Dr. Reynolds. "AI influencers represent the next evolution of this approach—more convincing, more engaging, and potentially more effective at shaping public opinion."

The scalability of AI influencers makes them particularly concerning in this context. A single team could potentially operate dozens or hundreds of virtual personalities, each targeting different demographic segments with tailored messaging.

"It's not hard to imagine a future where your social media feed includes multiple AI influencers that you follow for different reasons—fashion tips, workout advice, cooking recipes—all subtly pushing the same political narrative," says digital rights advocate Maria Gonzalez. "The cumulative effect could be powerful, especially if users don't realize these seemingly distinct personalities are actually coordinated."

Detecting the Digital: Can You Spot the Fakes?

As AI influencers become more sophisticated, identifying them becomes increasingly challenging. While early examples like Lil Miquela are openly acknowledged as virtual, future AI personalities may not be so transparent.

"We're approaching a point where the visual distinction between real and artificial humans in still images is becoming imperceptible to the average person," explains computer vision researcher Dr. Alan Zhang. "Video remains more challenging for AI to render convincingly, but that gap is closing rapidly."

This convergence creates a potential crisis of trust in digital spaces. If users cannot reliably distinguish between human and artificial content creators, the fundamental nature of online social interaction changes.

"The assumption that you're interacting with other humans is basic to how we understand social media," says digital sociologist Dr. Emma Richards. "When that assumption becomes unreliable, it undermines the entire social contract of these platforms."

Several technical approaches to identifying AI influencers are under development:

- **Behavioral analysis**: Examining posting patterns, interaction styles, and content consistency that might reveal non-human patterns
- **Metadata verification**: Creating systems to authenticate the origin of images and videos
- **Digital watermarking**: Requiring AI-generated content to include invisible markers identifying it as artificial
- **Blockchain verification**: Using distributed ledger technology to create tamper-proof records of content provenance

However, these technical solutions face significant challenges. As detection methods improve, generation technologies evolve to evade them, creating an ongoing arms race between authentication and deception.

> "The technical solutions are important, but ultimately insufficient," argues Dr. Richards. "What we really need is a cultural shift toward greater skepticism and media literacy. People need to approach all online content with a critical eye, questioning its origins and motivations rather than accepting it at face value."

The Human Response: Reclaiming Authentic Influence

As AI influencers proliferate, some see an opportunity for human influencers to differentiate themselves by emphasizing their authentic, unfiltered humanity.

> "There's a growing counter-trend toward raw, unedited content that embraces human imperfection," notes cultural trend analyst Jordan Kim. "Some influencers are deliberately posting without filters, showing their actual homes and bodies, and discussing real struggles— positioning themselves in direct opposition to the polished perfection of AI personalities."

> This authenticity movement suggests that while AI influencers may capture a significant portion of the commercial market, they may never fully replace the genuine human connection that draws people to social media in the first place.

> "Humans are wired to connect with other humans," says Kim. "We can be fooled temporarily, but there's something fundamentally different about knowing you're interacting with another conscious being who shares your capacity for joy, pain, and genuine emotional experience."

Others are calling for regulatory approaches that preserve this distinction. Proposed measures include:

- **Mandatory disclosure**: Requiring clear labeling of AI-generated personalities and content
- **Transparency in advertising**: Special requirements for commercial partnerships involving AI influencers
- **Ethical guidelines**: Industry standards for responsible creation and operation of virtual personalities
- **Platform policies**: Rules governing how social media companies handle and identify AI accounts

"The goal isn't to ban AI influencers, but to ensure they operate in a transparent ecosystem where users can make informed choices about who and what they follow," explains digital policy expert Samantha Chen. "People should know whether they're forming a parasocial relationship with a human being or a corporate-owned algorithm."

The Future of Synthetic Influence

As we look toward the future, several trends suggest where AI influence might be heading:

Hyper-Personalization

Future AI systems may be able to create personalized experiences for individual followers, adapting their appearance, personality, and content based on each user's preferences and interaction history.

"Imagine an AI influencer who looks slightly different to each follower, emphasizing the features that algorithm determines that specific person finds most attractive," suggests futurist Dr. Elijah Moore. "Or one that adjusts its personality to mirror your communication style and values. It's the ultimate form of personalized content."

Cross-Platform Integration

AI influencers are likely to expand beyond traditional social media into emerging digital environments like augmented reality, virtual reality, and the metaverse.

> "The logical evolution is for these digital personalities to become more interactive and immersive," says tech analyst Priya Sharma. "Imagine attending a virtual concert where you can actually interact with your favorite AI influencer, or using AR glasses that allow them to appear in your physical environment."

Human-AI Collaboration

Rather than a binary choice between human and artificial influencers, we may see increasing collaboration and hybridization between the two.

> "We're already seeing human influencers use AI tools to generate content or enhance their appearance," notes Sharma. "The line between human-created and AI-assisted content is blurring. We might eventually see human influencers licensing their likeness and personality to AI systems that can create content on their behalf, essentially becoming hybrid entities."

Democratization of Creation

As the technology becomes more accessible, the ability to create AI personalities may extend beyond major companies to smaller creators and even individuals.

"The tools to create convincing digital humans are becoming increasingly available to the average person," explains digital artist Marcus Wong. "We're approaching a point where anyone with basic technical skills could create their own AI influencer. This democratization could lead to an explosion of virtual personalities across the digital landscape."

Conclusion: The Human Value Proposition

As AI influencers become more sophisticated and prevalent, they force us to confront fundamental questions about influence, authenticity, and human connection in digital spaces. They represent perhaps the most advanced form of social media manipulation— entities specifically designed to build emotional connections that can be leveraged for commercial, political, or ideological purposes.

Yet they also highlight what remains uniquely valuable about human connection. In a world increasingly populated by artificial personalities optimized for engagement, genuine human authenticity—with all its messiness, unpredictability, and imperfection—may become more precious than ever.

"The rise of AI influencers doesn't mean the end of human influence," concludes Dr. Maya Johnson. "But it does mean we need to be more conscious about where we invest our attention and emotional energy online. As these technologies advance, the ability to distinguish between authentic human connection and manufactured engagement will become an essential skill for navigating digital spaces."

The battle for your attention and influence is no longer just between competing human voices—it's increasingly between humans and the algorithms designed to mimic them. Understanding this new landscape is crucial for maintaining agency in a world where the line between authentic and artificial influence grows increasingly blurred.

As we move forward, the question isn't whether AI influencers will transform social media—they already are. The question is whether we can develop the technological tools, regulatory frameworks, and personal discernment needed to ensure that this transformation serves human flourishing rather than simply corporate or political interests.

In the digital theater of war, AI influencers represent a powerful new weapon—one that targets not just what you think, but who you trust and connect with. Recognizing this reality is the first step toward reclaiming your digital autonomy in an age of synthetic influence.

Chapter 9: Case Study: The 2020 U.S. Election and Beyond

The 2020 United States presidential election stands as a watershed moment in the evolution of information warfare. Taking place amid a global pandemic, unprecedented social unrest, and growing political polarization, it became the perfect laboratory for testing and deploying the most sophisticated influence operations ever witnessed. While previous elections had seen their share of manipulation attempts, 2020 represented a quantum leap forward in both the scale and sophistication of these efforts. This chapter examines what happened, who was involved, and what it tells us about the future of democracy in an age of artificial intelligence.

The Battlefield: America Divided

As Americans prepared to vote in the 2020 election, they did so in a nation already deeply fractured. The COVID-19 pandemic had upended daily life, claiming hundreds of thousands of lives and devastating the economy. The murder of George Floyd had sparked nationwide protests against racial injustice. And years of increasingly partisan media consumption had created two Americas living in separate information ecosystems, each with its own version of reality.

> "The conditions couldn't have been more perfect for information warfare," explains Dr. Samantha Bradshaw, a researcher at the Stanford Internet Observatory. "You had a population that was scared, isolated, spending unprecedented amounts of time online, and deeply distrustful of traditional institutions. It was fertile ground for manipulation."

> These divisions were not accidental. They were the result of years of targeted efforts to fragment American society—efforts that had been accelerated and amplified by social media algorithms designed to maximize engagement by showing users content that provoked strong emotional reactions. By 2020, many Americans were primed to believe the worst about their political opponents and to dismiss any information that contradicted their existing beliefs.

"What we saw in 2020 was the culmination of a long-term strategy," says former NSA analyst Marcus Chen. "Foreign adversaries had spent years studying American society, identifying fault lines, and developing sophisticated techniques to exploit them. The election was just the moment when all of these efforts converged."

The Players: A Multi-Front Assault

According to the declassified Intelligence Community Assessment released in March 2021, multiple foreign actors attempted to influence the outcome of the 2020 election. The report identified Russia, Iran, and to a lesser extent China as the primary state actors involved, though their goals and methods differed significantly.

Russia: The Veteran Manipulator

Russia's interference in the 2020 election represented an evolution of tactics first deployed in 2016. According to the intelligence assessment, "Russian President Putin authorized, and a range of Russian government organizations conducted, influence operations aimed at denigrating President Biden's candidacy and the Democratic Party, supporting former President Trump, undermining public confidence in the electoral process, and exacerbating sociopolitical divisions in the US."

Unlike in 2016, however, Russian operatives did not attempt to hack election infrastructure directly. Instead, they focused on a more sophisticated approach: using proxies linked to Russian intelligence to push influence narratives into U.S. media organizations and to prominent individuals close to the Trump administration.

"The Russians learned from 2016 that direct hacking attempts left too many fingerprints," explains cybersecurity expert Alicia Montgomery. "In 2020, they operated more like a public relations firm, crafting narratives and finding ways to insert them into legitimate channels where they could spread organically."

These narratives often centered around unsubstantiated allegations about Biden's family, particularly his son Hunter. Russian operatives amplified and sometimes created content suggesting corruption, which was then picked up by sympathetic media outlets and spread through social networks.

Iran: The Emerging Threat

While Russia's activities received the most attention, Iran conducted what the intelligence community described as "a multi-pronged covert influence campaign intended to undercut former President Trump's reelection prospects." Iranian efforts included sending spoofed emails designed to intimidate voters, creating a website aimed at inciting violence against election officials, and disseminating content that exploited existing social divisions.

"Iran's approach was more direct and less sophisticated than Russia's," notes political scientist Dr. James Wilson. "But it demonstrated their growing capabilities in this space and their willingness to target American democracy directly."

China: The Cautious Observer

Interestingly, the intelligence assessment concluded that China "considered but did not deploy influence efforts intended to change the outcome of the US Presidential election." While Chinese officials had a preference for Biden over Trump, they assessed that direct interference carried too many risks and could backfire.

"China played the long game," explains foreign policy analyst Dr. Elena Vasquez. "They recognized that overt interference could strengthen Trump's position by validating his claims about Chinese hostility. Instead, they focused on more traditional forms of influence through economic and diplomatic channels."

The Weapons: From Bots to Deepfakes

The 2020 election saw the deployment of a wide range of digital weapons, from relatively simple automated social media accounts to sophisticated AI-generated content. While true deepfakes did not play a major role in 2020, the groundwork was being laid for their use in future elections.

Bot Networks and Coordinated Campaigns

Bot networks—collections of automated social media accounts controlled by a central entity—were deployed at unprecedented scale during the 2020 election. These networks amplified divisive content, spread misinformation, and created the illusion of widespread support for particular narratives.

"What made the 2020 bot networks different was their sophistication," explains social media researcher Dr. Priya Sharma. "These weren't just simple automated accounts posting the same message over and over. They were carefully crafted to appear authentic, with unique profiles, posting histories, and behavioral patterns that made them difficult to distinguish from real users."

These bot networks were often supplemented by human-operated "sock puppet" accounts—fake personas managed by real people who could engage more naturally with other users and adapt their messaging in real-time. The combination of automated scale and human nuance created a powerful force for spreading targeted narratives.

"The most effective campaigns blended automation with human touch," says disinformation researcher Thomas Nguyen. "A bot network might initially amplify a piece of content, making it appear popular and driving it into trending topics. Then human operators would step in to engage with real users who encountered the content, reinforcing the message and lending it credibility."

Synthetic Media and the Specter of Deepfakes

While fully convincing deepfakes were not widely deployed in 2020, the election saw increasing use of manipulated media. This included selectively edited videos, out-of-context clips, and "cheap fakes"—content that was manipulated using basic editing techniques rather than sophisticated AI.

"The 2020 election was a transitional moment for synthetic media," explains Dr. Claire Reynolds, an expert in computational propaganda. "The technology wasn't quite ready for prime time, but we saw early examples of what was coming. More importantly, we saw how even the possibility of deepfakes could be weaponized to cast doubt on authentic content."

Indeed, one of the most insidious effects of the growing awareness of deepfakes was the emergence of what researchers call the "liar's dividend"—the ability of bad actors to dismiss authentic evidence by claiming it had been fabricated. Several times during the campaign, politicians or their supporters responded to damaging authentic recordings by suggesting they might be deepfakes, sowing confusion among voters.

Microtargeting and Psychological Profiling

Perhaps the most sophisticated weapon deployed in 2020 was not content creation but content targeting. Using vast amounts of data harvested from social media platforms, data brokers, and other sources, political campaigns and foreign actors alike were able to identify and target highly specific segments of the population with tailored messaging.

"The real innovation in 2020 was the precision of the targeting," says data scientist Dr. Marcus Williams. "Operators could identify not just demographic groups but psychological profiles—people who were susceptible to particular types of messaging or who held specific combinations of beliefs that made them valuable vectors for spreading certain narratives."

This microtargeting allowed influence operations to focus their resources on the most vulnerable or valuable segments of the population, maximizing impact while minimizing the risk of detection. It also enabled the creation of highly personalized content designed to resonate with specific individuals or small groups.

"What we saw in 2020 was just the beginning," warns Dr. Williams. "As AI continues to advance, the ability to create and target personalized content at scale will only grow more sophisticated."

The Battlegrounds: Where the War Was Fought

The information war surrounding the 2020 election played out across multiple platforms and media environments, each with its own dynamics and vulnerabilities.

Social Media: The Primary Front

Social media platforms remained the primary vector for influence operations in 2020, with Facebook, Twitter (now X), YouTube, and increasingly TikTok serving as the main battlegrounds. These platforms offered several advantages for influence operations: massive reach, algorithmic amplification, and the ability to target specific user segments with precision.

> "The social media companies were caught in a difficult position," explains tech policy expert Dr. Rebecca Chen. "Their business models depend on engagement, which often means amplifying emotionally provocative content—exactly the kind of content that influence operations produce. And their scale makes comprehensive content moderation nearly impossible."

> While the major platforms had implemented new policies and detection systems following the 2016 election, these measures proved inadequate to the challenge. Influence operators adapted their tactics, finding new ways to evade detection and exploit loopholes in platform policies.

> "It was a classic arms race," says Dr. Chen. "The platforms would identify and counter a particular tactic, and the operators would evolve their approach. The fundamental asymmetry is that it's much easier to create misleading content than to detect and remove it."

Traditional Media: The Amplification Vector

While social media served as the primary incubator for disinformation, traditional media outlets often unwittingly amplified these narratives, lending them credibility and expanding their reach.

> "One of the most effective strategies we observed was what we call 'narrative laundering,'" explains media analyst Jordan Rivera. "An influence operation would plant a story on social media or a fringe website, which would then be picked up by increasingly mainstream outlets, gaining legitimacy at each step. By the time it reached major news platforms, its dubious origins had been obscured."

This process was facilitated by the increasing pressure on news organizations to produce content quickly and generate engagement in a highly competitive media environment. The rush to report breaking news often meant that claims spreading on social media were repeated before they could be thoroughly verified.

"The relationship between disinformation and media coverage was unidirectional," notes Dr. Koen Pauwels, a distinguished professor of marketing at Northeastern University who studied the 2020 election. "Disinformation drove media coverage, but not the reverse."

Private Messaging: The Dark Battlefield

While public platforms received the most attention, some of the most effective influence operations in 2020 took place in private messaging apps and closed groups, where content could spread rapidly without oversight or fact-checking.

"WhatsApp, Telegram, and private Facebook groups became key vectors for spreading misinformation," says digital anthropologist Dr. Sophia Kim. "These closed environments create a sense of trust and intimacy that makes people more likely to believe and share content, even if it would seem dubious in a more public context."

The private nature of these channels also made them particularly difficult for researchers and platform moderators to monitor, creating blind spots in efforts to track and counter influence operations.

"We only saw the tip of the iceberg on public platforms," warns Dr. Kim. "Much of the most damaging content was spreading in spaces we couldn't observe."

The Aftermath: Eroding Trust in Democracy

The most significant impact of the information warfare surrounding the 2020 election was not its effect on the outcome—which remains difficult to quantify—but its erosion of trust in democratic institutions and processes.

In the weeks following the election, false claims of widespread fraud spread rapidly across social media and alternative news outlets, fueled by a mix of domestic political actors, foreign influence operations, and algorithmic amplification. These claims found fertile ground among voters already primed by years of messaging about the vulnerability of election systems.

"What we witnessed was a perfect storm," says election security expert Dr. Michael Thornton. "You had authentic concerns about election security that had been raised by experts for years, partisan actors willing to exploit those concerns for political gain, foreign entities happy to amplify anything that caused chaos, and a significant portion of the population already distrustful of institutions and living in information bubbles."

The result was a profound crisis of confidence in the electoral system itself—one that culminated in the January 6, 2021, attack on the U.S. Capitol but continues to reverberate through American politics today.

"The most successful influence operation isn't one that changes how people vote," observes political psychologist Dr. Rachel Goldman. "It's one that makes people question whether voting matters at all, or whether they can trust the results regardless of who wins. That's the real victory for those seeking to undermine democracy."

The Future: AI Supercharges the Threat

As we look beyond 2020, the emergence of increasingly sophisticated AI tools presents both new challenges and opportunities in the battle against information warfare. The rapid advancement of generative AI since 2020 has dramatically lowered the barriers to creating convincing fake content, making it possible for virtually anyone to produce realistic images, videos, and text that can be used to manipulate public opinion.

"What we saw in 2020 was just the beginning," warns AI ethics researcher Dr. Eliza Montgomery. "The tools available today make the disinformation of 2020 look primitive by comparison. We're entering an era where the line between real and fake content is increasingly blurred, and our existing defenses are woefully inadequate."

Already, we've seen examples of how these new capabilities can be deployed in political contexts. In January 2024, a political consultant used AI to generate a deepfake robocall mimicking President Biden's voice, which reached thousands of New Hampshire voters and discouraged them from participating in the state's presidential primary. The consultant claimed he spent only about $500 on the operation but generated an estimated $5 million worth of media coverage.

Similarly, during the 2024 election cycle, a deepfake video circulated showing Vice President Kamala Harris appearing to make inflammatory remarks about an assassination attempt against Donald Trump. The video, which Microsoft's threat intelligence team attributed to Russian influence actors, received tens of thousands of views on social media platforms.

"These examples demonstrate how AI-generated content can be used not just to spread false information but to suppress voter participation and inflame tensions," says election security expert Maria Vasquez. "And they represent just the tip of the iceberg in terms of what's possible with today's technology."

Perhaps most concerning is the way in which the mere existence of convincing AI fakes allows all authentic content to be called into question. During the 2024 campaign, genuine photos of a Kamala Harris rally were dismissed by opponents as AI-generated, despite forensic image experts confirming their authenticity.

"We're entering what some scholars call the 'reality crisis,'" explains digital media professor Dr. Jason Chen. "When any content can plausibly be fake, and determining authenticity requires specialized expertise, truth itself becomes contested territory. This is the ultimate goal of information warfare—not just to spread specific falsehoods but to undermine the very concept of shared reality."

Defending Democracy: A Multi-Layered Approach

In the face of these evolving threats, protecting democratic processes requires a comprehensive strategy that addresses both the technical and social dimensions of information warfare.

Technical Solutions: Authentication and Transparency

One promising approach involves developing and implementing standards for content provenance and authenticity. Initiatives like the Coalition for Content Provenance and Authenticity (C2PA) aim to create technical standards that can help verify the origin and integrity of digital content.

"Think of it as a digital watermark or passport for content," explains cybersecurity expert Dr. Robert Chen. "These systems can help establish when and how content was created, making it easier to identify manipulated or synthetic media."

However, technical solutions alone are insufficient. They face significant challenges in terms of adoption, user experience, and the fundamental asymmetry between the ease of creating misleading content and the difficulty of verifying authenticity.

"We can't rely solely on technical fixes," cautions Dr. Chen. "They're an important part of the solution, but they need to be complemented by regulatory frameworks, platform policies, and media literacy efforts."

Regulatory Approaches: Setting Boundaries

Governments around the world are increasingly exploring regulatory responses to the threats posed by AI-generated disinformation. These range from transparency requirements for political advertising to outright bans on certain types of synthetic media in political contexts.

"Regulation is tricky because it needs to balance multiple competing values," notes digital rights attorney Sarah Johnson. "We want to protect democratic processes from manipulation, but we also need to preserve free expression and avoid creating systems that could be used for censorship."

Effective regulation requires international cooperation, as influence operations frequently cross national boundaries. It also demands careful design to ensure that rules can be meaningfully enforced without creating undue burdens on legitimate speech and innovation.

Media Literacy: Empowering Citizens

Perhaps the most important line of defense is an informed and critical citizenry. Media literacy education can help people identify potential manipulation and make more informed judgments about the content they encounter.

> "We need to move beyond simple checklists for spotting fake news," argues education researcher Dr. Maria Rodriguez. "Modern media literacy needs to include understanding how algorithms shape what we see, how our own biases affect how we process information, and how to verify claims using multiple sources."

> This kind of education needs to reach people of all ages and backgrounds, not just students. It also needs to evolve continuously as the tactics used in influence operations change.

> "Media literacy isn't a one-time vaccination against misinformation," says Dr. Rodriguez. "It's more like regular exercise—a set of skills that need to be practiced and updated throughout life."

Conclusion: Democracy at a Crossroads

The 2020 election represented a critical moment in the evolution of information warfare, demonstrating both the vulnerability of democratic systems to manipulation and the resilience of institutions when properly defended. As we move forward, the threats will only grow more sophisticated, driven by advances in AI and deepening understanding of human psychology.

"We're at a crossroads," reflects democracy advocate Elena Martinez. "The tools of manipulation are becoming more powerful and accessible, but our awareness of the threat is also growing. The question is whether we can develop and implement solutions quickly enough to preserve the integrity of our information ecosystem and, by extension, our democratic processes."

The battle for the future of democracy will not be fought primarily at the ballot box but in the digital spaces where public opinion is shaped. It will require coordination between technologists, policymakers, educators, and citizens, all working together to build systems that promote truth and transparency over manipulation and division.

"The 2020 election showed us what's at stake," concludes Martinez. "Now it's up to all of us to ensure that the lessons learned are translated into effective action before the next major test of our democratic resilience."

Chapter 10: Operation Shadow Influence

In the digital battlefield of social media, influence operations don't happen by accident. They are meticulously planned, expertly executed campaigns designed to shape public opinion, manipulate behavior, and ultimately achieve strategic objectives. This chapter examines how these campaigns are structured, the playbooks they follow, and the sophisticated strategies that make them so effective—and so dangerous.

The Anatomy of an Influence Operation

When Russia's Internet Research Agency (IRA) targeted the 2016 U.S. presidential election, it wasn't simply posting random content. It was executing a carefully orchestrated campaign with clear objectives, defined targets, and sophisticated tactics. The same is true of China's efforts to shape global narratives about Hong Kong's democracy protests, Iran's campaigns to influence Middle Eastern politics, and countless other operations conducted by state and non-state actors around the world.

> "These operations follow a military-style structure," explains Dr. Elena Vasquez, a researcher specializing in computational propaganda. "They have command hierarchies, specialized units, training protocols, and battle plans. The only difference is that instead of physical territory, they're fighting for control of the information space."

Understanding how these operations work requires looking beyond individual posts or accounts to see the larger strategic framework. While each campaign has its unique characteristics, they typically follow a similar operational structure:

Phase 1: Planning and Preparation

Before a single post appears online, extensive planning takes place. This includes:

- **Objective Setting**: Defining clear goals, whether it's promoting a specific narrative, discrediting opponents, sowing division, or influencing an election outcome.

- **Target Audience Analysis**: Identifying and researching the demographics, psychographics, and behavioral patterns of the intended audience.

- **Resource Allocation**: Determining the human, technical, and financial resources needed for the operation.

- **Infrastructure Development**: Creating the technical foundation for the campaign, including registering domain names, setting up servers, acquiring SIM cards and burner phones, and establishing VPN connections.

- **Account Creation and Cultivation**: Registering and developing social media accounts that will be used in the operation, often months or years in advance.

"The preparation phase is critical," says cybersecurity expert Marcus Chen. "The more thorough the groundwork, the more effective and resilient the operation will be. Sophisticated actors might spend years developing their digital infrastructure and building credible online personas before activating them for a specific campaign."

Phase 2: Account Credibility Building

For influence operations to succeed, the accounts they use must appear authentic and trustworthy. This requires deliberate cultivation through techniques that researchers at Trustwave SpiderLabs have identified:

- **Engagement Farming**: Accounts post content designed to maximize visibility and engagement within platform algorithms. This often involves addressing polarizing topics that spark debate or using emotionally charged headlines to provoke reactions.

- **Follower Farming**: Operators build follower counts through various means, including follow-unfollow strategies, purchasing followers, or hosting giveaways that require users to follow the account.

- **Hate Farming**: Some accounts deliberately post inflammatory content on divisive topics like race, religion, gender, or politics to generate emotional responses and engagement.

"These techniques serve a dual purpose," explains social media researcher Dr. Priya Sharma. "They build the account's credibility metrics—followers, engagement rates, account age—while also training the algorithms to show the account's content to more users. By the time the actual influence operation begins, these accounts have already established themselves as 'legitimate' voices in their target communities."

Phase 3: Deployment and Execution

Once the groundwork is laid, the operation moves into active deployment. This is when the carefully cultivated accounts begin executing specific influence strategies. Based on research by Pastor-Galindo and colleagues at the University of Murcia and Universidad Politecnica de Madrid, we can identify seven primary strategies employed in modern influence operations:

Strategy 1: Narrative Release

The first step in many influence operations is introducing a narrative into the social network that aligns with the operation's objectives. This involves posting original content—text, images, videos, or links—designed to establish an anchor point for influence.

> "Narrative release is about planting the seed," says disinformation researcher Thomas Nguyen. "The content needs to be carefully crafted to resonate with the target audience's existing beliefs and values while introducing new elements that serve the operator's goals."

> For example, during the COVID-19 pandemic, Russian state media introduced narratives suggesting that Western vaccines were dangerous or ineffective, while promoting Russian alternatives. These initial posts established frames that could later be amplified and reinforced through other strategies.

Strategy 2: Narrative Support

Once a narrative is introduced, it needs reinforcement to gain credibility and acceptance. This strategy involves amplifying the narrative by leveraging existing content and creating the impression of widespread support.

> "The goal here is to make the narrative seem more legitimate by showing that others believe it," explains Dr. Claire Reynolds, an expert in computational propaganda. "This often involves techniques like coordinated liking and sharing, or having multiple accounts post similar messages to create the illusion of consensus."

A common tactic is forced engagement, where networks of accounts interact with the narrative to increase its visibility and perceived reliability. This might include commenting on posts with supportive messages, sharing content across multiple platforms, or creating the appearance of organic discussion around the topic.

Strategy 3: Narrative Amplification

While narrative support focuses on building credibility, narrative amplification aims to maximize reach and virality. This strategy employs techniques designed to expand the audience exposed to the narrative and increase its perceived importance.

"Amplification is about gaming the algorithms," says social media analyst Jordan Rivera. "Operators use techniques like incentivizing sharing, creating search-optimized content, and designing clickbait to push the narrative to as many users as possible."

These techniques might include creating provocative Instagram reels with eye-catching visuals and emotional captions, developing hashtag campaigns that encourage user participation, or crafting content specifically designed to trigger platform recommendation algorithms.

Strategy 4: Counter-Narrative Reaction

Not all influence strategies focus on promoting a particular narrative; some aim to undermine competing perspectives. Counter-narrative reaction involves challenging, weakening, or redirecting attention from opposing viewpoints through strategic commenting and engagement.

"This is where we see the most direct confrontation in the information space," notes political scientist Dr. James Wilson. "Operators flood comment sections, reply threads, and discussion forums with content designed to derail conversations, attack credibility, or simply drown out opposing voices."

A typical example is the coordinated flooding of YouTube comment sections with either supportive messages for content that aligns with the operation's goals or critical and dismissive comments on content that challenges their narrative. The goal is to shape how other users perceive the discussion and to control which perspectives appear dominant.

Strategy 5: Narrative Manipulation

Rather than simply promoting or countering narratives, this strategy involves actively distorting existing information to reshape public perception. Narrative manipulation uses techniques like selective editing, decontextualization, and outright falsification to transform reality in service of the operation's objectives.

"This is perhaps the most insidious strategy," says media literacy educator Maria Rodriguez. "It takes advantage of real events or statements but twists them in ways that completely change their meaning or implications."

Common tactics include creating misleading headlines that misrepresent article content, editing videos to remove important context, or establishing fake news websites that mix factual reporting with strategic distortions. Social media advertising is often used to target specific user segments with this manipulated content, customized to exploit their particular biases and concerns.

Strategy 6: Target Degradation

Some influence operations focus not on promoting particular narratives but on silencing or discrediting specific individuals or groups who pose a threat to their objectives. Target degradation employs harassment, intimidation, and reputation attacks to diminish the influence of these targets.

> "This strategy is about removing obstacles," explains digital rights advocate Sarah Johnson. "If certain journalists, experts, or public figures are effectively countering an operation's narratives, they become targets for coordinated attacks designed to silence them or destroy their credibility."

> These attacks often begin with detailed intelligence gathering on the target, identifying vulnerabilities that can be exploited. The operation might then deploy personalized harassment campaigns, doxxing (revealing private information), or coordinated reporting of accounts to platform moderators in attempts to get them suspended.

Strategy 7: Information Pollution

The final strategy takes a broader approach, focusing not on specific narratives but on degrading the overall information environment. Information pollution—what Trustwave SpiderLabs calls "Distributed Denial of Truth" (DDoT)—floods social networks with excessive or conflicting content to create confusion and erode trust in all information sources.

> "This strategy doesn't necessarily promote a particular viewpoint," says cybersecurity researcher Alicia Montgomery. "Instead, it creates an environment where users become overwhelmed and unable to distinguish reliable information from falsehoods. When people can't tell what's true anymore, they become more susceptible to accepting simple but false explanations that align with their existing beliefs."

Tactics include generating massive volumes of low-quality content, creating multiple contradictory narratives around the same events, and deliberately introducing confusion into public discourse. The goal is to produce information fatigue, where users simply give up on trying to determine what's true.

Case Study: The Patriots Run Project

To understand how these strategies work together in practice, consider the case of the Patriots Run Project (PRP), a sophisticated influence operation uncovered by Meta's security team in 2024.

The operation created a network of 96 Facebook accounts, 16 pages, 12 groups, and 3 Instagram accounts, along with several domains including "patriotsrunproject.com" and a presence on X (formerly Twitter) through the account "PRPNational." While the accounts originated in Bangladesh, they crafted a false narrative of a widespread grassroots political advocacy group with chapters in several U.S. states.

"What made this operation particularly sophisticated was its patient approach to building credibility," explains social media researcher Dr. Sophia Kim. "The operators used AI to create initial profile pictures, which were later replaced with more personalized images. They carefully cultivated relationships with real users and established a seemingly legitimate organizational structure before beginning to push political content."

The operation employed multiple strategies from our framework:

- **Narrative Release**: Creating original content presenting PRP as a legitimate political movement with broad support across the United States.

- **Narrative Support**: Using the network of accounts to interact with each other's content, creating the appearance of an active community.

- **Narrative Amplification**: Establishing multiple "chapter" pages to make the movement appear more widespread than it actually was.

- **Narrative Manipulation**: Presenting foreign operators as American citizens concerned about domestic political issues.

- **Information Pollution**: Contributing to the cluttered political advocacy space, making it harder for users to distinguish genuine grassroots movements from artificial ones.

"What's particularly concerning about cases like PRP is how they blur the line between foreign and domestic influence," notes Dr. Kim. "By creating the appearance of a legitimate American political movement, foreign actors can inject their preferred narratives into domestic discourse while hiding their true origins and motives."

The Playbook in Action: How Campaigns Unfold

While understanding individual strategies is important, the real power of influence operations comes from how they combine these approaches into coordinated campaigns. Let's examine how a typical operation might unfold, drawing on real-world examples.

Stage 1: Establishing Presence

The operation begins with narrative release, introducing key themes and frames that will define the campaign. This often involves creating "anchor content" that subsequent activities can reference and build upon.

> During the 2016 U.S. election, for example, the Internet Research Agency created pages like "Heart of Texas" and "United Muslims of America," establishing seemingly authentic community spaces focused on specific identity groups. These pages initially posted relatively benign content related to state pride or religious identity, establishing their presence and building follower bases before pivoting to more divisive political content.

> "The initial content rarely reveals the operation's true objectives," explains disinformation researcher Dr. Rachel Goldman. "It's designed to attract followers, establish credibility, and begin building communities that can later be mobilized for influence purposes."

Stage 2: Building Momentum

As the operation progresses, it employs narrative support and amplification strategies to increase reach and engagement. This might involve coordinated action across multiple platforms, with content flowing from more permissive spaces to more mainstream ones.

> "There's often a clear pipeline," says technology policy expert Dr. Rebecca Chen. "Content might originate on fringe platforms with limited moderation, get refined based on engagement metrics, and then be repackaged for distribution on mainstream platforms like Facebook, Twitter, or YouTube."

> This stage frequently involves creating the illusion of organic virality, with networks of accounts strategically amplifying content to trigger recommendation algorithms. The goal is to reach a tipping point where real users begin sharing the content, providing authentic engagement that further boosts visibility and credibility.

Stage 3: Controlling the Conversation

Once a narrative gains traction, the operation shifts to maintaining control of how it's discussed and perceived. This involves counter-narrative reaction strategies to suppress or discredit opposing viewpoints while continuing to amplify supportive voices.

> "At this stage, we often see the deployment of what researchers call 'conversational AI,'" notes Dr. Chen. "These are automated systems designed to monitor discussions across platforms and deploy counter-messaging whenever the narrative is challenged. They might post pre-prepared talking points, engage in whataboutism to deflect criticism, or simply flood discussion spaces with noise to derail productive conversation."

> This stage might also involve target degradation tactics against particularly effective opponents. Journalists investigating the operation, fact-checkers debunking its claims, or influential figures speaking out against it may find themselves subjected to coordinated harassment or smear campaigns designed to neutralize their impact.

Stage 4: Adapting and Evolving

Sophisticated operations continuously monitor their effectiveness and adapt their approaches based on results. This might involve refining messaging, shifting platforms as moderation increases, or pivoting to new narratives when existing ones lose effectiveness.

> "The most advanced operations employ A/B testing and data analytics just like any digital marketing campaign," explains data scientist Dr. Marcus Williams. "They track engagement metrics, monitor sentiment, and continuously optimize their content and tactics based on what's working."

This adaptability makes influence operations particularly challenging to counter. By the time platforms or researchers identify and respond to specific tactics, operators have often already evolved their approaches to evade detection.

The AI Advantage: How Technology Is Transforming Influence Operations

While influence operations have existed for decades, the integration of artificial intelligence is dramatically enhancing their capabilities and impact. AI technologies are transforming every phase of influence operations, from planning to execution to analysis.

Content Generation at Scale

Perhaps the most obvious impact of AI is in content creation. Large language models and generative image models can produce vast quantities of high-quality, contextually appropriate content that would previously have required teams of human operators.

"The economics of influence operations have completely changed," says AI ethics researcher Dr. Eliza Montgomery. "What once required hundreds of staff working around the clock can now be accomplished with a handful of operators directing AI systems. This makes sophisticated influence campaigns accessible to a much wider range of actors, from smaller states to non-state groups and even individuals with sufficient technical knowledge."

These AI systems can generate content that is linguistically and culturally appropriate for specific target audiences, overcoming limitations that previously hampered influence operations targeting foreign populations. They can also rapidly adapt messaging based on current events, creating timely content that feels relevant and authentic.

Personalization and Targeting

AI also enables unprecedented levels of personalization in influence operations. By analyzing vast amounts of user data, these systems can identify specific psychological vulnerabilities and tailor content to exploit them.

"Modern influence operations don't just target demographic groups; they target psychological profiles," explains Dr. Williams. "They can identify users who are particularly susceptible to fear-based messaging, conspiracy theories, or appeals to specific values, and then deliver precisely calibrated content designed to resonate with those individuals."

This capability allows operators to segment audiences with remarkable precision, delivering different versions of the same narrative to different user groups based on what will most effectively influence each one. The result is a form of mass customization that maximizes impact while maintaining overall narrative coherence.

Detection Evasion

As platforms have improved their ability to identify and counter influence operations, AI has become crucial for evading these defenses. Advanced systems can analyze patterns of content that trigger platform detection algorithms and then modify their outputs to avoid these patterns while preserving the underlying message.

"It's an arms race," notes cybersecurity expert Robert Chen. "As detection systems improve, influence operations employ increasingly sophisticated evasion techniques. AI allows them to continuously test and refine their approaches, identifying what triggers detection and adjusting accordingly."

This capability extends to mimicking authentic human behavior patterns, avoiding the regularities in posting schedules, language use, or engagement patterns that might flag accounts as inauthentic. The result is influence operations that are increasingly difficult to distinguish from genuine user activity.

Real-time Adaptation

Perhaps most significantly, AI enables influence operations to adapt in real-time based on audience responses and changing circumstances. These systems can monitor engagement metrics, sentiment analysis, and broader conversation trends to continuously optimize their approaches.

"The feedback loop has become nearly instantaneous," says Dr. Montgomery. "Modern influence operations can test dozens of narrative variations simultaneously, identify which ones are gaining traction, and rapidly pivot resources to amplify the most effective messaging. This makes them far more responsive and adaptive than traditional influence campaigns."

This capability allows operators to capitalize on emerging opportunities and abandon unsuccessful approaches before investing significant resources. It also enables them to rapidly counter opposition narratives or adapt to changing platform policies that might otherwise disrupt their operations.

The Future of Shadow Influence

As we look ahead, several trends suggest that influence operations will become even more sophisticated, pervasive, and difficult to counter.

Multimodal Manipulation

While current operations primarily focus on text and static images, the rapid advancement of video and audio generation technologies is enabling new forms of manipulation that are even more persuasive and difficult to detect.

> "We're entering an era where seeing and hearing will no longer be believing," warns digital forensics expert Dr. Jonathan Park. "As these technologies improve, influence operations will increasingly incorporate synthetic video and audio content that is virtually indistinguishable from authentic recordings."

> This capability will enable more convincing impersonations of public figures, more emotionally impactful narrative delivery, and new forms of evidence fabrication that could fundamentally undermine trust in digital media.

Cross-platform Integration

Future influence operations will likely become more seamless in their integration across platforms, creating cohesive information ecosystems that guide users through carefully orchestrated journeys.

"We're already seeing operations that use different platforms for different phases of influence," notes Dr. Chen. "They might use TikTok for initial awareness, YouTube for deeper narrative development, Telegram for community building, and Twitter for mainstream amplification. As these operations become more sophisticated, they'll create even more integrated cross-platform experiences."

This approach makes operations more resilient to platform-specific countermeasures and allows them to leverage the unique affordances of each platform for maximum impact.

Human-AI Collaboration

The most effective future operations will likely involve close collaboration between human operators and AI systems, combining the strategic thinking and cultural understanding of humans with the scale and efficiency of artificial intelligence.

"The model we're moving toward is one where human operators provide strategic direction and quality control, while AI systems handle content generation, distribution, and adaptation," explains Dr. Montgomery. "This hybrid approach overcomes the limitations of both purely human and purely automated operations."

Such collaborations will enable more nuanced and contextually appropriate influence campaigns that can respond to complex social and political dynamics while maintaining the scale and efficiency that make modern influence operations so powerful.

Defensive Asymmetry

Perhaps most concerning is the growing asymmetry between offensive and defensive capabilities in the influence space. While the tools and techniques for conducting influence operations are becoming more accessible and powerful, our collective ability to detect and counter these operations is not advancing at the same pace.

> "The fundamental challenge is that it's inherently easier to create confusion than to create clarity," says democracy advocate Elena Martinez. "Influence operations don't need to convince everyone of a particular narrative; they just need to create enough doubt and division to prevent effective collective action. This gives them a structural advantage that is difficult to overcome."

> Addressing this asymmetry will require not just technical solutions but also social, educational, and institutional responses that build societal resilience to manipulation and foster healthier information ecosystems.

Conclusion: The Shadow War Continues

As we've seen throughout this chapter, influence operations represent a sophisticated form of information warfare that is continuously evolving in response to technological advancements, platform countermeasures, and changing social dynamics. Understanding the strategies and structures that underpin these operations is essential for recognizing and responding to them effectively.

> "What makes modern influence operations so dangerous is not just their technical sophistication but their deep understanding of human psychology and social dynamics," reflects Dr. Vasquez. "They exploit fundamental features of how we process information, form beliefs, and relate to others. This makes them particularly difficult to counter through purely technical means."

As AI continues to enhance the capabilities of influence operations, the challenge of maintaining a healthy information environment will only grow more complex. Meeting this challenge will require collaboration between technology platforms, government agencies, civil society organizations, and individual users, all working together to build more resilient digital communities and information systems.

In the next chapter, we'll explore how these influence operations manifest in one of their most powerful forms: the manipulation of crowd behavior and the creation of artificial social movements designed to advance strategic objectives while appearing to represent authentic grassroots activism.

Chapter 11: When the Mob Is Machine-Led

The crowd gathered quickly outside the courthouse. Within an hour, hundreds of protesters had assembled, their signs bearing identical slogans, their chants perfectly synchronized. Social media exploded with hashtags supporting their cause, thousands of accounts sharing the same message with minor variations. News outlets scrambled to cover what appeared to be a spontaneous uprising of public sentiment.

But something wasn't quite right.

A closer look revealed strange patterns. The protesters seemed oddly coordinated, their movements almost choreographed. Many couldn't articulate why they were there when interviewed. The social media accounts supporting the movement had thin profiles, created just weeks earlier. And when analysts examined the timing of posts, they found an unnatural synchronicity—thousands of messages appearing within seconds of each other.

This wasn't a grassroots movement. It was a synthetic one—a machine-led mob manufactured through artificial intelligence.

The Rise of Synthetic Social Movements

Throughout history, social movements have been the engines of change, from civil rights to environmental activism. These movements traditionally grew organically, spreading through human connections and shared grievances. But in the age of AI, we're witnessing something new: synthetic social movements that appear organic but are actually orchestrated by centralized entities using sophisticated technologies.

"What we're seeing now is fundamentally different from traditional propaganda or influence operations," explains Dr. Eliza Montgomery, a researcher specializing in computational propaganda at Oxford University. "These aren't just fake news stories or misleading advertisements. They're entire fabricated social movements complete with seemingly real participants, coordinated messaging, and the appearance of widespread public support."

The concept builds upon what political scientists have long called "astroturfing"—creating fake grassroots movements to give the appearance of widespread public support. The term itself is a play on "grassroots," implying something artificial designed to look natural, like AstroTurf. But while traditional astroturfing required significant human resources and coordination, AI has transformed this practice into something far more sophisticated and dangerous.

"Traditional astroturfing might involve hiring a few dozen people to show up at a protest or write letters to politicians," explains former intelligence analyst Marcus Chen. "Today's synthetic movements can involve thousands of AI-generated personas operating across multiple platforms simultaneously, creating the illusion of a massive public uprising with minimal human oversight."

The Anatomy of a Machine-Led Mob

To understand how synthetic social movements operate, we need to examine their components and the technologies that enable them.

Digital Foot Soldiers: Bots and Sock Puppets Evolved

The foot soldiers of synthetic movements are no longer simple bots posting repetitive messages. They've evolved into sophisticated AI-powered personas that can generate original content, engage in conversations, and adapt their behavior to avoid detection.

"What we're seeing now are hyper-realistic digital personas," explains social media researcher Dr. Aisha Johnson. "These aren't just accounts posting pre-written messages. They're AI systems that can generate unique content, respond to current events, and even engage with real humans in seemingly authentic ways."

These digital personas often have complete backstories, profile pictures generated by GANs (Generative Adversarial Networks), and posting histories that make them appear like genuine users. Some even have fabricated personal details—jobs, hobbies, family members—all generated by AI to create the appearance of authentic human accounts.

In Burma following the 2021 military coup, researchers identified networks of AI-driven bots that harassed activists and flooded social media with pro-junta narratives. These weren't simple automated accounts but sophisticated personas that could generate contextually relevant content and engage with real users, creating the impression of widespread support for the military government.

Coordination Through Artificial Intelligence

What distinguishes synthetic movements from genuine grassroots activism is their coordination patterns. Research published in Nature found that on average, 74% of accounts involved in astroturfing campaigns engaged in coordination behaviors like co-tweeting and co-retweeting—posting identical or similar content within very short time windows.

"Genuine social movements show organic patterns of information diffusion," explains network scientist Dr. David Schoch, one of the authors of the Nature study. "Information cascades through networks of real people at varying speeds as individuals see content, decide whether to share it, and then do so at their convenience. Synthetic movements, by contrast, show unnatural synchronization that betrays their centralized control."

This coordination extends beyond timing. Synthetic movements often display consistent messaging across platforms, with identical talking points appearing simultaneously on Twitter, Facebook, Instagram, and TikTok. The language may vary slightly, but the core narratives remain consistent in ways that organic movements rarely achieve.

The Command Structure: AI as Campaign Manager

At the heart of synthetic movements lies a sophisticated AI system that functions as a campaign manager, analyzing public sentiment, crafting messages, coordinating digital personas, and adapting strategies in real-time.

"These systems are essentially running influence operations that would have required dozens of human operatives just a few years ago," explains cybersecurity expert Rajiv Patel. "They can monitor news cycles, identify trending topics, generate content tailored to specific audiences, and deploy it through their networks of digital personas—all with minimal human oversight."

These AI campaign managers can:

- Monitor social media for trending topics and public sentiment
- Generate content optimized for emotional impact and virality
- Coordinate the activities of thousands of digital personas
- Adapt messaging based on audience responses
- Target specific demographic groups with customized content
- Identify and counter opposing narratives

The result is a synthetic movement that can respond to events and evolve its tactics far more quickly than traditional influence operations.

Case Studies in Synthetic Activism

The Anti-Vaccine "Parents' Coalition"

In 2023, a group calling itself the "National Parents' Coalition for Medical Freedom" seemingly emerged overnight, with thousands of social media accounts claiming to be concerned parents opposed to school vaccination requirements. The movement appeared to have chapters in dozens of cities, with local Facebook groups, Twitter accounts, and even physical protests outside school board meetings.

Investigation by the Digital Forensic Research Lab revealed that the entire movement was synthetic—created by a political consulting firm using AI tools to generate content, coordinate messaging, and even produce deepfake videos of supposed "parent testimonials." The operation included:

- Over 5,000 AI-generated social media profiles with fabricated backstories
- Coordinated posting schedules managed by an AI system
- Deepfake videos of "concerned parents" sharing emotional stories
- AI-generated "local chapter" websites with fabricated leadership teams
- Small paid protests supplemented by manipulated images to appear larger

"What made this operation particularly effective was how it blended digital deception with small real-world elements," explains disinformation researcher Emma Torres. "They would hire a handful of people to show up at a protest, then use AI to generate images making the crowd look ten times larger. This created the impression of a massive movement that simply didn't exist."

The "Citizens for Economic Justice" Campaign

In the lead-up to a major financial regulation vote, a seemingly grassroots movement called "Citizens for Economic Justice" emerged, advocating against new banking regulations. The movement appeared to represent ordinary citizens concerned about economic freedom, with thousands of social media accounts sharing personal stories about how the regulations would harm small businesses and families.

Analysis by researchers at Stanford's Internet Observatory revealed that the movement was entirely synthetic, created by a financial industry lobbying group using advanced AI tools. The operation included:

- AI-generated "citizen testimonials" tailored to specific congressional districts
- Coordinated social media campaigns targeting the constituents of key legislators
- Fake local business owners created using GAN-generated images and AI-written backstories
- Automated systems for generating personalized emails to legislators that appeared to come from real constituents

"What was particularly sophisticated about this operation was how it targeted specific geographic areas," notes political scientist Dr. James Wilson. "The AI system would generate content that referenced local landmarks, businesses, and concerns, making the messages appear to come from genuine local constituents rather than a centralized campaign."

The Technology Behind the Deception

The creation of synthetic social movements relies on several key technologies that have advanced dramatically in recent years.

Large Language Models as Content Factories

At the core of synthetic movements are large language models (LLMs) that can generate human-like text at scale. These models can produce thousands of unique posts, comments, articles, and emails that appear to come from different individuals while maintaining consistent messaging.

"The latest generation of language models can generate content that's nearly indistinguishable from human-written text," explains AI researcher Dr. Maya Patel. "They can adopt different writing styles, incorporate local references, and even simulate different personality types and educational backgrounds. This allows operators to create the illusion of diverse supporters all independently arriving at the same conclusions."

These models can also be fine-tuned to mimic specific demographics or political orientations, allowing operators to create content that resonates with particular target audiences. A synthetic movement targeting conservative voters, for instance, might use language models trained on conservative media to generate content that uses familiar phrases and references.

Generative Adversarial Networks for Visual Deception

The visual components of synthetic movements—profile pictures, event photos, and video testimonials—are increasingly generated using GANs and other generative AI technologies. These systems can create images of non-existent people, fabricate crowd scenes, or even produce deepfake videos of fictional supporters.

"The quality of AI-generated imagery has improved exponentially," notes visual forensics expert Dr. Carlos Mendez. "Just a few years ago, GAN-generated faces had obvious tells—asymmetrical features, strange backgrounds, weird artifacts. Today's systems produce images that can fool even trained observers without specialized tools."

This visual deception extends beyond static images. Deepfake technology allows operators to create video testimonials from fictional supporters, complete with emotional delivery and personal stories. These videos can be particularly persuasive, as humans are naturally inclined to trust visual evidence and emotional appeals.

Coordination Algorithms for Orchestrating Campaigns

Behind every synthetic movement is a sophisticated coordination system that manages the activities of thousands of digital personas across multiple platforms. These systems schedule posts, monitor responses, and adapt strategies based on public engagement.

> "These coordination systems are essentially AI campaign managers," explains computational propaganda researcher Dr. Sophia Chen. "They can track which messages are resonating, which platforms are generating the most engagement, and which audiences are most receptive to particular narratives. They then adjust the campaign in real-time to maximize impact."

> These systems also incorporate sophisticated timing algorithms that avoid the unnatural synchronization patterns that might trigger detection systems. Rather than having all accounts post simultaneously, they might stagger posts in patterns that mimic organic human behavior while still achieving the desired amplification effect.

Detecting the Machine-Led Mob

As synthetic movements become more sophisticated, detecting them becomes increasingly challenging. However, researchers and platform security teams have developed several approaches for identifying these operations.

Network Analysis: Finding the Patterns in Chaos

One of the most effective methods for detecting synthetic movements is network analysis—examining the patterns of connections and interactions between accounts to identify unnatural coordination.

> "Genuine social movements have organic network structures," explains data scientist Dr. Rebecca Liu. "Information flows through existing social connections, creating patterns that reflect real human relationships. Synthetic movements, by contrast, often show distinctive patterns of coordination that betray their artificial nature."

> These patterns might include:

- Clusters of accounts that consistently interact with each other but have few connections to the broader network
- Unnatural timing patterns, with multiple accounts posting similar content within seconds of each other
- Coordinated amplification, where the same content is shared by multiple accounts in predictable sequences

By mapping these interaction patterns, analysts can identify the telltale signatures of synthetic movements even when the individual accounts appear convincing.

Linguistic Analysis: Finding the Machine's Voice

Despite their sophistication, AI-generated content often contains subtle linguistic patterns that distinguish it from human-written text. Researchers have developed tools that can analyze large volumes of content to identify these patterns.

> "AI-generated text often has statistical properties that differ from human writing," explains computational linguist Dr. Jonathan Park. "These include patterns in sentence structure, word choice, and stylistic consistency that might not be obvious to casual readers but can be detected through computational analysis."

These linguistic markers become particularly evident when analyzing large volumes of content from a synthetic movement. While individual posts might appear convincing, patterns emerge across the collective output that reveal their shared origin.

Temporal Analysis: The Rhythm of Deception

The timing of activity within synthetic movements often betrays their artificial nature. Genuine social movements show organic patterns of activity that reflect human behavior—surges during waking hours, lulls overnight, variations based on weekdays versus weekends.

> "Synthetic movements often show unnatural temporal patterns," notes social media researcher Dr. Michael Chen. "Even when they try to mimic human activity cycles, they typically lack the natural variability of genuine movements. They might show too much consistency, too little regional variation, or suspicious coordination across time zones."

By analyzing these temporal patterns, researchers can identify movements that don't follow natural human rhythms, suggesting centralized coordination rather than organic growth.

The Future of Synthetic Social Movements

As AI technology continues to advance, synthetic social movements will become increasingly sophisticated and difficult to detect. Several emerging trends point to the future evolution of this phenomenon.

Hybrid Operations: Blending Real and Synthetic Elements

Future synthetic movements will likely blend AI-generated elements with genuine human participation, creating hybrid operations that are particularly difficult to detect and counter.

"The most effective disinformation campaigns have always combined elements of truth with fabrication," explains strategic communications expert Dr. Natalia Ivanova. "Future synthetic movements will likely recruit genuine believers to serve as the public face of the movement, while using AI to amplify their message and create the impression of widespread support."

These hybrid operations might start with a small core of genuine believers, then use AI to identify and target potential sympathizers with personalized messaging. As real humans join the movement, the operation gains authenticity while still benefiting from AI-powered amplification and coordination.

Personalized Persuasion at Scale

Advances in AI will enable increasingly personalized targeting, with synthetic movements tailoring their messages to individual psychological profiles and personal concerns.

"The future of synthetic movements isn't just about creating fake supporters—it's about personalizing persuasion for each target," warns digital ethics researcher Dr. Thomas Wright. "By analyzing your digital footprint, these systems can identify your specific concerns, values, and psychological triggers, then generate content designed specifically to resonate with you."

This personalization could make synthetic movements particularly effective at recruiting genuine supporters who don't realize they're being manipulated by an AI-orchestrated campaign.

Cross-Platform Coordination

Future synthetic movements will operate seamlessly across multiple platforms and media channels, creating an immersive information environment that's difficult to escape.

> "The most sophisticated operations won't be limited to social media," explains media researcher Dr. Sophia Rodriguez. "They'll coordinate messaging across platforms, traditional media, email, messaging apps, and even physical spaces, creating an impression that 'everyone is talking about this' from multiple independent sources."

> This cross-platform approach makes synthetic movements more convincing by creating the impression of independent verification—when in fact, all the messages are coming from the same centralized operation.

Defending Against the Machine-Led Mob

As synthetic movements become more sophisticated, developing effective countermeasures becomes increasingly important. Several approaches show promise for detecting and countering these operations.

Platform-Level Detection and Enforcement

Social media platforms are developing increasingly sophisticated systems for detecting coordinated inauthentic behavior, including the patterns associated with synthetic movements.

"The platforms have a vested interest in maintaining user trust," notes platform policy expert Maria Gonzalez. "They're investing heavily in systems that can identify unnatural coordination patterns, suspicious account creation patterns, and other indicators of synthetic movements."

These detection systems increasingly use the same AI technologies that power synthetic movements, creating an ongoing technological arms race between those creating deception and those trying to detect it.

Media Literacy and Public Education

Educating the public about the existence and methods of synthetic movements is crucial for building societal resilience against these operations.

"People are much less susceptible to manipulation when they understand how it works," explains media literacy educator Dr. James Wilson. "Teaching people to recognize the signs of synthetic movements—like sudden emergence, perfect message discipline, and unnatural coordination—can help them approach viral content with appropriate skepticism."

This education needs to reach beyond traditional media literacy to include specific information about how AI is used to create synthetic movements and the warning signs that might indicate artificial coordination.

Transparency and Authentication Systems

New technologies for verifying the authenticity of content and accounts could help distinguish genuine expression from synthetic manipulation.

"We need systems that can verify the provenance of content and the identity of those creating it," argues digital rights advocate Elena Kuznetsova. "This doesn't mean eliminating anonymity, but rather creating mechanisms that can distinguish between genuine human expression and machine-generated content without necessarily revealing personal identities."

These systems might include digital watermarking for AI-generated content, blockchain-based authentication for verified human accounts, or platform features that indicate the age and activity patterns of accounts sharing viral content.

The Ethical Battlefield

The rise of synthetic social movements raises profound ethical questions about the nature of public discourse, political participation, and democratic processes.

"We're entering an era where the line between genuine public opinion and manufactured sentiment is increasingly blurred," warns political philosopher Dr. Marcus Johnson. "This threatens the foundational assumption of democracy—that governance should reflect the authentic will of the people."

When public discourse can be manipulated through synthetic movements, how do we determine what the public truly wants? When politicians respond to what appears to be constituent pressure but is actually a machine-led mob, whose interests are really being served?

These questions have no easy answers, but they highlight the importance of developing both technological and social responses to the challenge of synthetic movements. The future of authentic public discourse—and perhaps democracy itself—may depend on our ability to distinguish between genuine grassroots activism and the machine-led mob.

As we navigate this new landscape, one thing is clear: the battle between authentic human expression and synthetic manipulation will be one of the defining conflicts of the digital age. And it's a battle we cannot afford to lose.

Chapter 12: Weaponized Virality

The video appeared on TikTok on a Tuesday morning. By Wednesday afternoon, it had been viewed over ten million times. By Friday, it had spread to Twitter, Facebook, and Instagram, accumulating another thirty million views. News outlets began covering the story. Politicians issued statements. Public outrage mounted.

> The video showed a prominent politician making inflammatory remarks about immigrants—remarks that seemed wildly out of character but were delivered with convincing authenticity. The timing couldn't have been worse: just three weeks before a contentious election.

> There was just one problem: the video was entirely fabricated. The politician had never said those words. The video was a sophisticated deepfake, created using AI tools and strategically released to exploit social media algorithms and trigger maximum virality.

> But by the time fact-checkers could debunk the video, the damage was done. The algorithms had already worked their magic, propelling the content to millions of users who were primed to believe it. The video had achieved what its creators intended: weaponized virality.

The Virality Machine

Social media platforms run on engagement. Every like, share, comment, and click feeds into sophisticated algorithms designed to maximize user attention—the most valuable commodity in the attention economy. These algorithms aren't passive conduits of information; they're active shapers of what content spreads and how quickly it travels.

"The fundamental architecture of social media platforms is built to amplify content that generates engagement," explains Dr. Samantha Chen, a digital media researcher at Stanford University. "This isn't inherently problematic, but when combined with sophisticated AI tools designed to manipulate these systems, it creates a perfect storm for weaponized virality."

Weaponized virality refers to the deliberate exploitation of social media algorithms to rapidly spread manipulative content to vast audiences. It's not merely about creating compelling content; it's about understanding and manipulating the invisible machinery that determines what content gets seen.

How Algorithms Decide What Goes Viral

To understand weaponized virality, we first need to understand how social media algorithms work. While each platform has its own proprietary algorithms, they share common principles.

"Social media algorithms are essentially prediction machines," explains former Facebook engineer Marcus Williams. "They analyze countless signals—what content you engage with, how long you watch videos, what your friends are sharing, what's generating engagement across the platform—to predict what will keep you scrolling."

These algorithms typically consider several key factors:

- **Engagement metrics**: Likes, shares, comments, and other interactions signal content value to algorithms.
- **User relationships**: Content from accounts you frequently interact with gets prioritized.
- **Content type**: Different platforms favor different formats (videos on TikTok, images on Instagram).
- **Recency**: Newer content generally gets preference over older posts.

- **Time spent**: How long users view or interact with content influences its spread.
- **Completion rate**: Whether users watch videos to completion or read entire posts.

But perhaps most importantly, these algorithms are designed to maximize emotional engagement. Content that triggers strong emotional responses—whether outrage, fear, amusement, or inspiration—tends to generate more engagement and thus receives algorithmic amplification.

> "The algorithms don't care if content is true, balanced, or socially beneficial," notes digital ethics researcher Dr. Elena Rodriguez. "They only care if it captures and holds attention. This creates a fundamental vulnerability that manipulators can exploit."

The Dual Role of AI in Algorithmic Manipulation

Artificial intelligence plays a dual role in the ecosystem of social media virality—both as a tool for manipulation and as a mechanism for algorithmic decision-making.

AI as the Manipulator

Advanced AI systems now enable manipulators to create content specifically designed to trigger algorithmic amplification. These systems analyze vast datasets of previously viral content to identify patterns and characteristics that correlate with high engagement.

> "It's like having a cheat code for social media algorithms," explains cybersecurity expert Rajiv Patel. "These AI tools can predict with remarkable accuracy what types of content will go viral on specific platforms, allowing manipulators to craft their messages accordingly."

These AI systems can:

- Generate emotionally provocative headlines and captions
- Identify optimal posting times for maximum initial engagement
- Create content tailored to specific demographic groups
- Predict which hashtags will amplify content reach
- Craft visuals optimized for algorithmic preference

The result is content precision-engineered to exploit algorithmic vulnerabilities and trigger viral spread.

AI as the Gatekeeper

On the other side, the social media platforms themselves rely on AI systems to determine content ranking and distribution. These algorithms continuously learn from user behavior, adapting their predictions to maximize engagement.

> "The platform algorithms are essentially black boxes," notes digital media scholar Dr. James Wilson. "Even the engineers who build them can't fully predict how they'll behave in all circumstances because they're constantly learning and evolving based on user interactions."

> This opacity creates opportunities for manipulation. By studying how algorithms respond to different types of content, manipulators can reverse-engineer the system, identifying exploitable patterns and vulnerabilities.

Techniques of Algorithmic Exploitation

Manipulators employ several sophisticated techniques to weaponize virality and exploit algorithmic vulnerabilities.

Coordinated Inauthentic Behavior

One of the most effective techniques involves creating the illusion of organic engagement through coordinated networks of accounts. These networks—which may include both automated bots and human-operated accounts—work together to generate initial engagement that tricks algorithms into perceiving content as naturally viral.

> "The first few minutes after content is posted are critical," explains social media researcher Dr. Maya Patel. "Algorithms look for early engagement signals to identify potentially viral content. By using coordinated networks to generate these signals artificially, manipulators can essentially jump-start the virality process."

> A 2023 internal Facebook report revealed that disinformation campaigns from Eastern Europe had used this technique to reach nearly half of all Americans before the 2020 election. These campaigns produced some of the most popular pages for Christian and Black American content, reaching 140 million U.S. users monthly—despite the fact that 75% of exposed users hadn't followed any of the pages. They saw the content because Facebook's recommendation system put it into their feeds after detecting high engagement signals.

Emotional Exploitation

Another powerful technique involves crafting content specifically designed to trigger strong emotional responses. AI systems can analyze which emotional triggers generate the most engagement for specific audience segments and tailor content accordingly.

"Different emotions drive different types of engagement," notes psychologist Dr. Sarah Johnson. "Outrage and anger drive sharing. Awe and inspiration drive likes. Fear drives comments. By targeting specific emotional triggers, manipulators can optimize for the type of engagement that algorithms value most."

This emotional manipulation is particularly effective because it exploits fundamental human cognitive biases. Our brains are wired to pay attention to emotionally charged information—a survival mechanism that helped our ancestors respond quickly to threats and opportunities. In the digital environment, this natural tendency makes us vulnerable to manipulation.

Timing and Trend Exploitation

Sophisticated manipulators also exploit temporal patterns in algorithmic behavior, timing their content to coincide with periods of heightened algorithmic sensitivity or reduced moderation capacity.

"Platforms often adjust their algorithms in response to major events or at specific times of day," explains former Twitter engineer Alex Chen. "By studying these patterns, manipulators can identify windows of opportunity when content is more likely to receive algorithmic amplification."

Similarly, manipulators exploit trending topics and hashtags to piggyback on existing algorithmic attention. By connecting their manipulative content to trending conversations, they can hijack the algorithmic boost these trends receive.

Case Studies in Weaponized Virality

The abstract threat of weaponized virality becomes concrete when we examine specific cases where these techniques have been deployed with devastating effect.

The Biden Robocall: Exploiting Algorithmic Blind Spots

In January 2024, just days before the New Hampshire primary, thousands of Democratic voters received a robocall that appeared to be from President Biden, urging them not to vote in the primary and "save your vote for the November election." The call used AI voice cloning technology to mimic Biden's voice with remarkable accuracy.

While the call itself reached only a limited audience, recordings quickly spread across social media platforms. The initial posts came from accounts with suspicious patterns of activity—created recently, posting political content at unusual hours, and engaging primarily with divisive topics.

"What made this case particularly effective was how it exploited algorithmic blind spots," explains disinformation researcher Emma Torres. "The platforms' AI systems were trained to detect deepfake videos but were less effective at identifying audio deepfakes. By the time human moderators identified the problem, the content had already achieved viral spread."

The incident demonstrated how manipulators can identify and exploit gaps in platform detection systems, using one medium (phone calls) to seed content that then spreads virally through another (social media).

Operation Shadow Amplification: Manufacturing Consensus

In 2023, researchers uncovered a sophisticated influence operation targeting multiple European elections. Dubbed "Operation Shadow Amplification," the campaign used AI-generated content and coordinated networks to create the appearance of widespread public support for fringe political positions.

The operation employed a technique called "distributed denial of truth" (DDoT), flooding social media platforms with thousands of slightly varied messages promoting the same narrative. Each individual message received modest engagement, but collectively they created the impression of a groundswell of public opinion.

"What made this operation particularly insidious was how it exploited recommendation algorithms," notes political scientist Dr. Thomas Wright. "By generating content tailored to specific demographic groups and interests, they ensured that users would encounter these narratives through seemingly unrelated content recommendations."

The operation demonstrated how sophisticated understanding of algorithmic recommendation systems can be weaponized to create the illusion of consensus around fringe viewpoints.

The Future of Weaponized Virality

As AI technologies continue to advance, the techniques for weaponizing virality will become increasingly sophisticated and difficult to detect.

Personalized Manipulation at Scale

Future manipulation campaigns will likely employ increasingly personalized approaches, using AI to tailor content to individual psychological profiles and vulnerabilities.

> "The next frontier is hyper-personalized manipulation," warns digital ethics researcher Dr. Natalia Ivanova. "AI systems can analyze your digital footprint to identify your specific concerns, values, and psychological triggers, then generate content designed specifically to resonate with you and prompt sharing behavior."

> This personalization could make synthetic movements particularly effective at recruiting genuine supporters who don't realize they're being manipulated by an AI-orchestrated campaign.

Cross-Platform Coordination

Future campaigns will also likely employ sophisticated cross-platform strategies, coordinating content across multiple media channels to create an immersive information environment.

> "The most sophisticated operations won't be limited to social media," explains media researcher Dr. Sophia Rodriguez. "They'll coordinate messaging across platforms, traditional media, email, messaging apps, and even physical spaces, creating an impression that 'everyone is talking about this' from multiple independent sources."

> This cross-platform approach makes synthetic movements more convincing by creating the impression of independent verification—when in fact, all the messages are coming from the same centralized operation.

The Algorithmic Arms Race

As manipulation techniques evolve, platforms are developing increasingly sophisticated countermeasures, creating an ongoing technological arms race between those creating deception and those trying to detect it.

> "The platforms have a vested interest in maintaining user trust," notes platform policy expert Maria Gonzalez. "They're investing heavily in systems that can identify unnatural coordination patterns, suspicious account creation patterns, and other indicators of synthetic movements."

> These detection systems increasingly use the same AI technologies that power synthetic movements, creating an ongoing technological arms race between those creating deception and those trying to detect it.

Defending Against Weaponized Virality

As the threat of weaponized virality grows, developing effective countermeasures becomes increasingly important. Several approaches show promise for detecting and countering these operations.

Platform-Level Detection and Enforcement

Social media platforms are developing increasingly sophisticated systems for detecting coordinated inauthentic behavior, including the patterns associated with synthetic movements.

> These detection systems analyze multiple signals, including:

- Timing patterns of posts and engagement

- Network relationships between accounts
- Linguistic patterns in content
- Account creation and activity patterns
- Engagement distribution across content

By identifying suspicious patterns in these signals, platforms can flag potential manipulation campaigns for human review and enforcement action.

Adding Friction to Viral Spread

Another promising approach involves adding "friction" to slow down the process of spreading information, particularly for content showing viral potential.

"High-velocity sharing is often a red flag," explains social media researcher Dr. Michael Chen. "By adding verification steps or cooling-off periods for content that's spreading unusually quickly, platforms can reduce the effectiveness of manipulation campaigns without significantly impacting legitimate viral content."

These friction mechanisms might include CAPTCHA tests for sharing highly viral content, temporary limits on sharing frequency, or enhanced fact-checking for content showing unusual spread patterns.

Algorithmic Transparency and User Control

Perhaps most importantly, addressing weaponized virality requires greater transparency about how algorithms work and more user control over content recommendations.

"Users have a right to understand why they're seeing specific content," argues digital rights advocate Elena Kuznetsova. "Platforms should provide clear explanations for algorithmic recommendations and give users meaningful control over the factors that influence their feeds."

This transparency would not only empower users to make informed choices but also create accountability for platforms, encouraging them to design algorithms that prioritize accuracy and social benefit alongside engagement.

The Ethical Battlefield

The rise of weaponized virality raises profound ethical questions about the nature of public discourse, political participation, and democratic processes.

"We're entering an era where the line between genuine public opinion and manufactured sentiment is increasingly blurred," warns political philosopher Dr. Marcus Johnson. "This threatens the foundational assumption of democracy—that governance should reflect the authentic will of the people."

When public discourse can be manipulated through weaponized virality, how do we determine what the public truly wants? When politicians respond to what appears to be constituent pressure but is actually a machine-led campaign, whose interests are really being served?

These questions have no easy answers, but they highlight the importance of developing both technological and social responses to the challenge of weaponized virality. The future of authentic public discourse—and perhaps democracy itself—may depend on our ability to distinguish between genuine viral phenomena and weaponized manipulation.

As we navigate this new landscape, one thing is clear: the battle between authentic human expression and algorithmic manipulation will be one of the defining conflicts of the digital age. And it's a battle we cannot afford to lose.

Chapter 13: How to Spot Synthetic Influence

The email arrived on a Tuesday morning. It appeared to be from your bank, warning about suspicious activity on your account. The formatting looked perfect—the bank's logo, the right fonts, even the footer with all the legal disclaimers. The message conveyed urgency: "Click here to verify your identity and secure your account."

But something felt off. Maybe it was the generic greeting, or perhaps the subtle pressure tactics. You hesitated, examined the sender's email address more carefully, and noticed it wasn't quite right—close to your bank's domain, but with an extra character. You deleted the email, and later learned that thousands of customers had received the same AI-generated phishing attempt.

You just spotted synthetic influence in the wild. And in doing so, you protected yourself from potential financial harm.

In previous chapters, we've explored the sophisticated tools and techniques used to create synthetic influence campaigns. Now, we turn to perhaps the most crucial question: How can ordinary people detect these increasingly sophisticated deceptions? How can we develop the skills to distinguish between authentic human communication and artificial manipulation?

"The most powerful defense against synthetic influence is an informed public," explains Dr. Maya Patel, a digital literacy researcher at Stanford University. "When people understand what to look for, they become much harder to manipulate."

This chapter provides a comprehensive guide to spotting synthetic influence across various media types and contexts. While no single technique is foolproof—and detection becomes more challenging as AI technology advances—combining multiple approaches can significantly improve your ability to identify artificial manipulation.

The Visual Domain: Spotting AI-Generated Images

Images are perhaps the most visceral form of synthetic influence. A compelling picture can trigger emotional responses before our rational mind has time to analyze what we're seeing. And with the rapid advancement of generative AI tools, creating realistic fake images has never been easier.

The Telltale Signs of Synthetic Images

Despite their increasing sophistication, AI-generated images still contain subtle artifacts and inconsistencies that human creators wouldn't make. Training yourself to notice these details can help you identify synthetic images.

> "AI systems struggle with certain aspects of visual coherence that humans take for granted," explains computer vision researcher Dr. James Wilson. "The human visual system is exquisitely tuned to notice these inconsistencies, even if we can't immediately articulate what seems wrong."

> Here are the key visual elements to examine when assessing an image's authenticity:

1. Hands and Fingers

One of the most reliable indicators of AI-generated imagery is unnatural hand rendering. Even advanced AI systems struggle with the complex anatomy of human hands.

> "Hands are incredibly complex structures with 27 bones, 29 joints, and over 30 muscles," explains digital forensics expert Sarah Johnson. "They can move in countless ways, and AI systems often fail to render them correctly."

Look for these specific anomalies: - Extra fingers (six or more on one hand) - Fused or blended fingers that lack clear separation - Unnatural joint positions or impossible bends - Inconsistent lighting or texturing on hands compared to the rest of the body

These hand-related artifacts are so common that they've become something of an inside joke among AI researchers. But for the average person, they represent one of the most reliable ways to spot synthetic imagery.

2. Facial Features and Consistency

The human face is another area where AI systems often make subtle but detectable mistakes. Our brains are highly specialized for facial recognition, making us sensitive to even minor inconsistencies.

When examining faces in suspicious images, pay attention to:

- **Eyes and eyebrows**: Look for symmetry issues, unnatural reflections, or inconsistent gaze direction. AI-generated eyes may appear too perfect or lack the subtle asymmetries of real human eyes.

- **Skin texture**: AI often creates unnaturally smooth skin or applies aging inconsistently across the face. The forehead might show wrinkles while cheeks appear impossibly smooth.

- **Hair rendering**: Hair is particularly challenging for AI systems. Look for unnatural hairlines, hair that appears painted rather than consisting of individual strands, or hair that doesn't move naturally with the person's position.

- **Teeth and ears**: These features are often rendered with subtle flaws. Teeth might appear too uniform or unnaturally white, while ears may have unusual shapes or lack expected details.

"The uncanny valley effect—that sense of discomfort we feel when something looks almost but not quite human—is our brain's way of alerting us to these inconsistencies," explains cognitive psychologist Dr. Elena Rodriguez. "Trust that feeling when something seems off about a face, even if you can't immediately identify why."

3. Environmental Coherence

AI systems often struggle with maintaining physical and environmental coherence throughout an image. These inconsistencies can be subtle but revealing.

Look for:

- **Background anomalies**: AI often blurs backgrounds entirely to hide its inability to render complex scenes consistently. Unnaturally blurred backgrounds or backgrounds with warped perspectives can indicate synthetic creation.

- **Architectural impossibilities**: Buildings with physically impossible features, such as windows that don't align, doors of inconsistent sizes, or walls that curve unnaturally.

- **Lighting and shadow inconsistencies**: Multiple light sources creating contradictory shadows, or objects that don't cast shadows at all. Pay particular attention to how light interacts with glasses, jewelry, or reflective surfaces.

- **Text elements**: AI systems often struggle with text rendering. Look for gibberish text, inconsistent fonts, or text that doesn't follow the natural perspective of the surface it appears on.

"Environmental coherence requires understanding complex physical laws and spatial relationships," notes computer graphics professor Dr. Michael Chen. "Current AI systems can create convincing foregrounds but often fail to maintain consistency throughout the entire scene."

Tools for Image Verification

While developing your own visual detection skills is valuable, several tools can assist in identifying synthetic images:

- **Reverse image searches**: Services like Google Images, TinEye, or Bing Visual Search can help determine if an image appeared elsewhere online before being modified.

- **Metadata analysis**: Tools like ExifTool can reveal information about when and how an image was created, though sophisticated manipulators often strip or falsify this data.

- **AI detection platforms**: Services like Hive Moderation, Hugging Face's detection models, and Winston AI specifically analyze images for signs of AI generation.

"No single tool is foolproof," cautions digital forensics expert Thomas Wright. "The most effective approach combines multiple verification methods with your own critical assessment."

The Textual Domain: Identifying AI-Written Content

Text-based synthetic influence—from social media posts to news articles to emails—presents its own detection challenges. Modern language models like GPT-4 can produce remarkably human-like text, but subtle patterns and inconsistencies remain detectable.

Linguistic and Stylistic Indicators

When assessing whether text might be AI-generated, consider these factors:

1. Unnatural Perfection

AI-generated text often exhibits a level of grammatical perfection and consistency that human writers rarely achieve, especially in casual communication.

> "Human writing contains natural variations—occasional typos, inconsistent capitalization, or regional expressions," explains linguistics professor Dr. Sarah Thompson. "The absence of these human touches can be a red flag."

> Look for: - Consistently perfect grammar and punctuation across long texts - Absence of the stylistic quirks that characterize human writing - Overly formal language in contexts where humans would be casual - Unnaturally consistent tone throughout lengthy content

2. Repetitive Patterns and Phrasing

AI systems often fall into repetitive patterns, particularly in how they structure arguments or transition between ideas.

> "Language models are essentially sophisticated pattern-matching systems," explains NLP researcher Dr. James Wilson. "They tend to reuse successful patterns they've learned, creating subtle repetitiveness that human writers would avoid."

> Watch for: - Overuse of certain transition phrases ("moreover," "furthermore," "in addition") - Similar sentence structures repeated throughout the text - Predictable paragraph organization - Repetitive word choices or turns of phrase

3. Contextual Inconsistencies

AI systems sometimes struggle with maintaining consistent context throughout longer pieces, particularly regarding specific details or specialized knowledge.

"AI can hallucinate facts or contradict itself because it doesn't truly understand the content it's generating," notes AI ethics researcher Dr. Elena Martinez. "It's making statistical predictions about what words should come next, not reasoning from a coherent understanding."

Look for: - Factual contradictions within the same piece - Vague references to specific events without precise details - Anachronisms or references that don't align with the purported time frame - Misunderstanding of specialized terminology or concepts

4. Emotional Flatness

Despite improvements in emotional modeling, AI-generated text often lacks the authentic emotional depth and nuance of human writing, particularly when discussing personal experiences or controversial topics.

"Human writing reflects lived experience and genuine emotional complexity," explains digital psychology researcher Dr. Michael Brown. "AI can simulate these qualities but typically produces a flattened version that lacks true emotional resonance."

Watch for: - Balanced, measured takes on topics that typically evoke strong emotions - Generic descriptions of emotional experiences without specific, vivid details - Avoidance of truly controversial positions - Lack of personal voice or distinctive perspective

Tools for Text Verification

Several tools can help identify AI-generated text, though their reliability varies:

- **AI content detectors**: Services like GPTZero, Content at Scale AI Detector, and Copyleaks analyze text for patterns consistent with AI generation.

- **Stylometric analysis tools**: These examine writing style for consistency with an author's known work or for patterns typical of AI generation.

- **Cross-reference verification**: Fact-checking tools and services can verify specific claims made in suspicious text.

"The detection landscape is constantly evolving," notes digital forensics expert Dr. Lisa Chen. "As generation technology improves, detection tools must also advance. The most reliable approach combines technological tools with human judgment."

The Audio and Video Domain: Detecting Deepfakes

Perhaps the most concerning form of synthetic influence involves manipulated audio and video—so-called "deepfakes." These can be particularly convincing because they engage multiple senses simultaneously and leverage our inherent trust in what we see and hear.

Visual Cues in Deepfake Videos

When assessing video authenticity, pay attention to these elements:

1. Facial Anomalies

Deepfake technology typically focuses on face replacement or manipulation, making facial inconsistencies the most reliable indicators.

> "The face is in constant motion, with subtle micro-expressions and movements that are difficult to fake perfectly," explains computer vision researcher Dr. Thomas Lee. "These inconsistencies become more apparent in motion than in still images."

> Look for: - Unnatural blinking patterns (too frequent, too rare, or synchronized blinking) - Facial movements that don't match the emotional content of speech - Inconsistent skin tone or texture at the boundaries of the face - Unnatural head movements or positioning

2. Audio-Visual Synchronization

The coordination between audio and visual elements often reveals deepfakes.

> "Our brains are highly sensitive to audio-visual synchronization," notes neuroscientist Dr. Maria Garcia. "Even slight misalignments between what we see and hear can trigger our suspicion, even if we can't immediately identify why something seems off."

> Watch for: - Lip movements that don't precisely match the spoken words - Inconsistent audio quality compared to video quality - Unnatural mouth movements or positions when speaking - Mismatched emotional tone between voice and facial expressions

3. Contextual Inconsistencies

As with images, deepfake videos often contain contextual elements that don't maintain consistency throughout the recording.

Look for: - Objects that appear, disappear, or change unexpectedly - Lighting changes that don't correspond to apparent light sources - Inconsistent reflections in glasses or other reflective surfaces - Background elements that behave unnaturally

Audio Deepfake Detection

Voice cloning and audio deepfakes present their own detection challenges:

"Voice is as unique as a fingerprint, with subtle characteristics that AI systems struggle to maintain consistently," explains audio forensics expert Dr. James Wilson. "Training yourself to listen for these inconsistencies can help identify synthetic audio."

Listen for: - Unnatural breathing patterns or lack of breath sounds - Robotic or mechanical undertones to the voice - Inconsistent background noise - Unusual transitions between words or sentences - Emotional flatness or inappropriate emotional emphasis

Tools for Deepfake Detection

Several specialized tools can assist in identifying deepfake content:

- **Deepfake detection platforms**: Services like Sensity AI, Deeptrace, and Microsoft Video Authenticator specifically analyze videos for signs of manipulation.

- **Audio forensics tools**: Specialized software can analyze audio for signs of synthetic generation or manipulation.

- **Metadata analysis**: As with images, examining video metadata can sometimes reveal manipulation, though this data is often stripped or falsified.

"The technology for creating deepfakes and the technology for detecting them are in a constant arms race," notes digital security expert Dr. Elena Rodriguez. "What's detectable today may be undetectable tomorrow, making ongoing education and vigilance essential."

Social Media-Specific Detection Strategies

Social media platforms present unique challenges for synthetic influence detection, given their fast-paced nature and the mix of content types they contain. Several platform-specific strategies can help identify manipulation:

Account Analysis

The accounts spreading synthetic content often contain their own red flags:

> "Synthetic influence operations typically involve networks of accounts rather than isolated instances," explains disinformation researcher Dr. Thomas Wright. "Examining the accounts themselves can reveal patterns indicative of coordinated manipulation."

> Look for: - Recently created accounts with high activity levels - Profile photos that show AI-generation artifacts - Inconsistent or generic biographical information - Unusual posting patterns (such as 24/7 activity without breaks) - Disconnection between claimed identity and content knowledge

Engagement Patterns

How content spreads and engages users can provide clues about its authenticity:

> "Organic content typically follows natural engagement patterns, while manipulated content often shows unusual amplification signatures," notes social media researcher Dr. Sarah Johnson.

> Watch for: - Suspiciously rapid accumulation of likes, shares, or comments - Engagement that doesn't match the account's follower count - Comments that seem generic or could apply to any content - Coordinated sharing across multiple accounts simultaneously

Cross-Platform Verification

Information that appears across multiple platforms can be cross-checked for consistency:

> "Legitimate information typically maintains consistency across platforms, while synthetic influence campaigns may show variations or contradictions," explains digital literacy expert Dr. Michael Chen.

> Try: - Searching for the same claim or content on different platforms - Checking if the original source exists and contains the claimed information - Verifying if trusted news sources or fact-checkers have addressed the content - Examining whether the content appears in multiple languages with slight variations

Developing Your Synthetic Influence Radar

Beyond specific techniques, developing a general "synthetic influence radar" involves cultivating certain habits and mindsets:

Practice Critical Consumption

"The single most important defense against synthetic influence is slowing down your consumption and response," advises media literacy expert Dr. Elena Martinez. "The impulse to immediately react—to share, comment, or act on information—is exactly what manipulators count on."

> Develop these habits: - Pause before sharing emotional or surprising content - Ask yourself: "Who benefits if I believe this?" - Consider whether the content seems designed to trigger strong emotions - Look for confirming information from multiple reliable sources

Stay Informed About Evolving Techniques

"The synthetic influence landscape changes rapidly," notes technology journalist Marcus Williams. "What was cutting-edge six months ago may be commonplace today, and new techniques emerge constantly."

> To stay current: - Follow reputable technology news sources - Participate in digital literacy communities - Pay attention to platform announcements about new detection features - Learn from examples of recently identified synthetic influence campaigns

Trust Your Instincts

"Our intuition often detects anomalies before our conscious mind can articulate what seems wrong," explains cognitive psychologist Dr. Sarah Thompson. "That feeling that something is 'off' deserves attention and investigation."

When you experience that feeling: - Take time to analyze why something seems suspicious - Look more closely at the elements that triggered your concern - Seek verification from trusted sources - Consider reporting the content to the platform

The Future of Detection

As AI technologies continue to advance, the challenge of detecting synthetic influence will grow more complex. Several emerging approaches show promise for the future:

Provenance Infrastructure

"The most promising long-term solution may be building authenticity into our digital infrastructure," explains digital security expert Dr. James Wilson. "Rather than detecting fakes after the fact, we need systems that can verify content from its source."

Emerging approaches include: - Content credentials that travel with media from creation to consumption - Blockchain-based verification systems - Digital watermarking technologies - Platform-level authentication requirements

Collaborative Detection Networks

"No single individual or organization can keep pace with all forms of synthetic influence," notes disinformation researcher Dr. Elena Rodriguez. "The future lies in collaborative networks that share detection insights and techniques."

These networks include: - Researcher collaborations across institutions - Platform-spanning detection initiatives - Citizen science approaches to identifying new manipulation techniques - Open-source detection tools and databases

Augmented Detection Tools

"The same AI technologies used to create synthetic influence can be harnessed to detect it," explains AI researcher Dr. Michael Chen. "The future will likely involve AI-augmented tools that help ordinary people identify manipulation."

Promising developments include: - Browser extensions that automatically flag suspicious content - Camera apps that detect manipulation in real-time - Voice analysis tools for phone calls and voice messages - Integrated platform features that provide authenticity context

The Human Element Remains Essential

Despite technological advances in both creation and detection, the human element remains irreplaceable in identifying synthetic influence.

"Technology alone will never solve this problem," cautions digital ethics professor Dr. Sarah Johnson. "Critical thinking, media literacy, and a healthy skepticism toward emotionally manipulative content are skills we must cultivate as individuals and societies."

The most effective defense combines technological tools with human judgment—leveraging both our sophisticated pattern recognition abilities and our capacity for contextual understanding that AI still lacks.

By developing these skills and remaining vigilant, you can protect yourself and others from the growing tide of synthetic influence. In the digital battlefield of information warfare, awareness is your strongest shield and critical thinking your most powerful weapon.

In the next chapter, we'll explore how to protect your digital mind once you've identified synthetic influence—moving from detection to defense in the ongoing battle for information integrity.

Chapter 14: Protecting Your Digital Mind

The notification appeared on Maria's phone at 3:17 AM. A message from her sister, Sarah, who rarely texted this late: "I'm stranded at the airport. My wallet was stolen. Can you send $500 for a hotel and new flight? I'll pay you back tomorrow."

Maria's finger hovered over the payment app. Something felt off—the timing, the amount, the urgency. She decided to call Sarah directly. No answer. She tried again. Finally, a groggy voice answered. Sarah was home in bed, her phone beside her, and she certainly wasn't stranded at any airport.

The message had come from Sarah's actual number, but it wasn't Sarah. It was an AI-powered scam that had spoofed her sister's phone number and mimicked her texting style perfectly. Had Maria sent the money, it would have vanished instantly.

In the previous chapter, we explored how to spot synthetic influence. Now, we turn to the equally crucial question: How do we protect our minds once we've identified these manipulations? How do we build psychological defenses against increasingly sophisticated attempts to hijack our thoughts, emotions, and behaviors?

"Detecting synthetic influence is only half the battle," explains cognitive security expert Dr. James Wilson. "The other half is developing mental frameworks that make us resistant to manipulation, even when we encounter it."

This chapter provides practical strategies for protecting your digital mind in an age of AI-driven manipulation. These approaches combine technological tools with psychological techniques, creating layered defenses against synthetic influence.

Understanding Your Cognitive Vulnerabilities

The first step in protecting your digital mind is understanding how it can be exploited. We all have cognitive vulnerabilities—psychological tendencies that manipulators can target.

> "AI systems are increasingly designed to exploit specific cognitive biases," notes psychology professor Dr. Elena Rodriguez. "Understanding your own vulnerabilities is the foundation of effective defense."

Common Cognitive Biases Exploited by AI

Several cognitive biases make us particularly susceptible to synthetic influence:

1. Confirmation Bias

We naturally seek and accept information that confirms our existing beliefs while dismissing contradictory evidence. AI systems can exploit this tendency by serving content that aligns with and gradually intensifies our existing views.

> "Confirmation bias creates a pathway for radicalization," explains social psychologist Dr. Sarah Thompson. "AI systems can identify your beliefs and feed you increasingly extreme versions, moving you toward fringe positions without triggering your skepticism."

> To counter this vulnerability: - Deliberately seek out diverse viewpoints on important topics - Practice the "steel man" technique—articulating opposing arguments in their strongest form - Regularly audit your information sources for ideological diversity - Notice when you dismiss information solely because it contradicts your existing beliefs

2. Emotional Triggering

Our rational thinking can be bypassed when content triggers strong emotional responses, particularly fear, outrage, or tribal identity.

> "Emotional arousal narrows attention and reduces critical thinking," notes neuroscientist Dr. Michael Chen. "AI systems can identify your emotional triggers with remarkable precision and deliver content designed to activate them."

> To counter this vulnerability: - Practice the "emotional pause"—when content provokes a strong reaction, wait before engaging - Ask yourself: "Why am I feeling this emotion right now? Is it being deliberately provoked?" - Develop awareness of your specific emotional triggers - Limit exposure to content sources that regularly provoke extreme emotions

3. Authority Bias

We tend to trust information from perceived authorities or experts. AI systems can exploit this by impersonating authoritative sources or creating synthetic "experts."

> "The human brain uses shortcuts to determine trustworthiness," explains cognitive scientist Dr. Thomas Wright. "Traditional markers of authority—credentials, professional language, confident delivery—can all be simulated by AI."

> To counter this vulnerability: - Verify the identity of purported experts through multiple channels - Evaluate arguments based on evidence rather than credentials alone - Be especially cautious of "experts" who appear only in social media contexts - Remember that genuine expertise is typically nuanced, not absolute

4. Social Proof

We look to others' behaviors to determine what's correct or appropriate. AI can create the illusion of consensus through coordinated bot networks and synthetic engagement.

> "Social proof is a powerful influence mechanism," notes digital sociology professor Dr. Maria Garcia. "When we see many people supporting an idea, we naturally assume it has merit, even if those 'people' are actually AI-driven entities."

> To counter this vulnerability: - Question whether apparent consensus might be manufactured - Look beyond raw numbers to evaluate the quality of engagement - Be skeptical of sudden viral trends, especially on divisive topics - Remember that popularity doesn't equal accuracy or value

Building Your Cognitive Defense System

Understanding vulnerabilities is just the beginning. The next step is developing active defenses against manipulation attempts.

The ESCAPE Framework

The ESCAPE framework provides a practical approach to protecting your digital mind:

E: Emotional Awareness

Developing emotional awareness means recognizing when content is triggering emotional responses that bypass critical thinking.

"Emotions aren't inherently problematic," explains psychologist Dr. Elena Martinez. "The issue arises when emotions are deliberately triggered to manipulate behavior or beliefs."

Practice these techniques: - Mindfulness meditation to increase emotional awareness - Emotion labeling—naming the specific emotions you're experiencing - Body scanning to notice physical manifestations of emotional arousal - Creating a "cooling off" period before acting on emotionally charged content

S: Source Verification

Verifying information sources has never been more important than in the age of synthetic influence.

"Source verification isn't just about checking if a website is legitimate," notes digital literacy expert Dr. James Wilson. "It's about understanding who created the content, why, and what their potential biases might be."

Effective source verification includes: - Checking domain registration information - Verifying author credentials across multiple platforms - Examining an organization's funding sources and affiliations - Assessing whether a source has a history of accuracy and corrections

C: Context Consideration

Information stripped of context is easily manipulated. Restoring context helps protect against synthetic influence.

"AI systems excel at removing context that might trigger skepticism," explains media studies professor Dr. Sarah Johnson. "Actively seeking context is a powerful defense against manipulation."

To restore context: - Research the broader topic beyond the specific claim - Look for the original source of quotes or statistics - Consider historical patterns related to the information - Examine whether similar claims have been debunked previously

A: Alternative Explanations

Actively generating alternative explanations for information helps counter manipulation attempts.

"When we encounter information, we typically accept the framing provided," notes cognitive psychologist Dr. Michael Brown. "Deliberately considering alternative explanations disrupts this automatic acceptance."

Practice these approaches: - Ask "What other explanations could account for this?" - Consider what information might be missing - Imagine how the same facts might be presented from different perspectives - Think about who benefits from your acceptance of the provided explanation

P: Pattern Recognition

Developing pattern recognition skills helps identify manipulation techniques across different contexts.

"Synthetic influence campaigns often reuse successful techniques," explains disinformation researcher Dr. Thomas Lee. "Learning to recognize these patterns makes you less vulnerable to future manipulation."

To develop pattern recognition: - Study known disinformation campaigns to understand their structure - Notice similarities in emotional manipulation across different topics - Identify recurring narrative structures in synthetic content - Pay attention to timing patterns in information release

E: Engagement Control

Controlling how you engage with digital content is perhaps the most powerful defense against synthetic influence.

> "The attention economy is designed to maximize engagement, often at the expense of well-being and truth," notes digital ethics professor Dr. Elena Rodriguez. "Taking control of your engagement patterns disrupts manipulation attempts."

> Effective engagement control includes: - Setting specific times for social media use rather than constant checking - Using tools to remove algorithmic feeds and recommendations - Practicing intentional consumption— deciding what to consume rather than reacting to what's served - Creating friction before sharing content (e.g., "Will I still want to share this tomorrow?")

Technological Shields for Your Digital Mind

While psychological defenses are essential, technological tools can provide additional protection against synthetic influence.

Content Filtering and Verification Tools

Several tools can help filter and verify digital content:

- **Browser extensions**: Tools like NewsGuard, Factual, and SurfSafe provide real-time credibility assessments of websites and news sources.

- **Reverse image search**: Services like TinEye and Google Reverse Image Search can verify whether images have been manipulated or taken out of context.

- **Fact-checking aggregators**: Sites like AllSides and Media Bias/Fact Check help identify potential biases in news sources.

- **AI detection tools**: Emerging tools can identify potentially AI-generated content, though their reliability varies.

"These tools aren't perfect, but they add valuable layers to your defense system," notes digital security expert Dr. James Wilson. "Think of them as supplements to, not replacements for, your own critical thinking."

Digital Environment Design

How you configure your digital environment significantly impacts your vulnerability to synthetic influence.

> "Most people accept default settings that maximize their exposure to manipulation," explains digital well-being researcher Dr. Sarah Thompson. "Reconfiguring your digital environment is a powerful act of self-defense."

> Consider these approaches:

- **Curated information sources**: Replace algorithmic feeds with manually curated sources like RSS feeds or email newsletters from trusted providers.

- **Notification management**: Disable non-essential notifications to reduce reactive engagement with digital platforms.

- **Alternative platforms**: Consider platforms with less algorithmic manipulation and more chronological content presentation.

- **Digital minimalism**: Regularly audit and remove unnecessary apps, accounts, and digital services.

"Your digital environment should serve your goals and well-being, not the other way around," notes digital ethics professor Dr. Elena Martinez. "Designing it intentionally is a fundamental act of cognitive self-defense."

Social Network Curation

The people and organizations you connect with online significantly impact your exposure to synthetic influence.

"Your social network is both a potential vulnerability and a potential defense," explains social media researcher Dr. Michael Chen. "Curating it thoughtfully can dramatically reduce your exposure to manipulation."

Consider these strategies:

- **Network auditing**: Regularly review your connections and remove or mute sources of low-quality information.

- **Trusted verification circles**: Develop relationships with people who have complementary expertise for mutual verification of suspicious content.

- **Diverse viewpoints**: Intentionally include thoughtful people with different perspectives to avoid echo chambers.

- **Quality over quantity**: Prioritize meaningful connections over accumulating followers or friends.

"A well-curated social network acts as a distributed cognitive defense system," notes digital sociology professor Dr. Thomas Wright. "When you encounter potential manipulation, having trusted connections with diverse expertise allows for rapid verification."

Special Contexts: High-Risk Scenarios

Certain contexts require heightened vigilance against synthetic influence. Understanding these high-risk scenarios can help you deploy appropriate defenses.

Election Periods

Elections represent prime targets for synthetic influence operations, with potentially significant consequences for democratic processes.

"Election periods see massive spikes in synthetic influence attempts," explains political communication researcher Dr. Elena Rodriguez. "The stakes are high, emotions are elevated, and the information environment becomes increasingly polluted."

During election periods: - Be especially cautious of emotionally charged political content - Verify information through official election websites and established news sources - Watch for sudden emergence of divisive narratives or framing - Be skeptical of last-minute "revelations" about candidates - Report suspected manipulation to platform authorities and election officials

Crisis Events

Natural disasters, terrorist attacks, public health emergencies, and other crises create fertile ground for synthetic influence.

"Crisis situations compress decision-making time and elevate emotions," notes crisis communication expert Dr. Sarah Johnson. "This creates perfect conditions for manipulation."

During crises: - Rely on established emergency management sources for critical information - Be wary of unverified "eyewitness" accounts, especially those promoting unusual narratives - Watch for content that exploits fear or uncertainty to promote specific actions - Verify charity appeals before donating, as crises attract financial scams - Remember that initial reports are often incomplete or incorrect, even from legitimate sources

Personal Financial Decisions

Financial contexts often involve significant consequences, making them attractive targets for synthetic influence.

"Financial decisions combine high stakes with time pressure and technical complexity," explains financial psychology researcher Dr. James Wilson. "This creates multiple avenues for manipulation."

When making financial decisions: - Verify financial advice through multiple independent sources - Be extremely cautious of "urgent" investment opportunities - Confirm the identity of financial institutions through official channels before providing information - Remember that legitimate financial institutions rarely request sensitive information via email or text - Be skeptical of financial content that triggers fear of missing out (FOMO) or promises unusual returns

The Social Dimension: Collective Defense

While individual defenses are essential, synthetic influence also requires collective responses.

"No individual can detect all forms of manipulation alone," explains digital citizenship researcher Dr. Maria Garcia. "Effective defense requires social coordination and shared responsibility."

Community Verification Networks

Developing trusted networks for information verification provides strength beyond individual capabilities.

"Different people have different areas of expertise and different cognitive strengths," notes social psychology professor Dr. Thomas Lee. "Community verification leverages this diversity for stronger collective defense."

Consider these approaches: - Develop explicit verification protocols within friend and family groups - Participate in community fact-checking initiatives - Share verification resources rather than just sharing debunked content - Practice respectful skepticism when others share potentially manipulated content

Intergenerational Knowledge Transfer

Different generations have different digital vulnerabilities and strengths. Intergenerational knowledge sharing strengthens collective defense.

"Younger users often have greater technical fluency, while older users may have stronger critical thinking skills from pre-digital experience," explains digital sociologist Dr. Elena Martinez. "Bridging these generational divides creates more robust defenses."

Consider these approaches: - Create family discussions about digital manipulation techniques - Encourage older adults to share pre-digital verification strategies - Have younger users explain emerging platforms and their manipulation risks - Develop shared language for discussing potential synthetic influence

Institutional Support and Advocacy

Beyond individual and community efforts, institutional responses are essential for addressing synthetic influence at scale.

"Individual defense is necessary but insufficient," notes digital policy expert Dr. Michael Chen. "We also need institutional frameworks that reduce the burden on individuals."

Consider these approaches: - Support media literacy education in schools and communities - Advocate for platform design that reduces manipulation potential - Engage with policymakers on synthetic media regulation - Participate in public comment periods for relevant legislation

The Mindset Shift: From Consumer to Guardian

Perhaps the most fundamental protection for your digital mind involves shifting how you conceptualize your role in the information ecosystem.

"Most people see themselves as passive consumers of information," explains digital ethics professor Dr. Sarah Thompson. "Protecting your digital mind requires reconceptualizing yourself as an active guardian of information integrity."

This mindset shift involves:

- **Taking responsibility**: Recognizing that sharing information makes you part of its distribution chain, with associated responsibilities.

- **Practicing information stewardship**: Treating information as a resource to be protected and carefully managed, not just consumed.

- **Developing verification habits**: Making verification a routine part of information consumption, not an exceptional activity.

- **Embracing skepticism**: Viewing healthy skepticism as a civic virtue rather than a character flaw.

"When enough individuals make this mindset shift, the economics of synthetic influence begin to change," notes media economist Dr. James Wilson. "Manipulation becomes more costly and less effective, creating positive feedback loops that improve the information environment for everyone."

The Journey of Continuous Adaptation

Protecting your digital mind isn't a one-time task but an ongoing journey of adaptation and learning.

"The synthetic influence landscape evolves constantly," explains digital security researcher Dr. Elena Rodriguez. "Effective defense requires continuous learning and adaptation."

This journey involves:

- **Staying informed**: Following developments in synthetic influence techniques and defenses.

- **Regular practice**: Actively applying verification skills to maintain and strengthen them.

- **Community engagement**: Participating in communities focused on digital literacy and defense.

- **Self-reflection**: Regularly assessing your own vulnerabilities and defense strategies.

"The goal isn't perfect immunity to manipulation—that's impossible," notes cognitive psychologist Dr. Thomas Wright. "The goal is developing sufficient resilience that synthetic influence loses its power to significantly distort your understanding and behavior."

By combining the strategies in this chapter—understanding cognitive vulnerabilities, applying the ESCAPE framework, utilizing technological tools, navigating high-risk contexts, engaging in collective defense, and shifting your mindset—you can substantially strengthen your resistance to synthetic influence.

In the next chapter, we'll explore how these individual protections scale to broader cyber hygiene practices in an AI-driven world, extending defense from the mind to our digital lives as a whole.

Chapter 15: Cyber Hygiene in an AI-Driven World

David stared at his phone in disbelief. The banking app showed a balance of $17.42—down from over $5,000 the previous day. Somehow, someone had drained his account overnight. As the panic subsided and clarity returned, he traced his steps backward. Three days earlier, he'd clicked a link in what appeared to be an email from his bank about suspicious activity. The page looked identical to his bank's website, and he'd entered his credentials without hesitation. Only now did he realize his mistake.

"I should have known better," he later told his cybersecurity friend. "I work in tech. I read about these scams. But it looked so real, and I was distracted."

His friend nodded sympathetically. "That's the thing about AI-driven attacks. They're not targeting the uninformed anymore—they're designed to catch even vigilant people in moments of vulnerability."

In previous chapters, we explored how to spot synthetic influence and protect your digital mind. Now, we turn to the practical, day-to-day habits and tools that can shield you from manipulation in an AI-driven world. This is cyber hygiene—the digital equivalent of washing your hands and brushing your teeth—essential practices that significantly reduce your vulnerability to the sophisticated threats we've discussed throughout this book.

"Cyber hygiene isn't about achieving perfect security, which is impossible," explains digital security expert Dr. Elena Rodriguez. "It's about making yourself a harder target by implementing layers of protection that work together."

This chapter provides practical strategies and tools for maintaining robust cyber hygiene in an age of AI-powered manipulation. These approaches combine technological solutions with behavioral practices, creating a comprehensive defense system against synthetic influence.

Counter-AI Tools: Your Digital Shield

As AI-driven manipulation has evolved, so too have the tools designed to counter it. While no single tool provides perfect protection, a thoughtfully assembled toolkit can significantly reduce your vulnerability.

Content Verification Tools

Several tools can help verify the authenticity of digital content you encounter:

1. AI Content Detectors

AI content detectors analyze text to identify patterns consistent with machine generation. While these tools aren't infallible—especially against advanced AI systems designed to evade detection—they provide a useful first-line assessment.

> "AI detectors work by identifying statistical patterns in text that differ from typical human writing," explains NLP researcher Dr. James Wilson. "They're not perfect, but they can flag content that warrants closer scrutiny."

Notable AI content detection tools include:

- **GPTZero**: Developed specifically to identify text generated by large language models like GPT-4, with a focus on educational settings.

- **Content at Scale AI Detector**: Offers a "humanness" score for text, highlighting sections that appear machine-generated.

- **Winston AI**: Provides detailed analysis of text with probability scores for AI generation.

- **Originality.ai**: Combines plagiarism checking with AI detection, useful for verifying original human-created content.

"These tools should be used as advisory systems, not definitive judges," cautions digital forensics expert Dr. Sarah Thompson. "False positives and false negatives are inevitable, so human judgment remains essential."

2. Deepfake Detection Platforms

As deepfake technology has advanced, specialized tools have emerged to identify synthetic media:

- **Sensity AI**: Offers both consumer and enterprise solutions for detecting manipulated images and videos.

- **Microsoft Video Authenticator**: Analyzes videos to provide a confidence score about whether the content has been artificially manipulated.

- **Deeptrace**: Specializes in detecting deepfakes across various media types.

- **Intel FakeCatcher**: Claims 96% accuracy in detecting deepfakes by analyzing blood flow in video subjects.

"Deepfake detection is an arms race," notes computer vision researcher Dr. Michael Chen. "As generation technology improves, detection tools must evolve in response. Today's effective detector may be obsolete tomorrow."

3. Browser Extensions for Information Verification

Several browser extensions provide real-time assessment of online content:

- **NewsGuard**: Rates news websites based on transparency and credibility criteria, helping identify potentially unreliable sources.

- **SurfSafe**: Detects manipulated images by comparing them against a database of original versions.

- **Factual**: Highlights claims in articles and provides verification information from multiple sources.

- **TrustedNews**: Flags potential misinformation and provides context about news sources.

"Browser extensions create a layer of verification that works passively as you browse," explains digital literacy expert Dr. Elena Martinez. "They're not perfect, but they introduce helpful friction before you accept information at face value."

Privacy-Enhancing Tools

Beyond content verification, several tools can enhance your privacy and reduce your digital footprint—limiting the data available for AI systems to exploit:

1. VPNs and Encrypted Communication

Virtual Private Networks (VPNs) and encrypted messaging apps provide fundamental privacy protection:

- **Reputable VPN services**: Tools like ProtonVPN, Mullvad, and Windscribe mask your IP address and encrypt your internet traffic, making it harder to track your online activities.

- **End-to-end encrypted messaging**: Apps like Signal, Wire, and ProtonMail ensure that only the intended recipients can read your communications.

- **Encrypted email services**: Providers like ProtonMail and Tutanota offer encrypted email with additional privacy features.

"Encryption doesn't just protect against hackers," notes cybersecurity expert Dr. Thomas Wright. "It also limits the data available for AI systems to analyze and exploit for manipulation purposes."

2. Ad and Tracker Blockers

Advertising networks and trackers collect vast amounts of data that can be used for manipulation:

- **uBlock Origin**: An efficient, wide-spectrum blocker that filters out ads, trackers, and malware domains.

- **Privacy Badger**: Automatically learns to block invisible trackers based on their behavior.

- **DuckDuckGo Privacy Essentials**: Combines tracker blocking with private search and forced HTTPS connections.

- **Ghostery**: Identifies and blocks trackers, with detailed information about the companies tracking you.

"Tracker blockers don't just improve page load times and battery life," explains privacy researcher Dr. Sarah Johnson. "They fundamentally reduce the data available for building the psychological profiles used in targeted manipulation."

3. Alternative Browsers and Search Engines

Mainstream browsers and search engines often prioritize data collection over privacy:

- **Privacy-focused browsers**: Brave, Firefox (with privacy settings adjusted), and Tor Browser offer stronger privacy protections than mainstream alternatives.

- **Private search engines**: DuckDuckGo, Startpage, and Brave Search provide search results without tracking your queries or building a profile of your interests.

- **Containerized browsing**: Tools like Firefox's Multi-Account Containers isolate different parts of your online life, preventing cross-site tracking.

"The browser is your primary interface with the digital world," notes digital privacy advocate Dr. Elena Rodriguez. "Choosing one that prioritizes your privacy rather than monetizing your data creates a foundation for better cyber hygiene."

Clean Tech Practices: Building Digital Resilience

Beyond specific tools, certain practices can significantly enhance your digital resilience against AI-driven manipulation.

Platform Settings Optimization

Most digital platforms offer privacy and security settings that few users fully utilize:

1. Social Media Privacy Lockdown

Each social media platform offers various privacy controls that can reduce your vulnerability:

- **Audience controls**: Limit who can see your posts, profile information, and friends/connections list.

- **Data sharing settings**: Restrict how the platform shares your data with third-party apps and advertisers.

- **Activity visibility**: Control whether your online status, activity, and interactions are visible to others.

- **Search engine indexing**: Prevent search engines from indexing your profile and posts.

"Most social platforms default to maximum data collection and visibility," explains digital privacy researcher Dr. Michael Brown. "Taking 30 minutes to review and adjust these settings can dramatically reduce your attack surface."

2. Device Permission Management

Modern apps request extensive permissions, often beyond what they actually need:

- **Regular permission audits**: Review and revoke unnecessary permissions for apps on all your devices.

- **Microphone and camera controls**: Disable access for apps that don't genuinely need these sensors.

- **Location sharing limits**: Restrict location access to only when an app is in use, or disable it entirely when not needed.

- **Background data restrictions**: Limit which apps can access data and run processes in the background.

"App permissions are the gateway to your personal data," notes mobile security expert Dr. Thomas Lee. "Minimizing these permissions directly reduces the information available for potential manipulation."

3. Account Security Enhancements

Basic account security measures provide essential protection:

- **Multi-factor authentication (MFA)**: Enable MFA on all important accounts, preferably using authenticator apps rather than SMS.

- **Password managers**: Use a reputable password manager to create and store strong, unique passwords for each service.

- **Security questions**: Provide fictional answers to security questions, stored in your password manager, as the real answers are often publicly available information.

- **Regular security audits**: Periodically review account activity, connected applications, and active sessions.

"These basic security measures aren't just about preventing account takeovers," explains cybersecurity researcher Dr. Sarah Thompson. "They also help maintain the integrity of your digital identity, which is essential for countering synthetic influence."

Digital Detox and Mindful Consumption

Perhaps the most powerful cyber hygiene practice is consciously managing how, when, and why you engage with digital content:

1. Scheduled Engagement

Rather than constant, reactive engagement with digital platforms, consider a more structured approach:

- **Designated check-in times**: Set specific times for checking social media, news, and email rather than responding to every notification.

- **Digital sabbaticals**: Regularly disconnect completely for defined periods — whether hours, days, or longer.

- **Notification management**: Disable non-essential notifications to reduce reactive engagement.

- **Screen time limits**: Use built-in tools like Screen Time (iOS) or Digital Wellbeing (Android) to set daily limits for specific apps.

"Constant connectivity creates continuous vulnerability," notes digital wellbeing researcher Dr. Elena Martinez. "Scheduled engagement reduces your exposure window for manipulation attempts."

2. Information Diet Planning

Just as you might plan a healthy food diet, consider consciously designing your information diet:

- **Source diversification**: Intentionally include varied, high-quality information sources representing different perspectives.

- **Quality over quantity**: Focus on fewer, deeper, more substantive content sources rather than high-volume, shallow consumption.

- **Active versus passive consumption**: Choose specific content to engage with rather than passively consuming whatever algorithms serve.

- **Slow media consumption**: Adopt principles from the "slow media" movement, prioritizing thoughtful, in-depth engagement over rapid consumption.

"Your information diet shapes your understanding of reality," explains media literacy expert Dr. James Wilson. "Consciously designing this diet rather than outsourcing it to algorithms is perhaps the most powerful defense against manipulation."

3. Cognitive Breaks and Attention Protection

Protecting your attention creates space for critical thinking:

- **Pomodoro technique**: Work in focused intervals (typically 25 minutes) followed by short breaks, creating space for reflection.

- **Meditation and mindfulness**: Regular practice strengthens attention control and emotional awareness.

- **Single-tasking**: Focus on one digital task at a time rather than constant multitasking, which depletes cognitive resources.

- **Physical/digital boundaries**: Create physical spaces in your home that are device-free zones.

"Attention is your scarcest resource in the digital age," notes cognitive psychologist Dr. Michael Chen. "Protecting it isn't just about productivity—it's about maintaining the cognitive capacity needed to detect and resist manipulation."

Building a Personal Security Stack

Different individuals face different threat levels and have different privacy needs. Building a personalized security stack involves assessing your specific situation and implementing appropriate protections.

Threat Modeling for Everyday Life

Threat modeling—a practice borrowed from professional cybersecurity—can help you identify your specific vulnerabilities:

1. Asset Inventory

Begin by identifying what you're trying to protect:

- **Digital assets**: Important accounts, files, communications, and online identities.

- **Personal information**: Private data that could be used for manipulation or impersonation.

- **Reputation**: Your public and professional image that could be damaged by synthetic content.

- **Attention and agency**: Your ability to make decisions free from undue influence.

"Most people never conduct this basic inventory," notes security consultant Dr. Thomas Wright. "Without knowing what you're protecting, effective defense is impossible."

2. Threat Identification

Consider who might target you and how:

- **Mass threats**: Untargeted scams, phishing, and manipulation that affect everyone.

- **Categorical threats**: Attacks targeting groups you belong to (profession, political affiliation, demographic).

- **Personal threats**: Specific threats based on your individual profile or activities.

"Different threats require different countermeasures," explains security researcher Dr. Sarah Johnson. "Understanding your specific threat landscape helps prioritize your defensive efforts."

3. Vulnerability Assessment

Identify specific weaknesses in your current practices:

- **Technical vulnerabilities**: Outdated software, weak passwords, excessive permissions.

- **Behavioral vulnerabilities**: Habits that increase risk, such as clicking links without verification.

- **Knowledge gaps**: Areas where limited understanding increases vulnerability.

"Vulnerabilities are the intersection points where threats can affect your assets," notes cybersecurity educator Dr. Elena Martinez. "Identifying these points is essential for effective protection."

4. Countermeasure Implementation

Based on your threat model, implement appropriate protections:

- **High-priority protections**: Address the most serious vulnerabilities affecting your most important assets first.

- **Defense in depth**: Implement multiple layers of protection rather than relying on a single measure.

- **Usability balance**: Choose protections you can consistently maintain without excessive friction.

"The perfect security stack you abandon is worse than an imperfect one you actually use," explains digital security pragmatist Dr. James Wilson. "Sustainability matters more than theoretical perfection."

Specialized Protection for High-Risk Individuals

Some individuals face heightened risks due to their profession, public profile, or other factors:

1. Journalists and Activists

Those who challenge powerful interests often face sophisticated targeting:

- **Advanced anonymity tools**: Tor Browser for anonymous browsing, Tails operating system for leaving no digital traces.

- **Secure drop systems**: Tools like SecureDrop for receiving sensitive information securely.

- **Compartmentalization**: Strict separation between different digital identities and activities.

- **Physical security awareness**: Understanding that digital and physical security are interconnected.

"For those facing state-level adversaries or organized groups, standard protections may be insufficient," notes digital security trainer Dr. Michael Brown, who works with journalists in conflict zones. "More robust measures become necessary."

2. Public Figures and Influencers

Those with significant public platforms face unique risks:

- **Identity verification systems**: Establishing verified presences across platforms to counter impersonation.

- **Reputation monitoring**: Services that alert you to mentions or impersonations across the web.

- **Crisis response planning**: Prepared strategies for addressing synthetic content targeting your reputation.

- **Professional security consultation**: Expert assessment of specific threats and appropriate countermeasures.

"Public figures face a particularly high risk of synthetic impersonation," explains digital reputation expert Dr. Thomas Lee. "Proactive verification and monitoring are essential defenses."

3. Business Leaders and Executives

Those with access to valuable resources or information require enhanced protection:

- **Executive security training**: Specialized education about targeted threats and appropriate responses.

- **Advanced endpoint protection**: Enterprise-grade security for all devices.

- **Communication security protocols**: Established procedures for verifying sensitive requests, especially financial ones.

- **Regular security briefings**: Staying informed about emerging threats specific to your industry.

"Executives are high-value targets for sophisticated social engineering," notes corporate security consultant Dr. Sarah Johnson. "The potential return on investment makes attackers willing to deploy significant resources against these targets."

The Future of Personal Cyber Defense

As AI-driven threats evolve, personal cyber defense must evolve in response. Several emerging approaches show promise for the future:

Decentralized Identity Systems

Current digital identity systems create significant vulnerability. Decentralized alternatives may offer better protection:

- **Self-sovereign identity**: Systems where individuals control their own identity data rather than relying on centralized providers.

- **Blockchain-based verification**: Using distributed ledger technology to create tamper-resistant identity verification.

- **Zero-knowledge proofs**: Cryptographic methods that allow proving facts without revealing underlying data.

"The centralization of identity is a fundamental security weakness," explains digital identity researcher Dr. Elena Rodriguez.

"Decentralized approaches could significantly reduce vulnerability to synthetic impersonation."

AI-Powered Personal Defense

The same AI technologies driving manipulation can be repurposed for defense:

- **Personal AI guardians**: AI systems that monitor your digital environment for manipulation attempts.

- **Adaptive security systems**: Defenses that learn and evolve based on your specific threat landscape.

- **Cognitive security assistants**: AI tools that help identify cognitive biases and manipulation attempts in real-time.

"Fighting AI with AI may be necessary as threats become more sophisticated," notes AI security researcher Dr. James Wilson. "Human attention alone cannot keep pace with the volume and complexity of modern threats."

Collective Defense Networks

Individual defense has inherent limitations. Collective approaches offer additional protection:

- **Trusted verification networks**: Communities that share information about emerging threats and verify suspicious content.

- **Distributed detection systems**: Networks that pool resources to identify manipulation at scale.

- **Community education initiatives**: Collaborative efforts to improve digital literacy and security awareness.

"No individual can detect all forms of manipulation alone," explains digital community organizer Dr. Michael Chen. "Collective defense leverages diverse perspectives and expertise for stronger protection."

Case Study: The Secure Digital Citizen

To illustrate these principles in action, consider the case of Maya, a journalist who implemented comprehensive cyber hygiene practices after being targeted by a sophisticated spear-phishing campaign:

Before: Vulnerable Digital Life

Maya's digital life before the incident had several vulnerabilities:

- **Convenience over security**: Using the same password (with minor variations) across multiple accounts.

- **Default settings**: Never adjusting privacy or security settings on social media platforms.

- **Reactive consumption**: Constantly checking notifications and consuming whatever content algorithms served.

- **Limited verification**: Accepting messages and requests at face value without verification.

The Wake-Up Call

The targeting incident served as a catalyst for change:

- **Sophisticated impersonation**: Attackers created a convincing impersonation of Maya's editor, requesting she click a document link.

- **Contextual knowledge**: The message referenced actual stories she was working on, suggesting research or monitoring.

- **Psychological pressure**: The request conveyed urgency, limiting time for critical assessment.

- **Technical sophistication**: The link led to a convincing but fake login page designed to capture her credentials.

After: Resilient Digital Citizen

Following the incident, Maya implemented a comprehensive cyber hygiene system:

- **Technological protections**: Password manager, MFA on all accounts, VPN usage, privacy-focused browser with security extensions.

- **Behavioral changes**: Scheduled digital engagement, verification protocols for requests, regular security audits.

- **Cognitive practices**: Mindfulness meditation, emotional awareness training, critical thinking frameworks.

- **Social dimension**: Joining a journalist security collective for shared threat intelligence and verification assistance.

"The difference isn't just technical—it's psychological," Maya explained. "I feel in control of my digital life rather than controlled by it. That sense of agency is perhaps the most important protection against manipulation."

Practical Implementation: Your 30-Day Cyber Hygiene Plan

Transforming your digital habits can seem overwhelming. This 30-day plan breaks the process into manageable steps:

Week 1: Foundation Building

- **Day 1-2**: Conduct a personal threat model assessment
- **Day 3-5**: Implement a password manager and update critical passwords
- **Day 6-7**: Enable MFA on your most important accounts

Week 2: Privacy Enhancement

- **Day 8-10**: Audit and adjust privacy settings across major platforms
- **Day 11-12**: Install and configure privacy-enhancing browser extensions
- **Day 13-14**: Review and restrict app permissions on all devices

Week 3: Consumption Redesign

- **Day 15-17**: Establish a curated information diet from diverse, quality sources
- **Day 18-19**: Implement notification management and scheduled engagement
- **Day 20-21**: Create physical and digital boundaries for attention protection

Week 4: Advanced Protection

- **Day 22-24**: Explore and implement appropriate encryption tools
- **Day 25-27**: Develop verification protocols for sensitive requests
- **Day 28-30**: Create a maintenance schedule for ongoing security practices

"Small, consistent changes are more effective than ambitious plans that aren't sustained," advises digital wellbeing coach Dr. Elena Martinez. "This graduated approach builds new habits that become second nature over time."

Conclusion: Hygiene as Resistance

In a world where AI increasingly shapes our information environment, basic cyber hygiene becomes an act of resistance—a reclaiming of agency in the face of sophisticated manipulation.

"We shouldn't think of cyber hygiene as merely technical—it's deeply political and personal," argues digital ethics professor Dr. Thomas Wright. "Each time we take steps to protect our digital autonomy, we're asserting our right to cognitive liberty."

The practices outlined in this chapter won't provide perfect protection. No defense is impenetrable against the most sophisticated threats. But implementing these layers of protection significantly raises the cost and difficulty of manipulating you, making you a harder target in a world where attackers typically focus on the most vulnerable.

"The goal isn't paranoia or isolation," emphasizes digital wellbeing researcher Dr. Sarah Johnson. "It's mindful engagement—using technology intentionally rather than being used by it."

As we move into the final chapter, we'll explore the broader societal dimensions of this challenge: how regulation, education, and collective action might shape a future where synthetic influence serves human flourishing rather than manipulation and control.

Key Takeaways:

- Cyber hygiene combines technological tools with behavioral practices to create layered defenses against synthetic influence.
- Content verification tools, privacy-enhancing technologies, and security measures form the technical foundation of digital protection.
- Mindful consumption practices and attention management are equally important for maintaining cognitive autonomy.
- Personal threat modeling helps identify your specific vulnerabilities and appropriate countermeasures.
- Small, consistent changes implemented over time are more effective than unsustainable security maximalism.
- Collective approaches complement individual defenses, leveraging diverse perspectives for stronger protection.

Chapter 16: The Future: Regulation, Resistance, and the Real War Ahead

In April 2023, a deepfake video of Pope Francis wearing a stylish white puffer jacket went viral, accumulating millions of views before most people realized it wasn't real. While relatively harmless, this incident highlighted a disturbing reality: even religious leaders of global significance aren't immune to synthetic manipulation.

Just months later, in January 2024, a more sinister application emerged when AI-generated robocalls impersonating President Biden's voice targeted thousands of New Hampshire voters, instructing them not to vote in the primary election. The calls were sophisticated enough that many recipients initially believed they were authentic.

These incidents represent just the beginning of what promises to be an escalating battle over the integrity of our shared information environment. Throughout this book, we've explored the tools, tactics, and psychological mechanisms behind AI-driven manipulation. We've examined personal defenses and protective measures. But as we conclude, we must confront a sobering reality: individual action alone cannot solve this problem.

"We're facing a structural challenge that requires structural solutions," explains digital policy expert Dr. Elena Rodriguez. "While personal digital hygiene is essential, it's like asking individuals to solve air pollution by wearing masks. We need systemic approaches alongside individual ones."

This final chapter examines the broader landscape of potential solutions—from regulatory frameworks to technological countermeasures to educational initiatives. It explores the inevitable arms races ahead and offers a vision for how societies might navigate the treacherous waters of synthetic influence while preserving human autonomy and democratic values.

The Regulatory Frontier: Policy Approaches to Synthetic Influence

As synthetic influence capabilities have advanced, policymakers worldwide have begun developing regulatory frameworks to address these challenges. These efforts face significant hurdles but represent an essential component of any comprehensive solution.

Current Regulatory Landscape

The regulatory response to synthetic influence varies widely across different jurisdictions:

1. United States Approaches

The U.S. has taken a largely fragmented approach to regulating synthetic influence:

- **State-level legislation**: Several states, including California, Texas, and Virginia, have enacted laws addressing specific aspects of synthetic media, particularly deepfakes used in political contexts or pornography.

- **Federal proposals**: Various bills have been introduced in Congress, including the DEEPFAKES Accountability Act and the Identifying Outputs of Generative Adversarial Networks Act (IOGAN Act), though few have become law.

- **Sector-specific regulations**: The Federal Trade Commission (FTC) has begun addressing synthetic content under existing fraud and deception authorities, while the Federal Election Commission (FEC) has considered rules for political deepfakes.

"The U.S. approach has been piecemeal and reactive," notes digital policy researcher Dr. Thomas Wright. "Constitutional protections for free speech create additional complexity for American regulators compared to other jurisdictions."

2. European Union Framework

The EU has taken a more comprehensive approach through several interconnected regulations:

- **Digital Services Act (DSA)**: Imposes obligations on platforms regarding illegal content, transparent advertising, and algorithmic recommendations.

- **AI Act**: The world's first comprehensive AI regulation, which includes specific provisions for generative AI systems and synthetic content.

- **General Data Protection Regulation (GDPR)**: Provides some protections against the data harvesting that enables targeted manipulation.

"The EU model represents the most ambitious regulatory framework globally," explains EU policy expert Dr. Sarah Johnson. "It attempts to address the entire ecosystem rather than specific applications or harms."

3. Global Variations

Other nations have developed distinctive approaches based on their legal traditions and political systems:

- **China**: Has implemented strict regulations requiring that all deepfakes be clearly labeled and that generative AI systems align with "core socialist values."

- **Canada**: Focused on extending existing election laws to cover synthetic content while developing voluntary industry codes of practice.

- **Brazil**: Enacted legislation specifically targeting synthetic content in electoral contexts following manipulation incidents in recent elections.

"The global regulatory landscape is fragmented, creating challenges for both compliance and enforcement," notes international policy expert Dr. Michael Chen. "This fragmentation also creates opportunities for regulatory arbitrage, where manipulators operate from jurisdictions with the weakest oversight."

Key Regulatory Challenges

Several fundamental challenges complicate the regulatory response to synthetic influence:

1. The Attribution Problem

Determining who is responsible for synthetic influence operations is increasingly difficult:

- **Technical obfuscation**: Advanced techniques can mask the origins of synthetic content.

- **Jurisdictional complexity**: Operations often cross multiple national boundaries.

- **Proxy deployment**: State actors frequently operate through cutouts and proxies.

- **Plausible deniability**: The technical complexity provides cover for denying involvement.

"Attribution challenges undermine traditional regulatory approaches that depend on identifying responsible parties," explains cybersecurity policy expert Dr. Elena Martinez. "You can't hold someone accountable if you can't prove who they are."

2. The Definition Dilemma

Precisely defining what constitutes harmful synthetic influence is surprisingly difficult:

- **Context dependency**: The same content may be harmful in one context but legitimate in another (e.g., clearly labeled satire versus deception).

- **Intent challenges**: Determining the intent behind content creation is often impossible.

- **Harm measurement**: Quantifying the harm caused by synthetic influence is methodologically complex.

- **Cultural variations**: Different societies have different standards for acceptable communication.

"Regulators face a fundamental challenge in defining the problem they're trying to solve," notes legal scholar Dr. Thomas Lee. "Overly broad definitions risk chilling legitimate speech, while narrow ones create loopholes for manipulators."

3. The Enforcement Gap

Even well-designed regulations face significant enforcement challenges:

- **Technical expertise shortages**: Regulatory agencies often lack the specialized knowledge needed to evaluate synthetic content.

- **Scale problems**: The volume of potentially regulated content far exceeds regulatory capacity.

- **Cross-border limitations**: National regulators have limited reach beyond their borders.

- **Technological evolution**: Regulations quickly become outdated as technology advances.

"The gap between regulatory ambition and enforcement capability is perhaps the greatest challenge," explains digital governance expert Dr. Sarah Thompson. "Even the best-designed rules are meaningless without effective implementation."

Promising Regulatory Approaches

Despite these challenges, several regulatory approaches show promise:

1. Transparency Requirements

Rather than prohibiting synthetic content outright, transparency regulations require disclosure:

- **Content labeling**: Mandating clear labels for synthetic media.

- **Provenance infrastructure**: Technical systems that track the origin and modification history of content.

- **Disclosure requirements**: Obligations to reveal when AI systems are being used to generate content or interact with humans.

"Transparency approaches don't prevent synthetic content but enable informed decision-making," notes media policy expert

Dr. Michael Brown. "They preserve creative and beneficial uses while reducing deceptive applications."

2. Platform Accountability

Holding digital platforms accountable for the synthetic content they amplify:

- **Due diligence obligations**: Requirements that platforms take reasonable steps to identify and address harmful synthetic content.

- **Algorithmic accountability**: Regulations governing how recommendation systems amplify synthetic content.

- **Researcher access**: Mandated access for independent researchers to study platform dynamics.

"Platform accountability approaches recognize that amplification, not just creation, drives synthetic influence harms," explains platform governance researcher Dr. Elena Rodriguez. "They address the ecosystem rather than just the content."

3. Critical Infrastructure Protection

Treating core information systems as critical infrastructure deserving special protection:

- **Election systems safeguards**: Special protections for electoral information ecosystems.

- **Crisis communication protocols**: Protected channels for authoritative information during emergencies.

- **Media literacy funding**: Public investment in educational initiatives to build societal resilience.

"Some information contexts are so vital to democratic functioning that they warrant special protection," argues democracy technology expert Dr. Thomas Wright. "This approach prioritizes the most critical contexts without attempting to regulate all synthetic content."

The Tech Arms Race: Technological Countermeasures

Beyond regulation, technological approaches offer another avenue for addressing synthetic influence. These approaches are evolving rapidly in an ongoing arms race between manipulation and detection technologies.

Detection Technologies

Various technologies aim to identify synthetic content:

1. Watermarking and Fingerprinting

Embedding identifying information in AI-generated content:

- **Invisible watermarks**: Subtle patterns embedded in generated images or text that identify AI origins.

- **Robust hashing**: Creating "fingerprints" of known synthetic content to identify reuse or modification.

- **Model signatures**: Distinctive patterns that identify which specific AI model generated content.

"Watermarking approaches are promising but face significant challenges," notes AI security researcher Dr. Sarah Johnson.

"Determined adversaries can often remove or obscure watermarks, and not all generative systems implement them."

2. Forensic Analysis

Identifying synthetic content through technical analysis:

- **Statistical pattern analysis**: Identifying linguistic or visual patterns characteristic of AI generation.

- **Artifact detection**: Finding technical anomalies that reveal synthetic origins.

- **Consistency analysis**: Identifying logical or physical inconsistencies in synthetic content.

"Forensic approaches are in a constant arms race with generation technology," explains digital forensics expert Dr. Michael Chen. "As generators improve, detectors must evolve in response, creating a perpetual cycle."

3. Multimodal Verification

Combining multiple data sources to verify authenticity:

- **Cross-modal consistency**: Checking whether visual, audio, and textual elements align naturally.

- **External knowledge verification**: Comparing content claims against established facts.

- **Temporal analysis**: Examining the timeline of content creation and distribution for suspicious patterns.

"Multimodal approaches raise the bar for convincing deception," notes verification technology researcher Dr. Elena Martinez.

"Manipulators must maintain consistency across multiple dimensions, increasing the technical challenge."

Authentication Systems

Beyond detection, authentication systems aim to verify that content comes from claimed sources:

1. Content Credentials

Industry initiatives to establish content provenance:

- **C2PA standard**: The Coalition for Content Provenance and Authenticity's technical standard for tracking content origins.

- **Content credentials**: Metadata that travels with content, documenting its creation and modification history.

- **Verification indicators**: Visual signals in platforms and browsers that indicate authenticated content.

"Content credentials are promising but face adoption challenges," explains digital authentication expert Dr. Thomas Lee. "They require widespread implementation across the content ecosystem to be truly effective."

2. Decentralized Identity

Systems that provide stronger verification of human identity:

- **Self-sovereign identity**: Frameworks allowing individuals to control their digital identities without centralized authorities.

- **Blockchain verification**: Using distributed ledger technology to create tamper-resistant identity records.

- **Proof of personhood**: Systems that verify human users without compromising privacy.

"Identity is the foundation of trust online," notes digital identity researcher Dr. Sarah Thompson. "Stronger identity systems make impersonation and synthetic personas harder to deploy effectively."

3. Authenticated Channels

Creating protected communication channels with verified participants:

- **Verified communication platforms**: Systems with strong identity verification for sensitive contexts.

- **Authenticated journalism**: Verification systems for news content from legitimate sources.

- **Official information channels**: Protected distribution systems for government and institutional communications.

"Rather than trying to detect synthetic content everywhere, authenticated channels create islands of higher trust," explains communication security expert Dr. Michael Brown. "This approach is particularly valuable for critical information contexts."

The Inevitable Arms Race

The technological contest between synthetic influence and countermeasures shows clear signs of an accelerating arms race:

1. The Red Queen Effect

Both offensive and defensive technologies are advancing rapidly:

- **Generative improvement**: Each new generation of AI systems produces more convincing synthetic content.

- **Detection evolution**: Detection systems continuously adapt to identify new generation techniques.

- **Evasion advances**: Manipulators develop increasingly sophisticated methods to evade detection.

"We're seeing a classic Red Queen scenario—running faster and faster just to stay in place," notes AI security researcher Dr. Elena Rodriguez, referencing the character from Lewis Carroll's "Through the Looking-Glass." "Each advance on one side triggers adaptation on the other."

2. Asymmetric Advantages

The current technological landscape offers several advantages to manipulators:

- **Economic incentives**: There's more money in creating convincing synthetic content than in detecting it.

- **Computational asymmetry**: Generation often requires less computing power than comprehensive detection.

- **Specificity advantage**: Attackers can focus on specific vulnerabilities, while defenders must protect everything.

"The technological playing field currently tilts toward offense rather than defense," explains cybersecurity strategist Dr. Thomas Wright. "This imbalance makes technological solutions necessary but insufficient on their own."

3. Democratization of Capabilities

Advanced manipulation capabilities are becoming increasingly accessible:

- **Commercialization**: Powerful generative AI systems are available through commercial APIs.

- **Open-source proliferation**: Sophisticated models are being released as open-source projects.

- **Specialized tools**: Purpose-built tools for specific manipulation tasks are widely available.

"The barrier to entry for sophisticated manipulation is dropping rapidly," notes AI ethics researcher Dr. Sarah Johnson. "Capabilities that once required nation-state resources are now accessible to much smaller actors."

The Human Element: Education and Resilience

Beyond regulation and technology, human factors play a crucial role in addressing synthetic influence. Educational approaches aim to build societal resilience against manipulation.

Media and Information Literacy

Educational initiatives focused on critical information consumption:

1. Critical Evaluation Skills

Teaching fundamental skills for assessing information:

- **Source evaluation**: Frameworks for assessing the credibility of information sources.

- **Evidence assessment**: Methods for evaluating the quality of evidence supporting claims.

- **Logical analysis**: Identifying common logical fallacies and reasoning errors.

- **Emotional awareness**: Recognizing when emotional reactions are being deliberately triggered.

"These fundamental critical thinking skills have always been important, but AI-driven manipulation makes them essential," explains media literacy educator Dr. Michael Chen. "They're the cognitive equivalent of basic hygiene."

2. Technical Literacy

Understanding the technical aspects of synthetic influence:

- **AI capabilities awareness**: Realistic understanding of what AI systems can and cannot do.

- **Manipulation technique recognition**: Familiarity with common synthetic influence tactics.

- **Platform mechanics knowledge**: Understanding how social media algorithms and features work.

- **Verification tool use**: Practical skills for using content verification resources.

"Technical literacy doesn't require becoming an AI expert," notes digital education researcher Dr. Elena Martinez. "It means understanding enough about how these systems work to make informed judgments about the content they produce."

3. Institutional Trust Rebuilding

Addressing the erosion of trust in information institutions:

- **Transparency initiatives**: Efforts by news organizations and platforms to explain their processes.

- **Correction practices**: Normalized procedures for acknowledging and correcting errors.

- **Trust indicators**: Clear signals of adherence to professional standards and practices.

- **Institutional accountability**: Mechanisms for holding information providers accountable.

"Synthetic influence thrives in environments where institutional trust has collapsed," explains media studies professor Dr. Thomas Lee. "Rebuilding warranted trust in legitimate information sources is as important as identifying manipulation."

Cognitive Security

Emerging approaches focused specifically on protecting cognitive processes from manipulation:

1. Cognitive Bias Awareness

Programs that help people understand their own psychological vulnerabilities:

- **Bias recognition training**: Helping people identify their own cognitive biases.

- **Debiasing techniques**: Practical methods for counteracting common biases.

- **Metacognitive practices**: Thinking about how we think and make decisions.

- **Emotional regulation**: Strategies for maintaining critical thinking during emotional arousal.

"Understanding your own cognitive vulnerabilities is the foundation of resistance to manipulation," notes cognitive psychologist Dr. Sarah Thompson. "You can't defend against exploits you don't recognize."

2. Prebunking and Inoculation

Proactively preparing people to recognize manipulation:

- **Manipulation previews**: Exposing people to weakened forms of manipulation techniques.

- **Technique explanation**: Explicitly explaining how specific manipulation tactics work.

- **Guided practice**: Structured exercises in identifying manipulation attempts.

- **Real-world application**: Applying learned concepts to current information environments.

"Prebunking approaches are showing significant promise in research studies," explains misinformation researcher Dr. Michael Brown. "They prepare mental antibodies before exposure to the full manipulation attempt."

3. Collective Verification Practices

Building social norms around information verification:

- **Verification before sharing**: Normalizing checking before spreading information.

- **Collaborative assessment**: Pooling diverse perspectives to evaluate content.

- **Correction norms**: Making it socially acceptable to correct misinformation respectfully.

- **Epistemic humility**: Cultivating comfort with uncertainty and provisional knowledge.

"Individual verification has limits—collective practices leverage diverse expertise and perspectives," notes digital sociology researcher Dr. Elena Rodriguez. "Building these practices into social norms is as important as individual skills."

The Limits of Education

While educational approaches are essential, they face important limitations:

1. Cognitive Load Constraints

Human cognitive capacity is finite:

- **Attention limitations**: People cannot verify everything they encounter.

- **Cognitive fatigue**: Constant vigilance leads to exhaustion and shortcuts.

- **Expertise boundaries**: No individual can be expert enough to evaluate all claims.

- **Time constraints**: Thorough verification takes time that daily life doesn't always permit.

"We cannot expect perfect vigilance from individuals," explains cognitive load researcher Dr. Thomas Wright. "Educational approaches must acknowledge human limitations rather than expecting superhuman performance."

2. Motivated Reasoning

People's prior beliefs strongly influence how they process new information:

- **Confirmation bias**: The tendency to accept information that confirms existing beliefs.

- **Identity protection**: Rejecting information that threatens important identities.

- **Tribal epistemology**: Evaluating information based on group loyalty rather than evidence.

- **Emotional investment**: Resistance to changing emotionally significant beliefs.

"Even the most media-literate individuals are susceptible to motivated reasoning," notes political psychology researcher Dr. Sarah Johnson. "Education helps but doesn't eliminate these deeply human tendencies."

3. Unequal Access

Educational resources are not equally distributed:

- **Digital divide**: Unequal access to technology and connectivity.

- **Educational disparities**: Varying levels of basic educational preparation.

- **Language barriers**: Most media literacy resources are available in limited languages.

- **Time poverty**: Many people lack the time for additional educational pursuits.

"Educational approaches must address equity concerns to avoid creating two-tiered information societies," argues digital equity advocate Dr. Michael Chen. "The most vulnerable populations often have the least access to protective resources."

Building Cyber Resilience: National and Community Approaches

Beyond individual education, broader societal approaches can build collective resilience against synthetic influence.

National Security Frameworks

Many nations are beginning to treat information integrity as a national security concern:

1. Strategic Communication Capabilities

Developing the capacity to counter synthetic influence operations:

- **Rapid response teams**: Specialized units that can quickly identify and respond to influence operations.

- **Attribution capabilities**: Technical and intelligence resources for identifying the sources of synthetic influence.

- **Counter-narrative development**: Capacity to develop and deploy accurate information to counter manipulation.

- **International coordination**: Collaborative mechanisms for addressing cross-border influence operations.

"Information defense is becoming as important as physical defense for many nations," explains national security expert Dr. Elena Martinez. "The challenge is developing these capabilities while preserving democratic values."

2. Critical Information Infrastructure

Protecting essential information systems and processes:

- **Election system protection**: Special safeguards for electoral information ecosystems.

- **Crisis communication channels**: Protected systems for authoritative information during emergencies.

- **Public health information security**: Defending health communication systems against manipulation.

- **Economic information protection**: Safeguarding financial and market information integrity.

"Some information contexts are so vital that they warrant special protection," notes critical infrastructure expert Dr. Thomas Lee. "The challenge is defining these boundaries appropriately without overreach."

3. Public-Private Partnerships

Collaboration between government and private sector entities:

- **Threat intelligence sharing**: Mechanisms for sharing information about emerging threats.

- **Technical standard development**: Collaborative development of authentication and verification standards.

- **Research funding**: Government support for fundamental research on synthetic influence defense.

- **Regulatory coordination**: Alignment between regulatory approaches and industry capabilities.

"Neither government nor industry can address this challenge alone," explains public-private partnership researcher Dr. Sarah Johnson. "Effective solutions require unprecedented collaboration across traditional boundaries."

Community Resilience Initiatives

Beyond national approaches, community-level initiatives show significant promise:

1. Local Information Ecosystems

Strengthening trusted local information sources:

- **Local journalism support**: Funding and capacity building for local news organizations.

- **Community information hubs**: Trusted local sources for verified information.

- **Neighborhood verification networks**: Grassroots systems for collaborative fact-checking.

- **Local government transparency**: Open communication channels between officials and communities.

"Strong local information ecosystems provide a foundation of trust that's harder to manipulate," notes community media researcher Dr. Michael Brown. "They create context for evaluating broader information flows."

2. Civil Society Organizations

Non-governmental organizations focused on information integrity:

- **Independent fact-checking organizations**: Non-partisan entities verifying claims in public discourse.

- **Digital literacy nonprofits**: Organizations providing educational resources and training.

- **Democracy technology groups**: Developing and deploying tools to protect democratic processes.

- **Research consortia**: Collaborative research initiatives studying synthetic influence.

"Civil society organizations play a crucial role in addressing synthetic influence while maintaining independence from both government and commercial interests," explains civil society researcher Dr. Elena Rodriguez. "They help fill gaps that neither sector adequately addresses."

3. Professional Standards and Ethics

Strengthening ethical frameworks within influential professions:

- **Journalism ethics evolution**: Updated ethical standards addressing synthetic content challenges.

- **Technology professional codes**: Ethical frameworks for AI developers and platform designers.

- **Marketing and PR standards**: Industry norms regarding the use of synthetic content.

- **Political campaign pledges**: Commitments to avoid deceptive synthetic content in campaigns.

"Professional ethics provide an essential layer of defense that operates independently of legal requirements," notes professional ethics scholar Dr. Thomas Wright. "They establish norms that shape behavior even when regulation is absent or inadequate."

The Path Forward: A Multi-Layered Approach

Addressing synthetic influence effectively requires combining multiple approaches in a comprehensive strategy.

The Defense-in-Depth Model

Security experts advocate a layered approach to complex threats:

1. Complementary Protections

Different approaches address different aspects of the challenge:

- **Regulation**: Establishes boundaries and consequences for the most harmful applications.

- **Technology**: Provides scalable detection and verification capabilities.

- **Education**: Builds human capacity to identify and resist manipulation.

- **Institutional trust**: Creates contexts where authoritative information can be recognized.

"No single approach can address synthetic influence alone," explains security strategist Dr. Sarah Johnson. "The strongest protection comes from multiple layers working in concert."

2. Resilience Through Redundancy

When one defense fails, others remain active:

- **Technical detection failure**: Even when detection tools miss synthetic content, educated users may spot it.

- **Individual vigilance limits**: When individual attention flags, platform safeguards can provide protection.

- **Regulatory gaps**: Professional ethics can address areas where regulation hasn't yet reached.

- **Trust breakdowns**: Verification technologies can provide evidence when trust is questioned.

"Redundancy isn't inefficiency—it's essential protection against sophisticated threats," notes resilience researcher Dr. Michael Chen. "The goal is a system where multiple failures would be required for manipulation to succeed."

3. Adaptive Response

Defenses that evolve as threats change:

- **Continuous assessment**: Regularly evaluating the effectiveness of current approaches.

- **Threat intelligence**: Monitoring emerging manipulation techniques and technologies.

- **Cross-sector learning**: Sharing insights across different domains and contexts.

- **Rapid response capability**: Quickly deploying new defenses when vulnerabilities are identified.

"The synthetic influence landscape is constantly evolving," explains adaptive security expert Dr. Elena Martinez. "Static defenses will inevitably fail against dynamic threats."

Values-Based Approaches

Beyond specific techniques, the values guiding our response matter deeply:

1. Preserving Free Expression

Balancing protection against manipulation with free speech values:

- **Precision targeting**: Focusing interventions on demonstrable harms rather than content categories.

- **Procedural protections**: Ensuring due process in content moderation decisions.

- **Transparency requirements**: Making intervention criteria and processes public.

- **Proportional responses**: Matching the scale of intervention to the severity of harm.

"The cure cannot be worse than the disease," cautions digital rights advocate Dr. Thomas Lee. "Approaches that undermine fundamental freedoms in the name of protection ultimately fail both goals."

2. Maintaining Human Agency

Ensuring that humans remain the ultimate decision-makers:

- **Explainable systems**: Making detection and verification technologies understandable to users.

- **Meaningful choices**: Providing options rather than imposing protections.

- **Informed consent**: Ensuring people understand how protective systems work.

- **Contestability**: Allowing challenges to automated decisions about content.

"Technology should enhance human judgment, not replace it," argues AI ethics researcher Dr. Sarah Johnson. "Systems that remove human agency ultimately increase vulnerability rather than reducing it."

3. Equity and Inclusion

Ensuring protections work for everyone, not just privileged groups:

- **Universal design**: Creating solutions accessible across different abilities and resources.

- **Diverse testing**: Evaluating protections across different communities and contexts.

- **Multilingual approaches**: Developing solutions that work across language barriers.

- **Participatory development**: Including diverse perspectives in designing protections.

"Synthetic influence often targets vulnerable communities first," notes digital equity researcher Dr. Michael Brown. "Effective solutions must work for those most at risk, not just those with the most resources."

The Real War Ahead: Competing Visions of the Future

As we conclude, it's important to recognize that the challenge of synthetic influence reflects a deeper contest between competing visions of our technological future.

The Manipulation Economy

One possible future extends current trends toward increasingly sophisticated manipulation:

- **Attention harvesting**: Economic models based on capturing and monetizing human attention.

- **Persuasion profiling**: Increasingly precise psychological targeting of individuals.

- **Reality fragmentation**: The dissolution of shared facts into algorithm-curated realities.

- **Trust collapse**: Widespread inability to distinguish authentic from synthetic content.

"This path leads to what some scholars call 'the post-truth society,'" explains digital futurist Dr. Elena Rodriguez. "It's a world where manipulation becomes so pervasive that authentic human connection and democratic governance become increasingly difficult."

The Human-Centered Alternative

An alternative vision prioritizes human flourishing over manipulation:

- **Aligned incentives**: Economic models that reward authentic value creation rather than attention capture.

- **Augmented judgment**: Technologies that enhance human decision-making rather than exploiting vulnerabilities.

- **Shared reality maintenance**: Systems that help maintain a foundation of shared facts while allowing diverse perspectives.

- **Trust infrastructure**: Technical and social systems that enable warranted trust in digital contexts.

"This alternative isn't about rejecting technology but redirecting it," argues digital ethics philosopher Dr. Thomas Wright. "It's about technologies designed to serve human needs rather than exploit human weaknesses."

The Choice Before Us

The path we take isn't predetermined but depends on collective choices:

- **Design decisions**: How we design and deploy AI systems and digital platforms.

- **Economic incentives**: What business models we permit and encourage.

- **Regulatory frameworks**: What boundaries we establish through policy.

- **Social norms**: What behaviors we accept, reject, or celebrate.

"We stand at a crucial juncture," notes technology historian Dr. Sarah Johnson. "The decisions we make in the next few years will shape our information environment for decades to come."

Conclusion: Agency in the Age of AI

Throughout this book, we've explored how AI is being used to hijack social media, control thoughts, and manipulate the masses. We've examined the tools and tactics of synthetic influence, from deepfakes to bot networks to AI-generated personas. We've investigated the psychological vulnerabilities these technologies exploit and the defensive measures individuals and societies can employ.

The picture that emerges is both concerning and hopeful. The threats are real and growing. The asymmetries currently favor those who would manipulate rather than inform. The technological arms race shows no signs of slowing.

Yet there are also grounds for optimism. Awareness is growing. Defensive technologies are evolving. Educational approaches are showing promise. Regulatory frameworks are developing. Most importantly, the conversation about how we want our digital future to unfold is expanding beyond technical experts to include broader society.

"The greatest danger isn't the technology itself but fatalism about our ability to shape its impact," argues digital democracy advocate Dr. Michael Chen. "The moment we believe we're powerless is the moment we surrender our agency."

The real war ahead isn't primarily technical but philosophical and political. It's about what kind of digital environment we want to create and inhabit. It's about whether technology will enhance human potential or diminish human agency. It's about whether our tools will connect us through authentic understanding or divide us through manufactured outrage.

This isn't a war that can be won once and for all. It's an ongoing contest that will require vigilance, adaptation, and commitment to human values in the face of powerful technological and economic forces. But it's a contest worth engaging, because the stakes—our autonomy, our democracy, our shared reality—couldn't be higher.

As you close this book, remember that you're not merely a passive observer in this unfolding drama. Through your choices as a citizen, consumer, creator, and community member, you help determine which vision of the future prevails. By understanding the mechanisms of manipulation, protecting your digital mind, and advocating for human-centered technology, you become part of the solution.

The invisible war for your attention and beliefs is already underway. Now that you can see it, what will you do?

Key Takeaways:

- Addressing synthetic influence requires a multi-layered approach combining regulation, technology, education, and institutional trust-building.
- Current regulatory efforts face significant challenges including attribution difficulties, definition problems, and enforcement limitations.
- Technological countermeasures are evolving rapidly but face an ongoing arms race with increasingly sophisticated manipulation techniques.
- Educational approaches build essential resilience but must acknowledge cognitive limitations and address equity concerns.
- National and community approaches can create contexts of greater resilience against synthetic influence.
- The deeper challenge involves competing visions of our technological future—one centered on manipulation, the other on human flourishing.
- Individual and collective choices will determine which vision prevails, making informed engagement essential.

Appendix A: AI Tools Used in Propaganda

This appendix provides a comprehensive catalog of current AI technologies being deployed in influence operations. Understanding these tools is essential for recognizing and countering synthetic influence campaigns. While this list aims to be thorough, the rapid pace of AI development means new tools and capabilities emerge regularly.

Text Generation Technologies

Large Language Models (LLMs)

Large Language Models represent the foundation of many text-based influence operations:

GPT Models (OpenAI)

- **Capabilities**: Advanced text generation with human-like quality, contextual understanding, and adaptation to different writing styles
- **Use in Influence Operations**: Creating persuasive content at scale, generating personalized manipulation, crafting convincing impersonations
- **Detection Indicators**: Unusual fluency, lack of factual errors typical in human writing, subtle repetitive patterns
- **Example Application**: Generating thousands of unique, persuasive comments on news articles or social media posts

Claude (Anthropic)

- **Capabilities**: Sophisticated dialogue, nuanced content generation with strong reasoning capabilities

- **Use in Influence Operations**: Creating conversational agents for manipulation, generating complex argumentative content
- **Detection Indicators**: Excessive balance in controversial topics, unnaturally consistent reasoning
- **Example Application**: Developing scripts for social engineering attacks that adapt to target responses

Llama Models (Meta)

- **Capabilities**: Open-source models with strong performance across multiple languages
- **Use in Influence Operations**: Widely accessible foundation for building specialized manipulation tools
- **Detection Indicators**: Varies based on fine-tuning and deployment
- **Example Application**: Creating localized disinformation campaigns in multiple languages

Specialized Propaganda Models

- **Capabilities**: Fine-tuned models specifically optimized for persuasion and influence
- **Use in Influence Operations**: Generating content with specific emotional triggers or cognitive exploits
- **Detection Indicators**: Unusual emotional loading, specific narrative patterns
- **Example Application**: Models trained on successful propaganda to replicate persuasion techniques

Specialized Text Generation Tools

Beyond general-purpose LLMs, specialized tools target specific influence applications:

Narrative Generation Systems

- **Capabilities**: Creating coherent, extended narratives around specific themes or objectives
- **Use in Influence Operations**: Developing consistent disinformation storylines across multiple platforms
- **Detection Indicators**: Thematic consistency across seemingly unrelated sources
- **Example Application**: Generating coordinated narratives about election fraud across multiple platforms

Sentiment Manipulation Tools

- **Capabilities**: Generating text with precisely calibrated emotional content
- **Use in Influence Operations**: Creating content designed to trigger specific emotional responses
- **Detection Indicators**: Unusual emotional precision, effective emotional triggers
- **Example Application**: Generating outrage-inducing content calibrated to specific audience segments

Multilingual Adaptation Systems

- **Capabilities**: Adapting persuasive content across languages while preserving influence techniques
- **Use in Influence Operations**: Deploying similar influence campaigns across different linguistic communities
- **Detection Indicators**: Similar narrative structures appearing in multiple languages simultaneously
- **Example Application**: Translating successful disinformation campaigns from one language to others while preserving persuasive elements

Visual Manipulation Technologies

Image Generation and Manipulation

AI systems for creating and altering visual content:

Diffusion Models (Stable Diffusion, Midjourney, DALL-E)

- **Capabilities**: Generating photorealistic images from text descriptions
- **Use in Influence Operations**: Creating synthetic "evidence" for false narratives, generating misleading imagery
- **Detection Indicators**: Inconsistencies in fine details (hands, text, backgrounds), unusual lighting patterns
- **Example Application**: Creating "photographic evidence" of events that never occurred

GAN-Based Systems (StyleGAN, CycleGAN)

- **Capabilities**: Generating highly realistic faces and transforming images across domains
- **Use in Influence Operations**: Creating synthetic identities, manipulating existing imagery
- **Detection Indicators**: Symmetry issues, background inconsistencies, unusual artifacts
- **Example Application**: Creating convincing profile pictures for synthetic social media personas

Neural Radiance Fields (NeRF)

- **Capabilities**: Creating 3D representations from limited 2D images

- **Use in Influence Operations**: Generating novel perspectives of fabricated scenes
- **Detection Indicators**: Inconsistent physics, unusual lighting interactions
- **Example Application**: Creating multiple viewpoints of synthetic events to enhance credibility

Image Manipulation Tools

- **Capabilities**: Seamlessly altering existing images to change meaning or context
- **Use in Influence Operations**: Modifying real images to support false narratives
- **Detection Indicators**: Inconsistent shadows, perspective errors, metadata anomalies
- **Example Application**: Adding or removing people or objects from authentic photographs

Video Synthesis and Manipulation

Technologies for creating and altering video content:

Deepfake Systems

- **Capabilities**: Face swapping in videos with increasing realism
- **Use in Influence Operations**: Creating false video evidence, impersonating public figures
- **Detection Indicators**: Unnatural facial movements, inconsistent blinking, edge artifacts
- **Example Application**: Creating videos of political figures saying things they never said

Full-Body Synthesis

- **Capabilities**: Generating or manipulating entire human figures in motion
- **Use in Influence Operations**: Creating synthetic video evidence of events
- **Detection Indicators**: Unnatural movement patterns, inconsistent physics
- **Example Application**: Generating video of public figures in compromising situations

Video Diffusion Models

- **Capabilities**: Generating video content from text descriptions
- **Use in Influence Operations**: Creating synthetic video evidence for disinformation narratives
- **Detection Indicators**: Temporal inconsistencies, physics violations
- **Example Application**: Generating "eyewitness" video of fabricated incidents

Real-Time Facial Reenactment

- **Capabilities**: Manipulating facial expressions and mouth movements in real-time
- **Use in Influence Operations**: Live impersonation, manipulated interviews or statements
- **Detection Indicators**: Microexpression inconsistencies, unusual facial dynamics
- **Example Application**: Creating fake live streams of authority figures during crisis situations

Audio Manipulation Technologies

Voice Synthesis and Cloning

Technologies for creating and manipulating audio content:

Text-to-Speech Systems

- **Capabilities**: Converting text to natural-sounding speech
- **Use in Influence Operations**: Creating synthetic audio content at scale
- **Detection Indicators**: Unnatural prosody, consistent quality across utterances
- **Example Application**: Generating synthetic news broadcasts or announcements

Voice Cloning Tools

- **Capabilities**: Replicating specific voices from limited samples
- **Use in Influence Operations**: Impersonating public figures or trusted individuals
- **Detection Indicators**: Unusual cadence, limited emotional range, artifacts in certain phonemes
- **Example Application**: Creating fake phone calls or audio messages from political leaders

Emotional Voice Synthesis

- **Capabilities**: Generating speech with specific emotional qualities
- **Use in Influence Operations**: Creating emotionally manipulative audio content

- **Detection Indicators**: Inconsistent emotional patterns, unusual emphasis
- **Example Application**: Creating panic-inducing emergency announcements with synthetic voices

Real-Time Voice Conversion

- **Capabilities**: Transforming one voice into another during live conversation
- **Use in Influence Operations**: Live impersonation in calls or broadcasts
- **Detection Indicators**: Processing delays, inconsistent transformation quality
- **Example Application**: Impersonating officials in phone calls to journalists or public figures

Audio Manipulation and Generation

Beyond voice, other audio manipulation technologies:

Audio Deepfakes

- **Capabilities**: Creating or manipulating complete audio environments
- **Use in Influence Operations**: Fabricating recordings of events or conversations
- **Detection Indicators**: Inconsistent background noise, unusual acoustic properties
- **Example Application**: Creating synthetic recordings of private meetings or conversations

Ambient Sound Generation

- **Capabilities**: Creating realistic environmental audio

- **Use in Influence Operations**: Adding authenticity to synthetic recordings
- **Detection Indicators**: Inconsistent acoustic properties, repetitive patterns
- **Example Application**: Adding location-specific background sounds to fake recordings

Multi-Modal Systems

Integrated Generation Platforms

Technologies that combine multiple media types:

Multi-Modal Generation Systems

- **Capabilities**: Creating coordinated text, image, audio, and video content
- **Use in Influence Operations**: Developing comprehensive synthetic narratives across media types
- **Detection Indicators**: Unusual consistency across modalities, coordinated release patterns
- **Example Application**: Generating complete synthetic news packages with matching text, images, and video

Interactive Synthetic Agents

- **Capabilities**: Creating responsive, adaptive synthetic personas
- **Use in Influence Operations**: Deploying convincing interactive agents for manipulation
- **Detection Indicators**: Limited topic adaptation, repetitive interaction patterns

- **Example Application**: Creating synthetic "experts" who can respond to questions in specific domains

Distribution and Amplification Technologies

Automated Deployment Systems

Technologies for distributing synthetic content:

Bot Networks

- **Capabilities**: Coordinated posting and interaction across multiple accounts
- **Use in Influence Operations**: Amplifying synthetic content, creating impression of consensus
- **Detection Indicators**: Unusual coordination, activity patterns, account creation clustering
- **Example Application**: Simultaneously promoting synthetic content across hundreds of accounts

Cross-Platform Coordination Tools

- **Capabilities**: Synchronizing influence operations across different social platforms
- **Use in Influence Operations**: Creating comprehensive information environments
- **Detection Indicators**: Similar content appearing across platforms with timing patterns
- **Example Application**: Coordinating narrative deployment across Twitter, Facebook, YouTube, and TikTok

Algorithmic Exploitation Systems

- **Capabilities**: Identifying and exploiting recommendation algorithm vulnerabilities
- **Use in Influence Operations**: Maximizing visibility of synthetic content
- **Detection Indicators**: Unusual virality patterns, engagement anomalies
- **Example Application**: Manipulating trending algorithms to promote synthetic content

Targeting and Personalization Technologies

Audience Analysis and Targeting

Technologies for identifying and exploiting vulnerabilities:

Psychographic Profiling Tools

- **Capabilities**: Creating psychological profiles from digital footprints
- **Use in Influence Operations**: Identifying psychological vulnerabilities for exploitation
- **Detection Indicators**: Unusually effective psychological targeting
- **Example Application**: Identifying and targeting individuals susceptible to specific conspiracy theories

Micro-Targeting Systems

- **Capabilities**: Delivering highly personalized content to specific audience segments

- **Use in Influence Operations**: Tailoring manipulation to individual psychological profiles
- **Detection Indicators**: Unusual personalization precision, effective emotional triggering
- **Example Application**: Delivering different versions of manipulative content to different demographic groups

A/B Testing Frameworks for Manipulation

- **Capabilities**: Rapidly testing and optimizing persuasive content
- **Use in Influence Operations**: Identifying most effective manipulation approaches
- **Detection Indicators**: Systematic content variations, rapid tactical adaptation
- **Example Application**: Testing dozens of headline variations to identify most effective emotional triggers

Counter-Detection Technologies

Evasion and Obfuscation Tools

Technologies designed to evade detection systems:

Watermark Removal Tools

- **Capabilities**: Removing or obscuring AI-generated content markers
- **Use in Influence Operations**: Evading automated detection systems
- **Detection Indicators**: Unusual artifacts from removal process
- **Example Application**: Stripping metadata and watermarks from AI-generated images

Adversarial Perturbation Systems

- **Capabilities**: Adding subtle modifications to evade AI detection
- **Use in Influence Operations**: Bypassing content moderation systems
- **Detection Indicators**: Unusual noise patterns, subtle visual artifacts
- **Example Application**: Modifying deepfakes to bypass platform detection algorithms

Human-in-the-Loop Refinement

- **Capabilities**: Using human feedback to improve evasion of detection
- **Use in Influence Operations**: Creating content that passes both automated and human review
- **Detection Indicators**: Hybrid characteristics of human and AI content
- **Example Application**: Human editors refining AI-generated text to remove detectable patterns

Emerging Technologies

Next-Generation Capabilities

Technologies on the horizon with significant influence potential:

Multimodal Foundation Models

- **Capabilities**: Unified understanding and generation across text, image, audio, and video

- **Potential Impact**: Seamless creation of synthetic content across all media types
- **Expected Timeline**: Increasingly capable systems emerging 2024-2026
- **Defensive Considerations**: Will require integrated cross-modal detection approaches

Embodied AI Systems

- **Capabilities**: AI systems with physical or virtual embodiment and agency
- **Potential Impact**: More convincing synthetic personas with apparent autonomy
- **Expected Timeline**: Limited capabilities by 2025, more advanced by 2027-2028
- **Defensive Considerations**: Will require new frameworks for authenticity verification

Brain-Computer Interface Exploitation

- **Capabilities**: Leveraging neural interfaces for direct influence
- **Potential Impact**: Potential for bypassing conscious cognitive defenses
- **Expected Timeline**: Early research applications 2026-2030
- **Defensive Considerations**: Will require new paradigms for cognitive security

Detection and Defense Resources

For each technology category described above, corresponding detection tools and defensive approaches are being developed. See Appendix B: Detection Frameworks for Social Manipulation for detailed information on identifying and countering these technologies.

Conclusion: The Evolving Landscape

The technologies described in this appendix represent the current state of AI tools used in influence operations. However, this landscape is evolving rapidly, with new capabilities emerging regularly. Staying informed about these developments is essential for maintaining effective defenses against synthetic influence.

Several trends are worth monitoring:

1. **Increasing accessibility**: Advanced capabilities are becoming available to smaller actors through commercial APIs and open-source implementations.

2. **Cross-modal integration**: The boundaries between different media types are blurring as integrated systems emerge.

3. **Defensive evasion**: New technologies increasingly incorporate features specifically designed to evade detection systems.

4. **Personalization advancement**: Targeting is becoming more precise and psychologically sophisticated.

Understanding these tools and their capabilities is the first step in developing effective countermeasures against synthetic influence operations.

Appendix B: Detection Frameworks for Social Manipulation

This appendix provides structured approaches for identifying synthetic influence and social manipulation. These frameworks range from individual assessment tools to organizational methodologies to technical detection systems. While no single framework is foolproof, combining multiple approaches significantly improves detection capabilities.

Individual Assessment Frameworks

The SIFT Method

The SIFT method, developed by digital literacy expert Mike Caulfield, provides a straightforward four-step process for evaluating online information:

Stop

- **Purpose**: Pause before sharing or believing information
- **Key Questions**:
    - Does this content trigger a strong emotional reaction?
    - Am I being pressured to act quickly?
    - Does this confirm what I already believe?
- **Implementation**: Create a habit of pausing for at least 30 seconds when encountering new information
- **Example Application**: When seeing a shocking headline about a public figure, stop and check your emotional response before proceeding

Investigate the Source

- **Purpose**: Determine if the source is credible and appropriate for the claim

- **Key Questions**:
  - Who created this information?
  - What is their expertise on this topic?
  - What are their potential biases or motivations?
- **Implementation**: Use lateral reading (checking other sources about the source) rather than evaluating based on appearance
- **Example Application**: When encountering a health claim, check the author's credentials and whether they're recognized by legitimate medical organizations

Find Better Coverage

- **Purpose**: Seek additional sources to verify or contextualize the information
- **Key Questions**:
  - Have other reputable sources reported this information?
  - What additional context do other sources provide?
  - Are there significant differences in how this is reported elsewhere?
- **Implementation**: Search for the claim or topic on trusted news sites and fact-checking organizations
- **Example Application**: When seeing a claim about a new scientific discovery, check if major scientific publications or institutions have covered it

Trace Claims, Quotes, and Media to the Original Context

- **Purpose**: Verify that information hasn't been altered or taken out of context
- **Key Questions**:
  - What is the original context of this quote or image?
  - Has it been altered from its original form?
  - Does the original context change the meaning?

- **Implementation**: Use reverse image searches, quote searches, and tracking to original sources
- **Example Application**: When seeing a controversial quote attributed to a public figure, find the complete original statement to check for context

The ESCAPE Framework

The ESCAPE framework, introduced in Chapter 14, provides a comprehensive approach to evaluating potentially manipulative content:

Emotional Awareness

- **Purpose**: Recognize when content is triggering emotional responses that bypass critical thinking
- **Key Questions**:
  - What specific emotions am I feeling right now?
  - Are these emotions interfering with my critical assessment?
  - Is this content designed to provoke these specific emotions?
- **Implementation**: Practice mindfulness techniques to identify emotional reactions as they occur
- **Example Application**: Noticing feelings of outrage when reading political content and taking time to cool down before evaluating

Source Verification

- **Purpose**: Determine the credibility and reliability of information sources
- **Key Questions**:
  - Is this source transparent about its identity and funding?

- – Does this source have relevant expertise on this topic?
- – Does this source have a history of accuracy and corrections?
- **Implementation**: Develop a personal database of trusted sources and verification methods
- **Example Application**: Checking domain registration information for unfamiliar websites before trusting their content

Context Consideration

- **Purpose**: Restore context that might have been stripped from information
- **Key Questions**:
  - – What broader situation surrounds this specific claim?
  - – What came before and after the presented information?
  - – What related information might change my understanding?
- **Implementation**: Actively seek additional context for claims that seem surprising or provocative
- **Example Application**: When seeing a short video clip of a controversial statement, finding the complete video to understand the full context

Alternative Explanations

- **Purpose**: Consider different interpretations of the same information
- **Key Questions**:
  - – What other explanations could account for this?
  - – What information might be missing?
  - – Who benefits from my accepting the provided explanation?
- **Implementation**: Practice generating multiple explanations for any claim or situation

- **Example Application**: When presented with a conspiracy theory, systematically considering more mundane explanations for the same evidence

Pattern Recognition

- **Purpose**: Identify recurring manipulation techniques across different contexts
- **Key Questions**:
    - Have I seen this specific technique before?
    - Does this follow common patterns of manipulation?
    - Are there signature elements that indicate a specific source?
- **Implementation**: Study known disinformation campaigns to understand their structure
- **Example Application**: Recognizing the pattern of crisis exploitation when suspicious content emerges immediately after a disaster

Engagement Control

- **Purpose**: Manage how and when you engage with digital content
- **Key Questions**:
    - Is this worth my attention right now?
    - Should I verify before sharing?
    - Would delayed engagement improve my assessment?
- **Implementation**: Establish personal rules for engagement with different content types
- **Example Application**: Setting a personal rule to wait 24 hours before sharing breaking news on social media

The RADAR Method

The RADAR method focuses specifically on identifying synthetic media and deepfakes:

Review Metadata

- **Purpose**: Examine technical information about the content
- **Key Questions**:
    - When and how was this content created?
    - Has the metadata been stripped or altered?
    - Are there inconsistencies in the technical information?
- **Implementation**: Use metadata viewing tools for images and videos
- **Example Application**: Checking image EXIF data to see if the creation date matches claimed timing

Analyze Visual Anomalies

- **Purpose**: Identify visual indicators of manipulation
- **Key Questions**:
    - Are there unnatural elements in faces or bodies?
    - Do lighting and shadows behave consistently?
    - Are there artifacts around edges or in textures?
- **Implementation**: Develop familiarity with common AI generation artifacts
- **Example Application**: Looking closely at hands in suspected AI-generated images to check for anatomical errors

Detect Audio Inconsistencies

- **Purpose**: Identify audio manipulation or synthesis
- **Key Questions**:

- Does the voice maintain natural variations?
- Are breathing patterns and background noise consistent?
- Do emotional tones match the content?

- **Implementation**: Train your ear to notice unnatural speech patterns
- **Example Application**: Listening for consistent background noise in audio recordings that claim to be continuous

Assess Contextual Coherence

- **Purpose**: Evaluate whether the content makes sense in its broader context
- **Key Questions**:
    - Does this align with known facts about the subject?
    - Are there physical or logical impossibilities?
    - Does the content fit with the purported time and place?
- **Implementation**: Cross-reference with established facts and physical laws
- **Example Application**: Checking whether clothing or technology in an image matches the claimed time period

Research Provenance

- **Purpose**: Trace the origin and distribution path of the content
- **Key Questions**:
    - Where did this content first appear?
    - How has it spread across platforms?
    - Are there variations or earlier versions?
- **Implementation**: Use reverse image searches and chronological analysis of sharing patterns
- **Example Application**: Tracing a viral image back to its first appearance to determine if it was repurposed from another context

Organizational Detection Frameworks

The DISARM Framework

The DISARM (Disinformation Analysis and Risk Management) framework provides a structured approach for organizations to identify and counter influence operations:

Tactical Pattern Recognition

- **Purpose**: Identify specific manipulation techniques being employed
- **Key Components**:
  - Taxonomy of known influence tactics
  - Historical pattern database
  - Cross-campaign comparison methodology
- **Implementation**: Maintain a continuously updated catalog of tactics with examples
- **Example Application**: Identifying coordinated inauthentic behavior across multiple platforms using consistent narrative elements

Attribution Analysis

- **Purpose**: Determine the likely source of influence operations
- **Key Components**:
  - Technical indicators of origin
  - Linguistic and stylistic analysis
  - Strategic objective assessment
  - Infrastructure fingerprinting
- **Implementation**: Combine technical and content analysis to build attribution cases

- **Example Application**: Linking a disinformation campaign to specific actors through technical infrastructure, narrative themes, and timing patterns

Impact Assessment

- **Purpose**: Evaluate the reach and effectiveness of influence operations
- **Key Components**:
  - Engagement metrics analysis
  - Sentiment tracking
  - Narrative adoption measurement
  - Behavioral impact evaluation
- **Implementation**: Develop multi-factor impact scoring systems
- **Example Application**: Measuring how widely a synthetic narrative has been adopted across different communities and platforms

Countermeasure Development

- **Purpose**: Create appropriate responses to identified operations
- **Key Components**:
  - Response option catalog
  - Proportionality guidelines
  - Effectiveness metrics
  - Unintended consequences assessment
- **Implementation**: Maintain a decision framework for selecting appropriate countermeasures
- **Example Application**: Determining whether to directly debunk, strategically ignore, or deploy counter-narratives against a specific campaign

The ABC Framework

The ABC (Actor-Behavior-Content) Framework, developed by the Carnegie Endowment for International Peace, provides a structured approach for analyzing influence operations:

Actor Analysis

- **Purpose**: Identify who is behind influence operations
- **Key Components**:
    - Account network mapping
    - Technical attribution indicators
    - Motivation assessment
    - Capability evaluation
- **Implementation**: Combine technical and contextual analysis to build actor profiles
- **Example Application**: Linking seemingly disparate accounts through behavioral patterns and technical indicators

Behavior Analysis

- **Purpose**: Examine how influence operations are conducted
- **Key Components**:
    - Coordination patterns
    - Amplification mechanisms
    - Temporal signatures
    - Cross-platform activities
- **Implementation**: Develop detection systems for abnormal behavioral patterns
- **Example Application**: Identifying synchronized posting patterns across multiple accounts that indicate coordination

Content Analysis

- **Purpose**: Analyze what messages are being promoted
- **Key Components**:
  - Narrative tracking
  - Linguistic analysis
  - Emotional targeting assessment
  - Multimedia forensics
- **Implementation**: Combine automated content analysis with human expertise
- **Example Application**: Identifying consistent narrative themes across different media types and platforms

The AMITT Framework

The AMITT (Adversarial Misinformation and Influence Tactics and Techniques) Framework adapts cybersecurity methodologies to influence operations:

Preparation Phase Analysis

- **Purpose**: Identify early indicators of influence operation planning
- **Key Components**:
  - Infrastructure development detection
  - Audience research indicators
  - Resource mobilization signals
  - Preliminary testing patterns
- **Implementation**: Monitor for preparatory activities that precede full campaigns
- **Example Application**: Detecting the creation of networks of dormant accounts before they become active

Execution Phase Detection

- **Purpose**: Recognize active influence operations in progress
- **Key Components**:
  - Campaign launch indicators
  - Amplification pattern detection
  - Narrative deployment tracking
  - Platform exploitation monitoring
- **Implementation**: Develop real-time monitoring systems for campaign activities
- **Example Application**: Identifying the sudden activation of previously dormant networks around specific narratives

Impact Measurement

- **Purpose**: Assess the effectiveness and reach of influence operations
- **Key Components**:
  - Engagement metrics analysis
  - Narrative adoption tracking
  - Media coverage monitoring
  - Behavioral impact assessment
- **Implementation**: Develop multi-factor frameworks for measuring different types of impact
- **Example Application**: Measuring how synthetic narratives penetrate mainstream discourse through citation chains

Technical Detection Systems

Content-Based Detection

Technical approaches focused on analyzing the content itself:

AI-Generated Text Detection

- **Purpose**: Identify text created by large language models
- **Key Technologies**:
  - Statistical pattern analysis
  - Perplexity and burstiness measurement
  - Stylometric analysis
  - Watermark detection
- **Implementation**: Deploy multiple detection models with different approaches
- **Example Application**: Scanning comments on news articles to identify AI-generated content

Deepfake Detection Systems

- **Purpose**: Identify manipulated or synthetic visual media
- **Key Technologies**:
  - Facial inconsistency detection
  - Temporal coherence analysis
  - Biological signal monitoring (blinking, pulse)
  - Artifact identification
- **Implementation**: Combine multiple detection approaches for greater accuracy
- **Example Application**: Analyzing viral videos of public figures for signs of manipulation

Audio Synthesis Detection

- **Purpose**: Identify artificially generated or manipulated audio
- **Key Technologies**:
  - Voice pattern analysis
  - Spectral inconsistency detection
  - Emotional coherence assessment

- – Background noise analysis
- **Implementation**: Develop layered detection systems with multiple techniques
- **Example Application**: Verifying the authenticity of purported recordings of private conversations

Cross-Modal Consistency Checking

- **Purpose**: Identify inconsistencies between different elements of multimedia content
- **Key Technologies**:
  - – Audio-visual synchronization analysis
  - – Content-context alignment checking
  - – Multi-element coherence assessment
- **Implementation**: Develop systems that analyze relationships between different media elements
- **Example Application**: Detecting when audio has been added to video from a different source

Behavioral Detection Systems

Technical approaches focused on distribution and engagement patterns:

Coordinated Inauthentic Behavior Detection

- **Purpose**: Identify networks of accounts working together to amplify content
- **Key Technologies**:
  - – Network analysis algorithms
  - – Temporal coordination detection
  - – Content similarity measurement
  - – Account relationship mapping

- **Implementation**: Deploy continuous monitoring systems across platforms
- **Example Application**: Identifying bot networks promoting synthetic content through coordinated action

Anomalous Amplification Detection

- **Purpose**: Identify content receiving unnatural patterns of engagement
- **Key Technologies**:
    - Engagement velocity analysis
    - Distribution pattern modeling
    - Comparative baseline assessment
    - Temporal signature analysis
- **Implementation**: Develop models of natural versus manipulated content spread
- **Example Application**: Detecting when content is being artificially boosted through inauthentic means

Account Authenticity Assessment

- **Purpose**: Determine whether accounts represent genuine users
- **Key Technologies**:
    - Behavioral consistency analysis
    - Linguistic pattern assessment
    - Activity timing evaluation
    - Profile coherence checking
- **Implementation**: Develop multi-factor authenticity scoring systems
- **Example Application**: Distinguishing between human-operated accounts and AI-driven personas

Documentation and Reporting Frameworks

Evidence Collection Methodologies

Structured approaches for documenting suspected manipulation:

Digital Forensic Documentation

- **Purpose**: Create verifiable records of suspected synthetic influence
- **Key Components**:
    - Timestamped screenshots
    - Archived webpage versions
    - Metadata preservation
    - Chain of custody documentation
- **Implementation**: Develop standardized evidence collection procedures
- **Example Application**: Creating legally admissible documentation of election interference attempts

Pattern Documentation Systems

- **Purpose**: Record recurring manipulation techniques for future reference
- **Key Components**:
    - Standardized taxonomy
    - Cross-instance comparison methodology
    - Temporal evolution tracking
    - Attribution indicator documentation
- **Implementation**: Maintain searchable databases of manipulation techniques

- **Example Application**: Documenting the evolution of specific manipulation tactics across multiple campaigns

Reporting Mechanisms

Frameworks for reporting suspected manipulation:

Platform Reporting Protocols

- **Purpose**: Effectively report manipulation to hosting platforms
- **Key Components**:
    - Platform-specific reporting guides
    - Evidence formatting requirements
    - Follow-up procedures
    - Escalation pathways
- **Implementation**: Develop standardized reporting templates for different platforms
- **Example Application**: Creating comprehensive reports for platform trust and safety teams

Public Interest Disclosure Frameworks

- **Purpose**: Responsibly disclose manipulation to relevant authorities and the public
- **Key Components**:
    - Ethical disclosure guidelines
    - Harm minimization protocols
    - Evidence presentation standards
    - Timing considerations
- **Implementation**: Develop ethical frameworks for public disclosure decisions

- **Example Application**: Determining when and how to publicly disclose evidence of election interference

Collaborative Reporting Networks

- **Purpose**: Pool resources for more effective detection and reporting
- **Key Components**:
    - Secure information sharing protocols
    - Collaborative verification procedures
    - Coordinated response mechanisms
    - Cross-organizational communication channels
- **Implementation**: Establish trusted networks for sharing manipulation intelligence
- **Example Application**: Coordinating responses to cross-platform influence operations

Integrated Detection Approaches

Multi-Layer Detection Systems

Comprehensive approaches combining multiple detection methods:

The Concentric Defense Model

- **Purpose**: Create layered defenses against synthetic influence
- **Key Components**:
    - Content analysis layer
    - Behavioral detection layer
    - Network analysis layer
    - Contextual assessment layer

- **Implementation**: Deploy multiple detection systems that work together
- **Example Application**: Implementing a comprehensive defense system for election information ecosystems

The Human-Machine Collaboration Framework

- **Purpose**: Combine technological detection with human expertise
- **Key Components**:
  - Automated first-pass screening
  - Human expert review processes
  - Feedback loops for system improvement
  - Escalation protocols for complex cases
- **Implementation**: Develop workflows that leverage both AI and human capabilities
- **Example Application**: Using AI to flag potential synthetic content for human analyst review

The Distributed Detection Network

- **Purpose**: Leverage diverse perspectives and expertise for better detection
- **Key Components**:
  - Cross-organizational collaboration protocols
  - Specialized expertise integration
  - Distributed monitoring responsibilities
  - Centralized intelligence sharing
- **Implementation**: Build networks of organizations with complementary capabilities
- **Example Application**: Connecting technical detection teams with subject matter experts and platform representatives

Practical Implementation Guide

Individual Implementation

Steps for implementing detection frameworks as an individual:

1. **Select Complementary Frameworks**: Choose frameworks that address different aspects of synthetic influence (e.g., SIFT for general information evaluation, RADAR for deepfake detection)

2. **Develop Personal Checklists**: Create simplified versions of these frameworks for daily use

3. **Practice Regular Application**: Apply these frameworks consistently to build habitual use

4. **Join Collaborative Networks**: Connect with others using similar frameworks to share insights

5. **Continuously Update Knowledge**: Stay informed about evolving manipulation techniques

Organizational Implementation

Steps for implementing detection frameworks within organizations:

1. **Assess Specific Vulnerabilities**: Identify how synthetic influence could specifically impact your organization

2. **Select Appropriate Frameworks**: Choose frameworks that address your specific risk profile

3. **Adapt to Organizational Context**: Modify frameworks to fit your organizational structure and resources

4. **Develop Training Programs**: Create educational materials to build detection capabilities across the organization

5. **Establish Response Protocols**: Develop clear procedures for when manipulation is detected

6. **Create Feedback Loops**: Continuously improve detection capabilities based on experience

7. **Participate in Cross-Organizational Sharing**: Contribute to and benefit from broader detection communities

Future Developments in Detection

Emerging Detection Approaches

Promising new directions in synthetic influence detection:

Multimodal Detection Systems

- **Purpose**: Analyze relationships between different media elements simultaneously
- **Current Status**: Early research systems showing promise
- **Expected Evolution**: Increasingly sophisticated integration of text, image, audio, and video analysis
- **Implementation Considerations**: Requires significant computational resources and expertise

Provenance Infrastructure

- **Purpose**: Track content from creation through distribution
- **Current Status**: Industry coalitions developing standards (e.g., C2PA)

- **Expected Evolution**: Increasingly robust chain-of-custody tracking for digital content
- **Implementation Considerations**: Requires broad adoption across the content ecosystem

Cognitive Security Frameworks

- **Purpose**: Protect cognitive processes from manipulation
- **Current Status**: Emerging interdisciplinary field
- **Expected Evolution**: Integration of psychological, technical, and social approaches
- **Implementation Considerations**: Requires collaboration across traditionally separate domains

Conclusion: Building Detection Capabilities

Effective detection of synthetic influence requires combining multiple frameworks and approaches. No single detection method is foolproof, but layered approaches significantly improve identification capabilities. As synthetic influence technologies evolve, detection frameworks must continuously adapt.

The most effective approach combines:

1. **Individual Critical Assessment**: Personal frameworks for evaluating information

2. **Organizational Detection Systems**: Structured approaches for identifying manipulation at scale

3. **Technical Detection Tools**: Automated systems for identifying synthetic content

4. **Collaborative Networks**: Shared intelligence and diverse expertise

5. **Continuous Learning**: Ongoing adaptation to evolving manipulation techniques

By implementing these detection frameworks, individuals and organizations can significantly improve their resilience against synthetic influence operations.

Appendix C: Glossary of AI and Cyber Warfare Terms

This glossary provides clear definitions of key technical terms used throughout the book. Each entry includes a plain-language explanation, relevant context, and cross-references to chapters where the concept is discussed in detail.

A

Advanced Persistent Threat (APT)

Definition: A sophisticated, long-term cyber attack where an unauthorized actor gains and maintains access to a network while remaining undetected.

> **Plain Language**: Think of APTs as digital spies who break into systems, stay hidden for months or years, and continuously steal information or manipulate data.

> **Context**: APTs are often associated with nation-state actors and require significant resources and expertise. They frequently incorporate social engineering and AI-driven techniques.

> **Cross-Reference**: Chapter 4: Who's Fighting? The Actors of the Info War

Adversarial Example

Definition: Input data that has been subtly modified to cause AI systems to make mistakes or behave in unintended ways.

Plain Language: These are specially crafted inputs designed to trick AI systems, like subtle changes to an image that make a computer vision system misidentify it completely.

Context: Adversarial examples exploit vulnerabilities in how AI systems process information and are increasingly used to evade content moderation and detection systems.

Cross-Reference: Chapter 6: Deepfakes and Synthetic Reality

Algorithm

Definition: A step-by-step procedure or formula for solving a problem or accomplishing a task, especially by a computer.

Plain Language: Think of algorithms as recipes that tell computers exactly what steps to follow to complete a specific task.

Context: Social media algorithms determine what content users see and can be manipulated to amplify synthetic influence.

Cross-Reference: Chapter 3: Social Media as a Battlefield

Artificial General Intelligence (AGI)

Definition: A hypothetical type of AI that would have the ability to understand, learn, and apply knowledge across a wide range of tasks at a level equal to or exceeding human capabilities.

Plain Language: Unlike today's specialized AI systems, AGI would be able to perform any intellectual task that a human can do.

Context: While AGI doesn't currently exist, concerns about its potential development influence discussions about AI regulation and safety.

Cross-Reference: Chapter 16: The Future: Regulation, Resistance, and the Real War Ahead

Artificial Intelligence (AI)

Definition: Computer systems designed to perform tasks that typically require human intelligence, such as visual perception, speech recognition, decision-making, and language translation.

> **Plain Language**: AI refers to machines programmed to mimic human cognitive functions like learning, problem-solving, and pattern recognition.

> **Context**: Modern AI systems, particularly those based on machine learning, are increasingly capable of generating and manipulating content in ways that appear human.

> **Cross-Reference**: Chapter 2: What Is AI… and Why It's Dangerous Here

Astroturfing

Definition: The practice of masking the sponsors of a message or organization to make it appear as though it originates from and is supported by grassroots participants.

> **Plain Language**: Astroturfing makes orchestrated campaigns look like spontaneous public movements by hiding who's really behind them.

> **Context**: AI technologies have made astroturfing more sophisticated by enabling the creation of convincing synthetic personas and coordinated messaging at scale.

> **Cross-Reference**: Chapter 11: When the Mob Is Machine-Led

Attribution

Definition: The process of identifying the actor responsible for a cyber operation or influence campaign.

> **Plain Language**: Attribution is digital detective work that tries to determine who's behind an attack or manipulation campaign.

> **Context**: Attribution has become increasingly difficult as AI enables more sophisticated obfuscation techniques.

> **Cross-Reference**: Chapter 10: Operation Shadow Influence

B

Behavioral Targeting

Definition: The practice of delivering content to users based on their browsing behavior, interests, and other demographic information.

> **Plain Language**: This is how platforms show you ads and content based on your online activities, location, and personal details.

> **Context**: AI systems have dramatically enhanced behavioral targeting capabilities, enabling highly personalized manipulation.

> **Cross-Reference**: Chapter 12: Weaponized Virality

Black Box Problem

Definition: The difficulty in understanding how complex AI systems make decisions due to their opaque internal processes.

Plain Language: Even the creators of advanced AI systems often can't explain exactly how their systems reach specific conclusions or generate particular outputs.

Context: The black box nature of modern AI makes it difficult to predict, understand, or control potentially harmful outputs.

Cross-Reference: Chapter 2: What Is AI… and Why It's Dangerous Here

Bot

Definition: An automated software program that performs tasks on the internet without human intervention.

Plain Language: Bots are software robots that can post content, interact with users, and perform other online activities automatically.

Context: Social media bots range from simple automated accounts to sophisticated AI-driven personas that can engage in convincing conversations.

Cross-Reference: Chapter 5: Bot Armies and Sock Puppets

Botnet

Definition: A network of compromised computers or social media accounts controlled remotely to perform coordinated actions.

Plain Language: Think of botnets as armies of hijacked computers or accounts that can be commanded to act together.

Context: Modern influence operations often deploy sophisticated botnets to amplify messages and create the illusion of widespread support.

Cross-Reference: Chapter 5: Bot Armies and Sock Puppets

C

Cognitive Bias

Definition: Systematic patterns of deviation from norm or rationality in judgment that occur due to perceptual distortions, inaccurate judgments, or illogical interpretations.

>**Plain Language**: These are mental shortcuts and tendencies that can lead us to make irrational decisions or judgments.

>**Context**: AI-driven influence operations are specifically designed to exploit cognitive biases to maximize their effectiveness.

>**Cross-Reference**: Chapter 14: Protecting Your Digital Mind

Cognitive Security

Definition: The protection of the human mind from manipulation, exploitation, and influence operations.

>**Plain Language**: Cognitive security focuses on defending our thinking processes from being hijacked or manipulated.

>**Context**: As AI-driven manipulation becomes more sophisticated, cognitive security is emerging as a crucial aspect of overall security.

>**Cross-Reference**: Chapter 14: Protecting Your Digital Mind

Computational Propaganda

Definition: The use of algorithms, automation, and human curation to purposefully distribute misleading information over social media networks.

> **Plain Language**: This is propaganda that uses technology to spread manipulative content efficiently across digital platforms.

> **Context**: Modern computational propaganda increasingly incorporates AI-generated content and targeting.

> **Cross-Reference**: Chapter 1: The Digital Theater of War

Content Moderation

Definition: The practice of monitoring and applying a set of rules and guidelines to user-generated submissions to determine if the content should be published on the platform.

> **Plain Language**: Content moderation is how platforms decide what posts, comments, and media to allow, flag, or remove.

> **Context**: AI systems are increasingly used for content moderation, creating an arms race between moderation algorithms and evasion techniques.

> **Cross-Reference**: Chapter 3: Social Media as a Battlefield

Coordinated Inauthentic Behavior (CIB)

Definition: Activities where groups of accounts or pages work together to mislead people about who they are or what they're doing.

Plain Language: This occurs when networks of accounts pretend to be something they're not while working together to manipulate public opinion.

Context: Social media platforms have policies against CIB, but AI-powered techniques make detection increasingly difficult.

Cross-Reference: Chapter 10: Operation Shadow Influence

D

Data Mining

Definition: The process of discovering patterns, correlations, and insights from large datasets.

Plain Language: Data mining extracts valuable information from massive amounts of data to identify trends and relationships.

Context: Influence operations use data mining to identify vulnerabilities and optimize manipulation strategies.

Cross-Reference: Chapter 12: Weaponized Virality

Deepfake

Definition: Synthetic media in which a person's likeness is replaced with someone else's using artificial intelligence.

Plain Language: Deepfakes are AI-generated videos or audio that make it appear as if someone said or did something they never actually did.

Context: As deepfake technology improves, the potential for political manipulation, fraud, and disinformation increases.

Cross-Reference: Chapter 6: Deepfakes and Synthetic Reality

Disinformation

Definition: False information deliberately created and spread to influence public opinion or obscure the truth.

Plain Language: Unlike misinformation, which can be accidentally shared, disinformation is intentionally created to deceive.

Context: AI technologies have dramatically increased the scale, sophistication, and personalization of disinformation campaigns.

Cross-Reference: Chapter 1: The Digital Theater of War

Distributed Denial of Truth (DDoT)

Definition: A strategy that overwhelms information ecosystems with contradictory claims, making it difficult for people to determine what's true.

Plain Language: This approach floods the zone with so many conflicting narratives that people become exhausted and give up trying to find the truth.

Context: AI-generated content has made DDoT attacks more effective by enabling the rapid creation of massive amounts of conflicting information.

Cross-Reference: Chapter 10: Operation Shadow Influence

Echo Chamber

Definition: An environment where a person only encounters beliefs or opinions that coincide with their own.

> **Plain Language**: Echo chambers are digital spaces where you only hear viewpoints similar to your own, reinforcing existing beliefs.

> **Context**: AI recommendation systems often create or strengthen echo chambers by showing users content similar to what they already engage with.

> **Cross-Reference**: Chapter 3: Social Media as a Battlefield

Emergent Behavior

Definition: Complex patterns or properties that arise from relatively simple rules or interactions within an AI system that weren't explicitly programmed.

> **Plain Language**: These are unexpected capabilities or behaviors that AI systems develop that weren't intended or anticipated by their creators.

> **Context**: Emergent behaviors in advanced AI systems can lead to unpredictable and potentially harmful outcomes in influence operations.

> **Cross-Reference**: Chapter 2: What Is AI... and Why It's Dangerous Here

Engagement-Based Ranking

Definition: The practice of ordering content based on metrics such as likes, comments, shares, and click-through rates.

> **Plain Language**: This is how platforms decide what content to show you based on how much interaction similar content has received.

> **Context**: Engagement-based ranking often amplifies emotionally provocative content, including synthetic influence operations.

> **Cross-Reference**: Chapter 3: Social Media as a Battlefield

F

Filter Bubble

Definition: A state of intellectual isolation that can result from personalized searches and algorithms that selectively guess what information a user would like to see.

> **Plain Language**: Filter bubbles are personalized information environments that limit exposure to diverse viewpoints.

> **Context**: AI recommendation systems create increasingly sophisticated filter bubbles that can be exploited by influence operations.

> **Cross-Reference**: Chapter 3: Social Media as a Battlefield

Fine-Tuning

Definition: The process of taking a pre-trained AI model and further training it on a specific dataset to adapt it for a particular task.

> **Plain Language**: Fine-tuning is like taking a general-purpose AI and giving it specialized training for a specific job.

> **Context**: Malicious actors fine-tune language models to create more effective manipulation tools tailored to specific audiences or objectives.

> **Cross-Reference**: Chapter 7: LLMs in Social Engineering

G

Generative Adversarial Network (GAN)

Definition: A class of machine learning framework where two neural networks (generator and discriminator) compete against each other, resulting in the creation of new, synthetic instances of data.

> **Plain Language**: GANs work like a counterfeiter and detective in competition, with one network creating fake content and the other trying to spot it, both improving through this contest.

> **Context**: GANs are the technology behind many deepfakes and synthetic images used in influence operations.

> **Cross-Reference**: Chapter 6: Deepfakes and Synthetic Reality

Generative AI

Definition: AI systems that can create new content, including text, images, audio, and video, based on patterns learned from training data.

> **Plain Language**: These are AI systems that can create new things rather than just analyzing existing data.

> **Context**: Generative AI has dramatically lowered the cost and technical barriers to creating synthetic content for influence operations.

> **Cross-Reference**: Chapter 2: What Is AI… and Why It's Dangerous Here

H

Hallucination (AI)

Definition: When an AI system generates content that appears plausible but is factually incorrect or completely fabricated.

> **Plain Language**: AI hallucinations are confident-sounding but made-up information that has no basis in the AI's training data.

> **Context**: Hallucinations in language models can inadvertently generate misinformation that appears authoritative.

> **Cross-Reference**: Chapter 7: LLMs in Social Engineering

Hashing

Definition: A process that converts data of any size into a fixed-size value, often used to identify or verify content.

>**Plain Language**: Hashing creates a unique digital fingerprint for content that can be used to track or identify it.

>**Context**: Hashing is used in content authentication systems to identify known synthetic or manipulated media.

>**Cross-Reference**: Chapter 13: How to Spot Synthetic Influence

---

I

Information Operation

Definition: Coordinated efforts to influence opinions, beliefs, and behaviors through the dissemination of information.

>**Plain Language**: These are organized campaigns to shape what people think and do by controlling what information they receive.

>**Context**: Modern information operations increasingly incorporate AI-generated content and targeting.

>**Cross-Reference**: Chapter 10: Operation Shadow Influence

Information Warfare

Definition: The strategic use of information and communication technologies to gain advantages over adversaries.

Plain Language: Information warfare uses information as a weapon to influence, disrupt, or control what people know and believe.

Context: AI technologies have become central to modern information warfare strategies.

Cross-Reference: Chapter 1: The Digital Theater of War

L

Large Language Model (LLM)

Definition: A type of AI model trained on vast amounts of text data that can generate human-like text, answer questions, and perform various language tasks.

Plain Language: LLMs are AI systems that understand and generate human language after being trained on massive text datasets.

Context: Models like GPT-4, Claude, and Llama have dramatically increased the quality and scale of synthetic text generation.

Cross-Reference: Chapter 7: LLMs in Social Engineering

Liar's Dividend

Definition: The phenomenon where the existence of deepfakes allows people to dismiss authentic content as fake.

Plain Language: The liar's dividend occurs when real evidence can be dismissed as AI-generated, allowing guilty parties to escape accountability.

Context: As synthetic media becomes more common, the ability to deny authentic evidence increases.

Cross-Reference: Chapter 6: Deepfakes and Synthetic Reality

M

Machine Learning

Definition: A subset of artificial intelligence that enables systems to learn from data and improve from experience without being explicitly programmed.

Plain Language: Machine learning allows computers to learn patterns from examples rather than following specific instructions.

Context: Machine learning underlies most modern AI systems used in influence operations.

Cross-Reference: Chapter 2: What Is AI... and Why It's Dangerous Here

Metadata

Definition: Data that provides information about other data, such as when and how it was created.

Plain Language: Metadata is information about information, like timestamps, location data, or device information attached to digital content.

Context: Analyzing metadata can help identify synthetic content or trace the origins of influence operations.

Cross-Reference: Chapter 13: How to Spot Synthetic Influence

Microtargeting

Definition: The practice of delivering highly personalized content to specific individuals or small groups based on detailed data profiles.

> **Plain Language**: Microtargeting is like having thousands of different messages, each crafted for a specific person or tiny group.

> **Context**: AI has dramatically enhanced microtargeting capabilities, enabling manipulation tailored to individual psychological vulnerabilities.

> **Cross-Reference**: Chapter 12: Weaponized Virality

Misinformation

Definition: False or inaccurate information that is spread regardless of intent to deceive.

> **Plain Language**: Unlike disinformation, misinformation may be shared by people who believe it's true.

> **Context**: AI-generated content can rapidly accelerate the spread of misinformation through social networks.

> **Cross-Reference**: Chapter 1: The Digital Theater of War

N

Natural Language Processing (NLP)

Definition: A field of AI focused on the interaction between computers and human language, enabling machines to understand, interpret, and generate human language.

> **Plain Language**: NLP is what allows AI to understand, analyze, and create human language.
>
> **Context**: Advances in NLP have enabled increasingly sophisticated text generation and analysis for influence operations.
>
> **Cross-Reference**: Chapter 2: What Is AI... and Why It's Dangerous Here

Neural Network

Definition: A computing system inspired by biological neural networks that forms the foundation of many modern AI systems.

> **Plain Language**: Neural networks are computing systems that learn by analyzing examples, roughly inspired by how human brains work.
>
> **Context**: Deep neural networks power most advanced AI systems used in synthetic influence.
>
> **Cross-Reference**: Chapter 2: What Is AI... and Why It's Dangerous Here

Prompt Engineering

Definition: The practice of designing inputs to AI systems to elicit desired outputs or behaviors.

> **Plain Language**: Prompt engineering is the art of crafting instructions to get AI systems to produce specific results.

> **Context**: Sophisticated prompt engineering can be used to bypass safety measures in AI systems for malicious purposes.

> **Cross-Reference**: Chapter 7: LLMs in Social Engineering

Prompt Injection

Definition: A technique where carefully crafted inputs cause AI systems to ignore their intended constraints or instructions.

> **Plain Language**: Prompt injection is like hacking an AI by tricking it into ignoring its rules or following new ones.

> **Context**: Malicious actors use prompt injection to bypass safety measures in AI systems.

> **Cross-Reference**: Chapter 7: LLMs in Social Engineering

Propaganda

Definition: Information, especially of a biased or misleading nature, used to promote a political cause or point of view.

Plain Language: Propaganda is strategic communication designed to influence opinions and behaviors, often through emotional appeals rather than balanced information.

Context: AI technologies have transformed propaganda from mass messaging to personalized influence.

Cross-Reference: Chapter 1: The Digital Theater of War

Psychological Operations (PSYOPS)

Definition: Planned operations to convey selected information to audiences to influence their emotions, motives, objective reasoning, and behavior.

Plain Language: PSYOPS are organized campaigns to influence how people think, feel, and act through carefully crafted information.

Context: Modern PSYOPS increasingly incorporate AI-generated content and psychological targeting.

Cross-Reference: Chapter 1: The Digital Theater of War

R

Recommendation Algorithm

Definition: An algorithm that suggests content to users based on various factors such as past behavior, preferences, and similarity to other users.

Plain Language: These are the systems that decide what content to show you next on platforms like YouTube, TikTok, or Facebook.

Context: Recommendation algorithms can be manipulated to amplify synthetic content and influence operations.

Cross-Reference: Chapter 3: Social Media as a Battlefield

S

Sentiment Analysis

Definition: The use of natural language processing to identify and extract subjective information from text, such as opinions and emotions.

Plain Language: Sentiment analysis is how AI systems determine whether text expresses positive, negative, or neutral feelings.

Context: Influence operations use sentiment analysis to measure campaign effectiveness and adjust strategies.

Cross-Reference: Chapter 12: Weaponized Virality

Social Engineering

Definition: The psychological manipulation of people into performing actions or divulging confidential information.

Plain Language: Social engineering is the art of tricking people into doing things or revealing information by exploiting human psychology.

Context: AI has dramatically enhanced social engineering capabilities through personalization and automation.

Cross-Reference: Chapter 7: LLMs in Social Engineering

Sock Puppet

Definition: A false online identity created for deceptive purposes, typically to promote a specific viewpoint or manipulate public opinion.

> **Plain Language**: Sock puppets are fake online personas controlled by someone pretending to be someone they're not.

> **Context**: AI technologies have made sock puppets more convincing and easier to operate at scale.

> **Cross-Reference**: Chapter 5: Bot Armies and Sock Puppets

Synthetic Identity

Definition: A fictional online persona created using a combination of fabricated and real information.

> **Plain Language**: Synthetic identities are fake people created by combining made-up details with real stolen information.

> **Context**: AI-generated synthetic identities are increasingly difficult to distinguish from authentic online presences.

> **Cross-Reference**: Chapter 5: Bot Armies and Sock Puppets

Synthetic Media

Definition: Media content generated or manipulated by AI, including images, audio, video, and text.

> **Plain Language**: Synthetic media is any content created or altered by AI rather than captured from the real world.

Context: Advances in AI have dramatically improved the quality and reduced the cost of creating synthetic media.

Cross-Reference: Chapter 6: Deepfakes and Synthetic Reality

T

Transfer Learning

Definition: A machine learning technique where a model developed for one task is reused as the starting point for a model on a second task.

Plain Language: Transfer learning is like teaching someone a new job by building on skills they already have from previous experience.

Context: Transfer learning enables the rapid development of specialized AI systems for influence operations.

Cross-Reference: Chapter 2: What Is AI… and Why It's Dangerous Here

Transformer Architecture

Definition: A neural network architecture that uses self-attention mechanisms to process sequential data, forming the foundation of modern language models.

Plain Language: Transformer architecture is the breakthrough AI design that powers most advanced language models today.

Context: The development of transformer architecture in 2017 led to dramatic improvements in AI language capabilities.

Cross-Reference: Chapter 2: What Is AI... and Why It's Dangerous Here

Troll Farm

Definition: An organized operation where a group of individuals create and manage multiple fake online personas to influence public opinion.

> **Plain Language**: Troll farms are like factories where people are paid to create conflict and spread propaganda online using fake accounts.

> **Context**: Modern troll farms increasingly incorporate AI tools to increase efficiency and effectiveness.

> **Cross-Reference**: Chapter 9: Case Study: The 2020 U.S. Election and Beyond

V

Verification

Definition: The process of establishing the truth, accuracy, or validity of something.

> **Plain Language**: Verification is the process of confirming whether information is true and comes from a legitimate source.

> **Context**: AI-generated content has made verification increasingly challenging and important.

> **Cross-Reference**: Chapter 13: How to Spot Synthetic Influence

Viral Marketing

Definition: Marketing techniques that use pre-existing social networks to produce increases in brand awareness through self-replicating viral processes.

> **Plain Language**: Viral marketing creates content designed to spread rapidly through social sharing.

> **Context**: The techniques of viral marketing are increasingly applied to synthetic influence operations.

> **Cross-Reference**: Chapter 12: Weaponized Virality

W

Watermarking

Definition: The process of embedding digital information into content that can later be detected to verify its source or authenticity.

> **Plain Language**: Digital watermarking is like adding an invisible signature to content that can be detected later to prove where it came from.

> **Context**: Watermarking is being developed as a potential solution for identifying AI-generated content.

> **Cross-Reference**: Chapter 16: The Future: Regulation, Resistance, and the Real War Ahead

Weaponized Narrative

Definition: Strategic communication designed to undermine or manipulate public discourse, often by exploiting social divisions.

Plain Language: Weaponized narratives are stories crafted specifically to divide people or undermine trust in institutions.

Context: AI technologies have made weaponized narratives more persuasive and easier to personalize.

Cross-Reference: Chapter 10: Operation Shadow Influence

Z

Zero-Day Vulnerability

Definition: A software security flaw that is unknown to those who should be interested in mitigating it, including the vendor of the target software.

Plain Language: Zero-day vulnerabilities are security holes that even the software creators don't know about yet, making them particularly dangerous.

Context: Influence operations may exploit zero-day vulnerabilities in platforms or systems to deploy synthetic content.

Cross-Reference: Chapter 4: Who's Fighting? The Actors of the Info War

Zero-Shot Learning

Definition: The ability of AI systems to perform tasks they weren't explicitly trained on.

Plain Language: Zero-shot learning is when AI can do things it wasn't specifically taught to do by applying knowledge from related tasks.

Context: Zero-shot capabilities make modern AI systems more versatile for influence operations.

Cross-Reference: Chapter 2: What Is AI… and Why It's Dangerous Here

Appendix D: Recommended Tools, Courses, and Further Reading

This appendix provides a curated collection of resources for readers who wish to deepen their understanding of AI-driven manipulation and develop stronger defenses against synthetic influence. These recommendations are organized by category and include brief descriptions to help you select the most relevant resources for your specific needs.

Tools for Personal Defense

Content Verification Tools

Browser Extensions

- **NewsGuard**
    - **Description**: Rates news and information sites based on nine journalistic criteria, providing trust scores and detailed "nutrition labels" for news sources.
    - **Best For**: Everyday browsing to quickly assess the reliability of news websites.
    - **URL**: https://www.newsguardtech.com/
    - **Cost**: Free trial available, then subscription-based.
- **SurfSafe**

- Description: Browser extension that detects manipulated images by comparing them against a database of known originals.
  - Best For: Identifying manipulated images while browsing social media.
  - URL: https://www.getsurfsafe.com/
  - Cost: Free.
- **Factual**
  - Description: Highlights claims in articles and provides verification information from multiple sources.
  - Best For: Reading news articles with factual claims that require verification.
  - URL: https://factual.news/
  - Cost: Free.
- **TrustedNews**
  - Description: Flags potential misinformation and provides context about news sources.
  - Best For: Quick assessment of news content reliability.
  - URL: https://trusted-news.com/
  - Cost: Free.

AI Content Detection

- **GPTZero**
  - Description: Analyzes text to determine the likelihood it was generated by AI like ChatGPT.
  - Best For: Educators and professionals concerned about AI-generated content.
  - URL: https://gptzero.me/
  - Cost: Free basic version, premium features available.
- **Content at Scale AI Detector**
  - Description: Provides a "humanness" score for text, highlighting sections that appear machine-generated.

- **Best For**: Content creators and publishers screening submissions.
- **URL**: https://contentatscale.ai/ai-content-detector/
- **Cost**: Free.

- **Winston AI**
  - **Description**: Offers detailed analysis of text with probability scores for AI generation.
  - **Best For**: Detailed analysis of suspected AI-generated content.
  - **URL**: https://gowinston.ai/
  - **Cost**: Free trial, then subscription-based.

- **Originality.ai**
  - **Description**: Combines plagiarism checking with AI detection, useful for verifying original human-created content.
  - **Best For**: Content managers and educators.
  - **URL**: https://originality.ai/
  - **Cost**: Subscription-based.

Image and Video Verification

- **InVID Verification Plugin**
  - **Description**: Browser extension with tools for verifying the authenticity of images and videos.
  - **Best For**: Journalists and fact-checkers analyzing visual media.
  - **URL**: https://www.invid-project.eu/
  - **Cost**: Free.

- **Forensically**
  - **Description**: Online tool for detailed forensic analysis of images.
  - **Best For**: Detailed examination of potentially manipulated images.

- **URL**: https://29a.ch/photo-forensics/
- **Cost**: Free.

- **TinEye Reverse Image Search**
  - **Description**: Search engine that finds where an image appears online and when it first appeared.
  - **Best For**: Tracing the origin and modifications of images.
  - **URL**: https://tineye.com/
  - **Cost**: Free for basic use, commercial API available.

Privacy and Security Tools

VPNs and Encrypted Communication

- **ProtonVPN**
  - **Description**: Secure VPN service with a focus on privacy and security.
  - **Best For**: General browsing privacy and accessing geo-restricted content.
  - **URL**: https://protonvpn.com/
  - **Cost**: Free basic version, premium features available.

- **Signal**
  - **Description**: End-to-end encrypted messaging app with a focus on privacy.
  - **Best For**: Secure communication with friends, family, and colleagues.
  - **URL**: https://signal.org/
  - **Cost**: Free.

- **ProtonMail**
  - **Description**: Encrypted email service with a focus on privacy and security.
  - **Best For**: Secure email communication.
  - **URL**: https://proton.me/mail

      – **Cost**: Free basic version, premium features available.

Ad and Tracker Blockers

- **uBlock Origin**
  - **Description**: Efficient, wide-spectrum blocker that filters out ads, trackers, and malware domains.
  - **Best For**: General browsing privacy and security.
  - **URL**: https://ublockorigin.com/
  - **Cost**: Free.
- **Privacy Badger**
  - **Description**: Automatically learns to block invisible trackers based on their behavior.
  - **Best For**: Protection against tracking without manual configuration.
  - **URL**: https://privacybadger.org/
  - **Cost**: Free.
- **DuckDuckGo Privacy Essentials**
  - **Description**: Combines tracker blocking with private search and forced HTTPS connections.
  - **Best For**: Basic privacy protection for everyday browsing.
  - **URL**: https://duckduckgo.com/app
  - **Cost**: Free.

Password and Identity Management

- **Bitwarden**
  - **Description**: Open-source password manager with strong encryption and cross-platform support.
  - **Best For**: Secure password management across multiple devices.
  - **URL**: https://bitwarden.com/
  - **Cost**: Free basic version, premium features available.

- **Authy**
  - **Description**: Two-factor authentication app with cloud backup and multi-device support.
  - **Best For**: Securing accounts with two-factor authentication.
  - **URL**: https://authy.com/
  - **Cost**: Free.
- **Have I Been Pwned**
  - **Description**: Service that checks if your email or phone has been involved in a data breach.
  - **Best For**: Monitoring your personal information for potential exposure.
  - **URL**: https://haveibeenpwned.com/
  - **Cost**: Free for basic checks.

Digital Wellbeing Tools

Screen Time Management

- **Freedom**
  - **Description**: App blocker that works across devices to limit distracting apps and websites.
  - **Best For**: Focused work sessions and digital detox periods.
  - **URL**: https://freedom.to/
  - **Cost**: Subscription-based.
- **RescueTime**
  - **Description**: Tracks your digital activity and provides insights into your productivity and habits.
  - **Best For**: Understanding and improving your digital behavior patterns.
  - **URL**: https://www.rescuetime.com/

- **Cost**: Free basic version, premium features available.

- **Forest**
  - **Description**: Gamified app that encourages focus by growing virtual trees when you stay off your phone.
  - **Best For**: Building better focus habits through positive reinforcement.
  - **URL**: https://www.forestapp.cc/
  - **Cost**: Free basic version, premium features available.

Information Diet Management

- **Pocket**
  - **Description**: Save articles, videos, and content from any publication, page, or app for later consumption.
  - **Best For**: Creating a curated reading list instead of reactive consumption.
  - **URL**: https://getpocket.com/
  - **Cost**: Free basic version, premium features available.

- **Feedly**
  - **Description**: RSS reader that allows you to follow specific sources rather than algorithm-driven feeds.
  - **Best For**: Creating a personalized news feed from trusted sources.
  - **URL**: https://feedly.com/
  - **Cost**: Free basic version, premium features available.

- **Ground News**
  - **Description**: News comparison platform that shows how different outlets cover the same story and identifies media bias.
  - **Best For**: Understanding different perspectives on current events.
  - **URL**: https://ground.news/
  - **Cost**: Free basic version, premium features available.

Educational Resources

Online Courses

Media Literacy and Critical Thinking

- **MediaWise Digital Literacy Courses**
    - **Description**: Free online courses teaching how to spot misinformation online.
    - **Best For**: Beginners looking for practical verification skills.
    - **URL**: https://mediawise.org/
    - **Length**: Self-paced, approximately 2-3 hours per course.
    - **Cost**: Free.
- **Crash Course: Navigating Digital Information**
    - **Description**: YouTube series covering essential skills for evaluating online information.
    - **Best For**: Visual learners seeking engaging content on information literacy.
    - **URL**: https://www.youtube.com/playlist?list=PL8dPuuaLjXtN07XYqqWSKpPrtNDiCHTzU
    - **Length**: 10 episodes, approximately 15 minutes each.
    - **Cost**: Free.
- **University of Washington: Calling Bullshit**
    - **Description**: Course materials on data reasoning and identifying misleading information.
    - **Best For**: Those interested in statistical literacy and data visualization critique.
    - **URL**: https://www.callingbullshit.org/
    - **Length**: Self-paced, approximately 10-15 hours total.
    - **Cost**: Free.

AI and Technology Understanding

- **Elements of AI**
  - **Description**: Introduction to AI concepts and applications without requiring programming knowledge.
  - **Best For**: General audience seeking to understand AI fundamentals.
  - **URL**: https://www.elementsofai.com/
  - **Length**: Approximately 30 hours.
  - **Cost**: Free.

- **AI for Everyone (Coursera)**
  - **Description**: Non-technical course by Andrew Ng explaining AI concepts, applications, and implications.
  - **Best For**: Business professionals and non-technical individuals.
  - **URL**: https://www.coursera.org/learn/ai-for-everyone
  - **Length**: Approximately 10 hours.
  - **Cost**: Free to audit, certificate available for purchase.

- **Ethics of AI (edX)**
  - **Description**: Course exploring ethical questions raised by artificial intelligence.
  - **Best For**: Those interested in the societal implications of AI.
  - **URL**: https://www.edx.org/course/ethics-of-ai
  - **Length**: Approximately 25 hours.
  - **Cost**: Free to audit, certificate available for purchase.

Cybersecurity Fundamentals

- **Cybersecurity Fundamentals (edX)**
  - **Description**: Introduction to core cybersecurity concepts and practices.
  - **Best For**: Beginners seeking a comprehensive introduction to cybersecurity.

- **URL**: https://www.edx.org/professional-certificate/ritx-cybersecurity-fundamentals
- **Length**: Approximately 24 hours.
- **Cost**: Free to audit, certificate available for purchase.

- **SANS Cyber Aces Online**
  - **Description**: Free online course covering systems, networking, and operating system security.
  - **Best For**: Hands-on learners interested in technical aspects of security.
  - **URL**: https://www.cyberaces.org/
  - **Length**: Self-paced, approximately 15-20 hours.
  - **Cost**: Free.

- **FutureLearn: Introduction to Cyber Security**
  - **Description**: Course covering basic concepts and practices in cybersecurity.
  - **Best For**: General audience seeking practical security knowledge.
  - **URL**: https://www.futurelearn.com/courses/introduction-to-cyber-security
  - **Length**: 8 weeks, 3 hours per week.
  - **Cost**: Free to audit, certificate available for purchase.

Workshops and Training Programs

Digital Verification Training

- **First Draft's Training Programs**
  - **Description**: Training materials and courses on verification, responsible reporting, and tackling misinformation.
  - **Best For**: Journalists, researchers, and fact-checkers.

- – **URL**: https://firstdraftnews.org/training/
- – **Format**: Online courses and downloadable resources.
- – **Cost**: Free.
- **Bellingcat's Workshops and Online Courses**
  - – **Description**: Training in open-source investigation techniques and digital verification.
  - – **Best For**: Investigators and researchers seeking advanced OSINT skills.
  - – **URL**: https://www.bellingcat.com/workshops/
  - – **Format**: In-person workshops and online courses.
  - – **Cost**: Varies, some free resources available.
- **WITNESS Media Lab Training**
  - – **Description**: Resources for authenticating and verifying video content.
  - – **Best For**: Human rights defenders and citizen journalists.
  - – **URL**: https://lab.witness.org/
  - – **Format**: Online guides and training materials.
  - – **Cost**: Free.

Cognitive Security Training

- **IREX's Learn to Discern (L2D)**
  - – **Description**: Media literacy training program focused on building resilience to manipulation.
  - – **Best For**: Educators and community leaders.
  - – **URL**: https://www.irex.org/project/learn-discern-l2d-media-literacy-training
  - – **Format**: Training materials and curriculum guides.
  - – **Cost**: Free resources available.
- **Mind Over Media**
  - – **Description**: Educational platform for analyzing contemporary propaganda.
  - – **Best For**: Educators and students.

- URL: https://propaganda.mediaeducationlab.com/
- **Format**: Online platform with lesson plans and activities.
- **Cost**: Free.
- **Digital Citizenship Education**
    - **Description**: Council of Europe's resources for digital citizenship education.
    - **Best For**: Educators and youth workers.
    - **URL**: https://www.coe.int/en/web/digital-citizenship-education
    - **Format**: Handbooks and educational materials.
    - **Cost**: Free.

Further Reading

Books

Understanding AI and Its Impacts

- **"The Alignment Problem" by Brian Christian**
    - **Description**: Explores the challenge of aligning AI systems with human values and intentions.
    - **Best For**: Readers interested in AI safety and ethics.
    - **Publication Date**: 2020
    - **Pages**: 496
- **"Atlas of AI" by Kate Crawford**
    - **Description**: Examines the social, political, and environmental implications of artificial intelligence.
    - **Best For**: Those interested in the broader societal context of AI.
    - **Publication Date**: 2021

- Pages: 336
- **"Weapons of Math Destruction" by Cathy O'Neil**
  - **Description**: Explores how algorithms and data-driven decisions can reinforce discrimination and inequality.
  - **Best For**: Readers concerned about algorithmic bias and justice.
  - **Publication Date**: 2016
  - **Pages**: 272

Disinformation and Manipulation

- **"LikeWar: The Weaponization of Social Media" by P.W. Singer and Emerson T. Brooking**
  - **Description**: Examines how social media has transformed war and politics.
  - **Best For**: Understanding the strategic use of social media in conflict.
  - **Publication Date**: 2018
  - **Pages**: 432
- **"This Is Not Propaganda" by Peter Pomerantsev**
  - **Description**: Explores the global information war through personal stories and analysis.
  - **Best For**: Readers interested in first-hand accounts of information manipulation.
  - **Publication Date**: 2019
  - **Pages**: 256
- **"Network Propaganda" by Yochai Benkler, Robert Faris, and Hal Roberts**
  - **Description**: Analyzes media ecosystems and their role in political manipulation.
  - **Best For**: Those seeking data-driven analysis of media manipulation.
  - **Publication Date**: 2018
  - **Pages**: 474

Cognitive Security and Digital Literacy

- **"Digital Literacy For Dummies" by Faithe Wempen**
  - **Description**: Practical guide to essential digital literacy skills.
  - **Best For**: Beginners seeking practical digital skills.
  - **Publication Date**: 2014
  - **Pages**: 320
- **"The Psychology of Information" by Ira Hyman**
  - **Description**: Explores how people process information and why they fall for misinformation.
  - **Best For**: Understanding the psychological aspects of information processing.
  - **Publication Date**: 2020
  - **Pages**: 304
- **"The Hype Machine" by Sinan Aral**
  - **Description**: Examines how social media affects our decisions, relationships, and society.
  - **Best For**: Understanding the mechanics of social media influence.
  - **Publication Date**: 2020
  - **Pages**: 416

Academic Papers and Reports

AI and Synthetic Media

- **"The Malicious Use of Artificial Intelligence: Forecasting, Prevention, and Mitigation"**
  - **Authors**: Miles Brundage et al.
  - **Description**: Comprehensive report on potential malicious uses of AI and possible countermeasures.
  - **URL**: https://arxiv.org/abs/1802.07228

- **Publication Date**: 2018
- **"Deep Fakes: A Looming Challenge for Privacy, Democracy, and National Security"**
  - **Authors**: Robert Chesney and Danielle Keats Citron
  - **Description**: Legal and policy analysis of deepfake technology implications.
  - **URL**: https://papers.ssrn.com/sol3/papers.cfm?abstract_id=3213954
  - **Publication Date**: 2019
- **"The State of Deepfakes: Landscape, Threats, and Impact"**
  - **Authors**: Deeptrace Labs
  - **Description**: Research report on deepfake prevalence, technology, and potential impacts.
  - **URL**: Available through academic databases
  - **Publication Date**: 2019

Information Operations and Influence

- **"The Global Disinformation Order: 2019 Global Inventory of Organised Social Media Manipulation"**
  - **Authors**: Samantha Bradshaw and Philip N. Howard
  - **Description**: Comprehensive report on computational propaganda worldwide.
  - **URL**: https://comprop.oii.ox.ac.uk/research/posts/the-global-disinformation-order-2019-global-inventory-of-organised-social-media-manipulation/
  - **Publication Date**: 2019
- **"Disinformation, 'Fake News' and Influence Campaigns on Twitter"**
  - **Authors**: Knight Foundation
  - **Description**: Analysis of disinformation networks and their evolution on Twitter.

- URL:
  https://knightfoundation.org/reports/disinformation-
  fake-news-and-influence-campaigns-on-twitter/
- **Publication Date**: 2018

- **"Beyond Fake News: Content Confusion and Understanding the Dynamics of the Contemporary Media Environment"**
  - **Authors**: Claire Wardle
  - **Description**: Framework for understanding different types of problematic information.
  - **URL**: https://firstdraftnews.org/wp-content/uploads/2018/03/The-Disinformation-Ecosystem-20180207-v4.pdf
  - **Publication Date**: 2017

Cognitive Security and Resilience

- **"The Psychology of Fake News"**
  - **Authors**: David G. Rand and Gordon Pennycook
  - **Description**: Research on why people believe and share false information.
  - **URL**:
    https://www.sciencedirect.com/science/article/pii/S1364661320301704
  - **Publication Date**: 2021

- **"Inoculating the Public against Misinformation about Climate Change"**
  - **Authors**: Sander van der Linden et al.
  - **Description**: Research on prebunking as a strategy against misinformation.
  - **URL**:
    https://www.tandfonline.com/doi/full/10.1080/17524032.2016.1276278
  - **Publication Date**: 2017

- **"Digital Media Literacy in a Post-Fact Age"**

- **Authors**: danah boyd
- **Description**: Analysis of the challenges facing media literacy in contemporary information environments.
- **URL**: https://datasociety.net/pubs/dm/DataAndSociety_Media_Literacy_2018.pdf
- **Publication Date**: 2018

Websites and Ongoing Resources

News and Analysis

- **Bellingcat**
  - **Description**: Investigative journalism website specializing in fact-checking and open-source intelligence.
  - **Best For**: Case studies of digital investigations and verification techniques.
  - **URL**: https://www.bellingcat.com/
- **The Markup**
  - **Description**: Nonprofit newsroom investigating how technology affects society.
  - **Best For**: In-depth reporting on algorithmic impacts and data privacy.
  - **URL**: https://themarkup.org/
- **First Draft**
  - **Description**: Organization dedicated to supporting journalists, academics, and technologists working on challenges of trust and truth in the digital age.
  - **Best For**: Practical guides and research on verification and responsible reporting.
  - **URL**: https://firstdraftnews.org/

Research Centers and Organizations

- **Stanford Internet Observatory**
  - **Description**: Research center studying abuse in information technologies.
  - **Best For**: Academic research on platform governance and information operations.
  - **URL**: https://cyber.fsi.stanford.edu/io
- **Data & Society**
  - **Description**: Research institute focused on the social implications of data-centric technologies.
  - **Best For**: Research reports on media manipulation and AI ethics.
  - **URL**: https://datasociety.net/
- **Center for Humane Technology**
  - **Description**: Organization focused on realigning technology with humanity's best interests.
  - **Best For**: Resources on digital well-being and ethical technology design.
  - **URL**: https://www.humanetech.com/

Fact-Checking Resources

- **International Fact-Checking Network (IFCN)**
  - **Description**: Global network of fact-checking organizations.
  - **Best For**: Access to verified fact-checking organizations worldwide.
  - **URL**: https://www.poynter.org/ifcn/
- **Snopes**
  - **Description**: One of the oldest and largest fact-checking websites.
  - **Best For**: Verification of viral claims and urban legends.
  - **URL**: https://www.snopes.com/

- **FactCheck.org**
  - **Description**: Nonpartisan, nonprofit fact-checking website.
  - **Best For**: Political fact-checking and analysis.
  - **URL**: https://www.factcheck.org/

Communities and Support Networks

Professional Networks

- **Trust & Safety Professional Association**
  - **Description**: Professional association for those working in trust and safety roles.
  - **Best For**: Professionals working on content moderation and platform safety.
  - **URL**: https://www.tspa.org/
- **Information Professionals Association**
  - **Description**: Organization for professionals working in information operations and related fields.
  - **Best For**: Military, government, and private sector professionals in information domains.
  - **URL**: https://information-professionals.org/
- **Society of Professional Journalists**
  - **Description**: Organization dedicated to promoting and defending journalism.
  - **Best For**: Journalists seeking resources on verification and ethical reporting.
  - **URL**: https://www.spj.org/

Community Support Groups

- **Media Literacy Now**
  - **Description**: Advocacy organization working to bring media literacy education to all schools.
  - **Best For**: Parents and educators concerned about youth media literacy.
  - **URL**: https://medialiteracynow.org/
- **PEN America**
  - **Description**: Organization working to protect free expression and combat disinformation.
  - **Best For**: Writers, journalists, and free expression advocates.
  - **URL**: https://pen.org/
- **Digital Wellness Collective**
  - **Description**: Global community promoting digital wellness and ethical technology use.
  - **Best For**: Individuals seeking support for healthier digital habits.
  - **URL**: https://www.digitalwellnesscollective.com/

How to Stay Current

The field of synthetic influence and AI manipulation evolves rapidly. Here are strategies for staying informed about new developments:

Regular Information Sources

- **Subscribe to specialized newsletters** like The Markup's "Hello World," WIRED's "Plaintext," or First Draft's newsletter.

- **Follow key researchers and organizations** on social media platforms.

- **Join relevant professional groups** on LinkedIn and other platforms.

- **Set up Google Alerts** for key terms like "deepfake detection," "AI regulation," or "synthetic media."

Continuous Learning Practices

- **Allocate regular time** for updating your knowledge, such as a weekly "learning hour."

- **Participate in webinars and virtual events** hosted by organizations in this space.

- **Join online communities** where members share new resources and developments.

- **Practice new verification techniques** regularly to maintain skills.

Conclusion: Building Your Personal Defense Toolkit

The resources in this appendix provide a starting point for developing your defenses against synthetic influence. Consider creating a personalized toolkit based on your specific needs and context:

1. **Select core verification tools** that align with your daily digital activities.

2. **Develop a personal learning plan** focusing on areas most relevant to your situation.

3. **Join at least one community** where you can share insights and receive support.

4. **Establish regular practices** for maintaining your digital hygiene and information literacy.

5. **Share your knowledge** with friends, family, and colleagues to build collective resilience.

Remember that no single tool or approach provides complete protection. The most effective defense combines technological tools with critical thinking skills and supportive communities. By drawing on the resources in this appendix, you can develop a layered approach to protecting yourself and others from synthetic influence in the AI age.

By

Ahmed Awad